Reveal

Embody the True Self,
Beyond Trauma and Conditioning

A Self-Help Memoir
by Harmony Kwiker, MA

Dedication

This book is dedicated to my daughter, Mylah, and my son, Tobin.
May you always remember the wholeness of your True Self.
In loving memory of my mom, Elizabeth Kwiker, 1950–2007.

CONTENTS

ACKNOWLEDGMENTS

My heart overflows with gratitude for these amazing beings: my dad, Dr. Michael Kwiker, D.O., whose love and generosity has given me wings; my mom, Elizabeth Kwiker, for showing me the fierce power of the feminine; Taylor Smith for showing me how my journey was mapped out in the stars; Bonnie Rascon for your lifelong maternal compassion; Susan Nemcek for seeing and loving me with clarity; Ellen Vernon for always speaking your truth; Sue Thoele for your generous mentorship; Michael Porchelli for embodying Integral leadership; Colleen Buckman for bringing magic back into my life; Chelsea Brady for your visionary design talent; and Melissa Kirk and Karin Conlin, my editors, for seeing the beauty in my story and helping me to put it to paper.

To the many friends, teachers, and lovers who have provided me a place to practice showing up to life empowered and aligned with my True Self, thank you. I would especially like to express deep gratitude for Lyn Gregory, Uri Talmor, LPC, Julia Mikk, Alicia Hagge, LCSW, Lindsey Felt-Dalton, Annie Hines, L.Ac, Bonnie Slater, Dr. Jenny Kim, OB/GYN, Ashley Connelly, LPC, Whitney Allen, Ali Shanti, Jess Nichole, Carolyn Eberle, LPC, Tim Singelton, Deanna Reiter, and Jane Strauss.

To my clients who have chosen me as a guide on your journey of healing and personal growth, I am humbled and in awe of your process. Through pain, fear, and deep grief, your courage to transform and your dedication to your healing offers me deep learning about humanity and resiliency. I will forever be appreciative of you.

And lastly, to those beings who are working to shift the paradigm of the masculine and feminine divide, from relationships based on power struggle to ones of integration, honor, and dignity, thank you for being part of this very important shift of consciousness and restoration of planetary peace. I am deeply grateful.

PROLOGUE

Here, right now within you, the core of your being is peeking through the layers of your conditioned self. The essence of who you are lives beneath the beliefs and pain you have acquired throughout your life. Thoughts and feelings of being wounded, powerless, small, and not enough drive the impulses of the conditioned self. When you believe that this is who you are, your powerful essence is hidden.

The strategies of the conditioned self are here to try to find you safety, acceptance, love, and power. However, the more you follow the impulse of your conditioning, the more powerless and small you end up feeling. Looping in this habitual way of being feels familiar, so it is the path of least resistance. However, following this impulse keeps you asleep to your true nature.

In your wholeness, you are inherently powerful and expansive and radiant. This will never change no matter the degree of your trauma or how identified you are with your conditioned self. Stripping away the layers of everything that you have acquired in this (and previous) lifetimes that is not part of your True Self will allow you to embody the wholeness that is your birthright.

The first step is knowing who you are and who you are not. You are not your thoughts, your beliefs, your character or persona. You are not your roles, your family lineage, or your career. You are the embodiment of divinity. Your true nature is your unbreakable connection with the creative Source of all things. This is the essence of who you are, and this will never change.

Expansive, wise, loving, strong, and whole, you are more powerful than the mind can conceive. Taking your power back from your conditioned self is the most vulnerable and invigorating act of courage. Trusting yourself and your connection with divinity is what this leap is all about.

Through the center of your body, down to the core of the earth and up to the sky above you, there is a line. This line is the core of your being, your True Self. This is your alignment with Source, and it anchors you here on this earth so that you may embody this essence. When you embody the True Self, you embody your own divinity.

To the left side of your face there is an energetic mask. This is the mask of your conditioned self. This is the persona that you present to the world, the ideas you've picked up from other people about who you are and how life should be, misbeliefs about love, and so on. Your character structure lives here and guides a lot of your thinking and behavior.

If you drew a line from this mask down to the right side of your right shoulder, you would find a collection of shadows: your disowned parts. This is where you hide the things about yourself that you think make you unlovable, bad, deviant, and so on. Disowned desire, disowned power, disowned anger, disowned sadness, etc. live here. These shadows drive a lot of your thoughts and actions, but you are less aware of them because they lurk in the deep unconscious.

This line, from your mask to your shadow, is the line of distortion. Most people live from this place. When we live from our distortion, we continually loop through old patterns and limiting thoughts that keep us feeling disempowered. We choose relationships from our wounds, we make career choices from our ego, we don't speak on behalf of our authentic truth, we criticize and try to control life and people, and we do things that aren't in alignment with who we really are. Then we wonder why we aren't manifesting our dreams or why we keep getting sick or why people are so mean.

Living in alignment with the core of your being takes conscious awareness of your mask and your shadow. You need to claim these parts of you, get to know them intimately, welcome them, and integrate them into the wholeness of your being. Recognize that even though they are a part of your humanity, they are not who you really are.

Embodying the True Self can be the most vulnerable thing you ever do. The conditioned self works hard to stop you, telling you to stay small and do the familiar thing to find safety. But the paradox is that you end up feeling less safe and having less satisfying connection when you listen to the beliefs and impulses of your familiar yet false self.

All of us are born in full alignment with our expansive, powerful self, fully connected with the Source that beats our heart, fully connected to God. However, the trauma and conditioning of life have split us from our connection with Source. We become afraid of being in our full expression and standing in our truth and power, so we navigate life from a contracted, false place. Trying to figure out how to get back to our essence, we seek the powerful feeling of Source in work, relationships, community, drugs, our physical appearance, and so on.

As we attempt to feel powerful from this small place, we unknowingly perpetuate the patterns of our conditioned self. Wondering why life doesn't feel satisfying or why our relationships are dysfunctional, we stay blind to our own conditioning.

There is a Hindu proverb that says there are Three Great Mysteries: "Air to a bird, water to a fish, mankind to himself." Self-discovery, seeing the water that we've been swimming in, and remembering our true nature allows us to embody the higher frequency of our essence in all aspects of life. It takes a deep level of awareness and understanding between our false and our true selves to live in integrity with who we really are.

I have dedicated my life to healing old trauma, taking my power back from my conditioned self, and learning how to facilitate others in embodying their essence and loving from wholeness. Using each experience and every relationship as an opportunity to go deeper into my awakening, I become more solid in myself while also becoming softer and more fluid. Trusting myself to honor my truth, my whole system integrates in such a way that the old patterns and the old stories become outdated.

Although the journey has been long and painful, I've emerged more powerful and whole than I ever could have imagined. As a lifelong learner, I believe that there are no failures in relationships, in work, or in self-development. Every single experience we have is here to usher us to the next level of our evolution. The key is to use the information provided by the universe for our own self-awareness, growth, and healing.

In the pages of this book, I share with you my journey of learning to embody my True Self. The vulnerability that it took me to share my story with you almost felt too big to overcome. If, however, my pain and awakening offer you any bit of hope for your own healing, then every single painful experience I have ever had was worth it. To be revealed, to allow myself to be seen in both my light and my shadow, strips away layers of shame that caused me to hide for far too many years. Wanting all beings to feel empowered and fully self-expressed, this is my giant leap toward embodying this desire.

Love,
Harmony

1
THE LOST SELF

"Illusions are the truths we live by until we know better."
— Nancy Gibbs

HIDDEN TRUTH

A pervasive sense of embarrassment and fear followed me down the busy San Francisco street in the Castro district. It was the summer of 1986, and the Castro was bustling with people wearing flamboyant clothing, thematic tattoos, and unusual piercings. The entire place seemed unfamiliar – especially the blurred gender lines. Mesmerized, I watched two men in leather chaps make out against the graffiti smeared wall, but I tried to act casual, like I was totally cool with all of it. As a voyeur in a new land, I was afraid to be seen watching, but too curious to look away.

The Castro was one of the first gay neighborhoods in the United States, and in the 80s this was still very much a fringe culture. A 10-year-old girl from the suburbs of Sacramento, I awkwardly gawked in disbelief at a culture that my mind could not grasp.

No one here fit into the box that my mind had constructed as normal, including my own family. I was here with my mom, who was cheery and happy to be strolling this eccentric neighborhood. She held her girlfriend Kristin's hand as my sister, Grace, strutted the district in her cutoff jean shorts, black shirt, and dark black makeup. I was angry that my mom was a lesbian and horrified that Kristin lived with us, but I didn't express that to anyone. I held my dissonant perspective closely, trying to maintain some sense of harmony in my otherwise crazy family.

As I casually strolled ten feet behind my mom, Kristin, and my sister, I was clearly the only normal one in our group. With my white preppy shorts, pink polo T-shirt, and thick blonde hair with perfectly feathered bangs, I hoped no one would guess that I was with them. But really I just wanted to disappear altogether. I looked around, trying to assess who was judging me. I thought someone must have noticed our unconventional crew. However, the more I looked around, the more it seemed that I was the one who was abnormal — I was too wholesome to fit into this deviant culture.

I wanted to retreat to my suburban home where I could continue hiding the truth about my mom, even though existence was no easier for me there. I liked Kristin well enough, but as an image conscious, prepubescent girl, I was mortified by her obesity and mullet hair style. She was a butch lesbian and a painter, and her clothes were always splattered with various shades of pastels. To make matters worse, my mom loved to push boundaries, so she was not shy about being affectionate in public with Kristin.

Before this, before my mom came out as a lesbian, she and I were so close. With no boundaries between us, my identity was entangled with hers. My success was her success; my happiness was her happiness; my pain was her pain. Without an inkling of who I was as a separate person from her, I was convinced that if anyone found out that my mom was a lesbian they would automatically think I was, too. I lived in fear of my friends finding out about Kristin, so I fabricated many lies about why she lived with us: She was our nanny. She was renovating our house. She was my mom's old friend from high school. She was just staying with us until she found her own place. She was ANYTHING but my mom's lover.

I didn't want the thought of my mom being a lesbian to cross anyone's mind, so I preemptively told the lies to stop them from pondering how this woman fit into our lives. I couldn't handle the truth, so I was certain that other people couldn't, either.

Daily, I lived this fear of being cast out as different, but here in the Castro we were steeped in a culture that valued individual self-expression over conformity. Here, I couldn't ignore or hide the truth about my mom being a lesbian. Where in my normal world, my mom and her girlfriend were the outcasts, somehow today they fit right in as they held hands in public.

They seemed elated and enamored with the culture here, and Grace seemed good with it, too. She had always been more self-expressive and eccentric than me. She had an artistic style and was outspoken about everything, including what she didn't like about our upbringing.

The heated arguments between Grace and Mom were countless, and I could always count on my sister to speak on behalf of us. Where I was too scared to oppose the status quo, Grace was a master at defiance. But today I felt betrayed by her, like she was on Mom's side.

I felt like I was in a nightmare, like a wholesome child from "The Waltons" trapped in "The Addams Family."

With our nontraditional household, I always felt on edge, like I had to mitigate any potential social damage before it arose. I just wanted to get by unseen. At school and at home, I was quiet, hiding my emotions and my brilliance in order to not bring attention to myself. If nobody saw me, I couldn't be hurt.

To my mom, this trip to the Castro was a fun family getaway; to me, this was a horrific nightmare of being confronted with the shadow of our family. I was not ready for this, and no one cared to ask me how I felt about this experience. Because I was quiet and pretending to be okay with everything, my mom was oblivious to my discomfort. But even if she had asked me how I was feeling, I would have likely lied, anyway. Although painful, pretending that I was fine was preferable. It earned me approval and kept a sort of balance in our family.

We made our way to the Hard Rock Café for lunch, and then we all packed into my mom's 1985 silver Toyota Camry and drove across the Bay Bridge to my mom's best friend Jane's home in Oakland.

Jane and her husband, Lester, lived in a beautiful home in the Oakland hills that was decorated traditionally. Compared to our 1980s modern furniture with clean lines and pastel colors, Jane and Lester had Craftsman-style furniture with rich colors and dark wood.

I felt comfortable here because everything about Jane and Lester was normal. They had normal gender roles, they wore normal clothes, they had normal body weight, and they had normal evenings, with food they prepared and calm conversation. At my house we ate out most nights or heated up frozen meals; we watched a lot of TV and either ignored each other or argued. I had no bedtime at home, no one asking me how I was doing, and no one making sure I brushed my teeth or did my homework.

Jane was different. I felt seen by her and she always sat with me while I worked on my school projects. I called her "My Janie" and while at her house I could relax in safety, feeling secure in the normalcy of the way they lived and the way she cared about me. All children want to know that the adults around them offer a loving and safe presence. Emotionally responsive and attuned adults create an environment that children can explore the full range of their being in unconditional love. For me, Jane was the only adult who came close to offering this to me. She was the mature and embodied role model I needed.

That night, I slept in Jane's luxurious and cozy guest room. I felt relieved to finally be alone and to get away from my mom.

I slept well, and the next morning I drifted awake to an erotic dream/fantasy involving Sean Astin and Kirk Cameron. Their shirts were off and they were fighting over me. I was extremely aroused. "Goonies" was my favorite movie, and "Growing Pains" was my favorite TV show. I stayed in bed way past my normal waking time to indulge the pleasure of this fantasy.

Eventually, I was called to breakfast. I pulled the covers back and rolled out of bed. I thought the arousal of the dream had made my underwear wet, but when I got to the bathroom there was blood. A lot of blood. I stared at my underwear, stunned by the revelation that this blood had come from inside of me. I had no idea that it was possible for a kid to menstruate—I thought periods were for adults. I was only 10 years old, and I didn't know what to do.

My mind went straight to my mom. I didn't want her to find out. Everything about my mom embarrassed me, and her response would certainly be mortifying. If she knew I was on my period she would tell everyone. Literally: the grocer and the waiter, her friends and clients. Everyone would know.

I had to keep this a secret. After I cleaned myself, I rolled up some toilet paper and shoved it in my underwear. Just like with my pain and my truth, I would hide this from her for as long as I could.

In this moment, the moment of my coming into womanhood, I didn't even let myself acknowledge that I needed to talk with someone with whom I felt safe. I couldn't tell Jane because she would certainly tell my mom, so I quickly bypassed my needs and pretended that nothing unusual was happening. And because I was so skilled at lying and hiding, no one suspected a thing. I sat at the breakfast table listening to the morning chatter about what we were going to do that day, relieved that nobody noticed anything different about me.

A girl's entry into womanhood has a strong influence on the way she feels about her own femininity. Some people have ceremonies and celebrations and deep honoring of this glorious gift of fertility. Girls are encouraged to embrace their femininity with strength and grace while taught about cycling with the full moon for full creative power. Honoring one's menstrual cycle as sacred honors the sacred nature of the inner divine feminine. This supports young girls in fully embodying their healthy feminine expression.

Conversely, when we feel shame about our cycle and our bodies, we hide and feel insignificant and awkward. Collapsing around our femininity, the dignity and beauty of this transition is lost. We split from our connection with the divine feminine, and we feel disempowered and unworthy. This is what happened with me when I was 10, and this pattern of hiding and collapse became my habitual way of being a woman in the world.

PERPETUATING THE UNHEALTHY FEMININE

My first day with a period would be spent walking around San Francisco with toilet paper shoved in my underwear. Although I felt uncomfortable, that was way better than the squirmy feeling I knew I would have if my mom talked to me about my vagina.

My mom thought we were close, and I thought so, too. Neither of us could see that there wasn't room for me and my needs in our dynamic. I was so accustomed to the way she made everything about her, that I didn't even know I was bypassing my needs. We were only close in that I never disagreed with her or spoke my opposition to anything, ever. I was easy for her, and I was very skilled at hiding myself to make it look as if I were okay with everything.

It was confusing for me having my mom as a mom. Even though I didn't feel safe sharing my truth and needs with her, she was adored by her clients and our community. She was a progressive healer who specialized in survivors of sexual abuse. This was during a time when people were just starting to come out and talk about incest, molestation, and rape.

My mom, who was the oldest girl of eight children, was a survivor of sexual abuse. Her grandfather, who was an Italian immigrant, was the first to teach her that her body didn't belong to her. Her grandparents lived in her home, and she endured this abuse because she thought she was protecting her siblings from being victimized. The Catholic priest, her dad's friends, and other men from her community projected their shadow sexuality onto her, and she started to believe that her worth came from her sexuality and that her body was an object for men's pleasure. Even though she was still identified with her wound, her pain from this abuse was channeled into her work where she empowered survivors of incest and sexual victimization.

Her siblings and her clients all looked to her as a healthy mother figure, the woman they wished they could call "Mom." Although she was wise and powerful in her own right, my mom's parenting was confusing for me. She was polished and put together for her clients, but behind closed doors she'd be inappropriate and mean. It was as if everyone else got the best of her, and she saved her shadow for me.

"You are so lucky to have your mom as a mom," her clients would say to me.

Hearing this I would smile in agreement, believing there was no room for me to disagree. The harm she caused me was invisible, so I thought my pain wasn't valid. Emotionally erratic, without boundaries, and totally lacking attunement to me and my needs, my mom's unhealed pain was projected onto me and became mine.

As a healer, she started off as a rebirther (also known as a breathworker), teaching people how to use their breath to heal and return to wholeness. In rebirthing, a person lies down on a mat on the floor or in a bathtub and starts breathing in a particular rhythmic pattern. As they breathe, they might feel sensation in their hands or pain in their body, or see images of past trauma in their mind's eye. Whatever emerges in a session, the person simply keeps breathing. It is with the breath alone that one draws in life force energy to the stored pain. And in this simple act of breathing, a person's system returns to original wholeness and the old trauma patterns shift.

When a person is doing breathwork and moving through old pain, they might yell and scream and cry. My mom saw clients out of our home. Often, I would be watching cartoons in my living room while my mom was in the next room with a client. I could hear screaming and crying, and I wanted to know what was happening in there. At 5 years old, I asked my mom to rebirth me. Nervous and timid, I walked into her room and lay down on the mat on her floor. She told me that it was okay that I was nervous and that I could stop at any point if I didn't want to go on. I asked her if I could go get my stuffed unicorn from my bedroom, and she agreed that that would be a great idea.

When I returned with my favorite stuffy, I laid back down and she taught me the breathing pattern. I breathed for about five minutes, and I became so fearful that I asked to stop. I got up and went to my room, and I didn't try rebirthing again until I was 19 years old.

Without any education, she became a successful coach/counselor, and she and Jane, her best friend, created powerful personal growth workshops together. She had a huge following, and her clients felt empowered by her.

I didn't get it. I couldn't see her talent. I couldn't see her gifts. All I could see was how negligent she was as my mom and how afraid I was to tell her my truth, how I felt about her bursts of rage, her wild parties, and her eccentric and seductive way of being. I wanted a normal mom, someone I could trust to be there with a soft and quiet touch when I told her I had my first period.

It wasn't just my bloody underwear I didn't want to tell her about, nor was it just my opposition to her choice in her lover. Her obesity, her inappropriate sexual boundaries, her drug use, her domineering energy, her need for approval, and her inability to keep a secret hurt me in deep and perplexing ways. I so wanted to tell her this, I wanted her to know her impact on me, but she seemed unable to receive any kind of criticism.

The one time I tried to oppose her, telling her that I didn't like the gift she had given me, she screamed at me hysterically and locked herself in her room, threatening to kill herself. I sat outside her door apologizing profusely, terrified that I would never see her again.

I pleaded with her, assuring her that I did love her. I shoved love letters under her door, hoping that my love would stop her pain. I became terrified to speak my truth, because apparently my words could kill her. I learned how to please her. I earned love all day long by pretending everything was okay, like I had no pain, like her bad behavior wasn't a problem to me. I was unaware that I was being shaped to be manipulative. The payoff was too great to look at the distortion of this behavior.

We all learn how to navigate the world through the interactions we have with our parents and caregivers in childhood. We look to our parents as guides. When they are oblivious to our needs, lacking emotional attunement, blaming us for their emotional outbursts, or violate us and create an unsafe environment, we try to find safety and connection by hiding parts of ourselves. This is the birthplace of manipulation. This is the wound of shame, where we disown parts of ourselves and hide our shadow. When we identify with this wound, we unconsciously use past experiences to interact with the world. Not being practiced in speaking our truth and staying solid in ourselves, our distortion becomes the patterned way we interact with the world.

In part my mom's distortion was shaped in response to the sexual abuse she endured; however, her parents were not a loving, caring presence for her to turn to. Her mother would burn her with cigarettes in her drunken rages, and her father would weigh all of the girls and whip them with a belt if they weighed more than he thought they should. And as the oldest girl, my mom was more of a maternal presence to her younger siblings than her mother ever was. She was there for all of them, and they trusted her to care for them in a way they were all starving for.

She learned early on that it wasn't safe for her to be in a body, and as an adult, she became morbidly obese with a thick layer of self-protection. She was around 300 pounds when I was a kid. She would overeat in front of the TV every night and then wonder why she couldn't lose weight. And just as I thought people would think I was gay if they knew she was, I was desperately afraid that her body said something about me, too.

I thought this often, that her embarrassing behavior was a reflection of me. That she was me. That her bigness, her loud voice, her boisterous personality, her flamboyant skirts and low-cut tops, were in fact me. But really, there was no me. I had no sense of self. I was a chameleon. I was mute.

Silent. Although I could speak, I didn't. Not when it really mattered, anyway. My pain was locked away deep inside my heart. I shoved it in. There was no room out there in the world for my pain. Only hers. Her suffering took up too much room. So I silenced mine.

When my mom felt rejected by me, my sister, or anyone at all, she would become volatile. Although Grace was cool with the Castro, she never had a problem telling Mom the ways in which her mothering damaged us. And when she expressed her truth, there was always a huge fight.

Grace was three years older than me and since no one was listening to us, she resorted to voicing her pain with anger and violence, which supported my dawning realization that there was no room in this house for my voice. Although I agreed with my sister, I always sided with my mom because I was so afraid of conflict. Of course, this angered Grace. In my siding with Mom, I earned the place as the favorite child while she held the very challenging role as the dark truth teller.

She could see my manipulative tactic to earn love, and she hated me for it. She had an explosive temper, and I felt like I was always walking on eggshells to try to keep her stable. I would do anything she told me to do, which typically involved getting her food and cleaning up after her. A common game we played as children was "slave" where I would literally do everything she asked. I looked up to her with trust and admiration, so I was her willing slave, and I believed every bit of criticism and blame she put on me about how much better her life would be if I had never been never born or if I were different in some way.

When Grace was angry, fear would surge through my body and I thought she would kill me. I wanted someone to protect me from her, but my parents were afraid of her, too. I would run into my room, trying to escape her intense rage as she chased me. In our family, I had the role of victim, she of perpetrator. I was the light and loving one while she acted out the role of the dark and hateful one. Just as I believed that I needed to be quiet and accommodating for my mom's

21

happiness, I also believed that it was my job to keep Grace happy. I thought that my need for safety wasn't valid, and I thought that my pain was inconsequential.

When we think that other people are more important than us, it's because we're trying to find a sense of security in the world around us. Unconsciously we're trying to control the environment by getting the people in our world to be stable. *"If I stay quiet and complicit,"* the mind unconsciously reasons, *"then they will find stability and I'll be safe."* In childhood this makes sense because we really do need the adults in our lives to keep us safe and protected. However, when we carry this pattern into adulthood we use our conditioning to keep us in the role of victim. Unlearning this pattern and discovering how to give voice to our pain, claiming that we are also important, can be the most empowering act of self-love and dignity.

HIDDEN

So here I was, on the first day of my very first period, hiding parts of myself, trying to keep a modicum of dignity. I knew I could count on myself to handle my period because this was the way it had always been. Self-reliance and self-parenting kept me functional.

The thing about neglect is that it's insidious. I wasn't even aware that my needs weren't being met because I colluded so well in it. The denial of my own needs came easily to me; I had no idea I was even doing it. In fact, most of the time I didn't even know I had needs. I didn't even know I had preferences that could be voiced.

I did know, however, that I felt better at my dad's house than I did at my mom's.

I had been going back and forth since the age of 4. The chaos and disorganization and addiction to food and television at my mom's was depressing at best. Over at my dad's, things were clean and orderly: I had a bedtime, I had home-cooked meals, and I had physical outlets, like bikes and basketball. My mom was sedentary, so I was sedentary at her house. My dad was active, so we did physically active things at his house.

And like most Americans, he hid his addiction and dysfunction really well. No one would have guessed that he escaped his suffering with porn and alcohol and mistresses. I didn't know. And that's how I preferred it.

My dad was an osteopathic physician who empowered his clients to come into the full expression of health with nutritional and alternative medicine. He was born into a Jewish family where education and achievement were standard. Expected to become a physician, he found a way to incorporate his hippie values with his medical practice by developing a holistic approach. He was ahead of his time and was a genuinely caring doctor who was equally brilliant and generous. Although progressive and loved by his patients and staff, he rarely, if ever, gave me his undivided attention. With a successful private practice and a new wife named Tina, my dad was preoccupied. He had left my mom for Tina, who was a nurse that worked for him. Aside from being physically active with me, his lack of presence and emotional attunement made it so he seemed vacant. And since I saw him so infrequently, I often felt like I didn't have a dad at all.

The most confusing wound can be the wound of neglect. When a parent is absent in any way, they're not able to give us the thing we want most: attention. And when we're simply not given something, it's hard to see the impact that has on us. When we're conditioned in response to violence, abuse, alcoholism, and so on, it can be more obvious to see the impact on us. But neglect is its own variety of trauma and conditioning that is quiet and subversive and hard to give language to.

For me the neglect from my dad was made even more confusing by the fact that I preferred to be at his house. I only saw him every other weekend, but it always felt like a vacation from the chaos of my mom's erratic and inappropriate behavior. My step-mom, Tina was thin and blonde, and she cooked real food and took me shopping. I was used to sitting on the couch eating potato chips and ice cream and pizza to the point of pain at my mom's. There was no gluttony at my dad's. Only the freshest food prepared with love.

My dad seemed to care a lot about image, buying yuppie clothes and checking out attractive women at every chance he could get. I would be midsentence when he would pause me and say, "Hold on a minute." Then his gaze would go to a beautiful woman and I would sit there, feeling dropped and unimportant, waiting for his attention again. In order to gain a sense of approval I turned my focus to my image. I would often admire myself in the mirror, marveling at how sophisticated I looked. My style made me feel cool. Like I belonged. Like I mattered. My polished appearance hid my pain and darkness, and this, I thought, was where I earned my worth.

My superficial self-adoration was contrasted by deep self-loathing. My inner critic was desperately afraid of having no worth. Fear of being not enough kept me looking in the mirror to try to find my enoughness. The misbelief that I was completely unlovable drove me to pretend that I was superior. Untouchable. It was safer up there on my pedestal of perfection. No one could view my flaws if I couldn't see them for myself.

I would compulsively check mirrors or store windows to see if I was pretty. I wanted to make sure I wasn't fat like my mom, ensuring that my appearance would get me the approval I desperately wanted. I was a little heavy compared to other girls my age, but compared to my mom I was a Barbie.

"Did you borrow Harmony's shorts?" I heard my mom ask my sister one day. It had been almost a year since I had started my period in Oakland. I had managed to keep it a secret from everyone, using toilet paper and stealing pads when I could.

"Mom, let me handle this," I heard Grace say as she intercepted our mom.

I was sitting on my bed in my room when my sister knocked on the door. I tried to hide my excitement and anxiety from her as I put on a face of aloofness. I wished I could have kept this secret hidden forever but I was outed by my own blood.

When Grace walked in, she had a soft look on her face and I instantly felt her care. She sat down next to me and said, "When you get your period, if you get really bad cramps you can stay home from school." I was shocked at this simple and very cool take on what seemed like a catastrophic life change. I sat in silence as I took in this new revelation, the idea that I might get some benefit from having blood come out of my vagina every month.

Even though I was scared of Grace for her outspoken and eccentric ways and told by Mom that it was my job to keep her stable, she was in my corner when it mattered most. She went on to explain tampons to me, but the idea of putting anything inside of my vagina scared me. I wasn't ready to even explore that option. She told Mom to buy me pads and to not talk to me about my period, and I felt indebted to her. She understood what literally no else could possibly understand about having our mom as a mom. And even though I didn't side with her in the arguments, she still had my back when I needed her.

My body softened with deep relief when I finally got my own package of pads. And when I realized that my mom was respecting the boundary to not talk with me about it, I surrendered in total relaxation. I had needed these for the past twelve months, and I finally had this need met without having to ask for it. I would have been mortified if it had happened any other way.

It didn't even occur to me that there was something wrong with this picture: that my own mother—a healer!—didn't feel like a safe person for me to talk to about my transition into womanhood. Because my mom adored me and told me that I was amazing on a daily basis, I was mixed up when it came to the ways in which she failed me. I was totally fine placating and obeying her unspoken expectations of me all day long if that meant I earned the love and safety I desperately needed. And I was lauded for this behavior. I was the favorite and deemed "the easy one."

To develop a sense of security in the world, children need to know that their parents can be a secure base for them. Children need to know that when they reach out to their primary caregiver they will be received with compassion, love, and tenderness. When a child has a responsive and safe parent who is emotionally attuned, that child learns that they matter, that what is happening within them matters. However, when the adults have unhealed wounds themselves, it can be nearly impossible to consistently be a secure base for a child. Children's needs can seem constant and unending, so having clean and clear boundaries is part of being a secure base. However, when a parent is still being driven by a wounded young one within them, they are less resilient and unconsciously pass on their wounding.

Of course no parent wants to pass on their wounding. In fact, many want to have kids so that they can do it differently. However, the acquired patterns of trauma and conditioning go way back in the family lineage and can be hard to decipher until we have our own children. Unintentionally passing on attachment wounds is the transgenerational pattern of ancestral trauma. Because these patterns live both in the DNA and actual experience, it's common to believe that they are part of one's identity. It's common to see our parents as wounded and to unknowingly identify with our own wounds.

These traumas and patterns were learned and acquired, so they can certainly be unlearned and healed. Wounds and misbeliefs from trauma and conditioning are not an inherent aspect of a person's true nature, so the work is about differentiating from the pattern and wounding. When we differentiate from our wounds, we can cultivate an identity with the True Self, the part of us that is untouched by the pattern. Differentiation is different from spiritual bypassing, which is the use of spiritual ideas to avoid facing unresolved pain. Differentiation is simply getting space from the wounds, recognizing that they are not who we are, that our conditioned self is not our identity. When we're in our wounds, identified with them, we can't even see them clearly and feel like we're drowning in them. With the space afforded by differentiation, we can see them more clearly, begin to heal them, and develop mastery over how we want to show up for our life.

SHAPED

My early childhood experiences taught me that I needed to be a certain way in order to garner a sense of stability and safety in my life. With all the chaos around me, I was shaped to interact with the world from a distorted place where I contorted my authentic truth to try to fit what others wanted. We are all shaped by the experiences that we have early in life, and these experiences form our conditioned self—the habitual way we engage with the world. We create beliefs about who we are based on these early experiences, and then we use this misinformation to guide our thinking and behavior. We use other people's values, unconscious behavior, and words as information about who we are. We wear this as our own personality, and then this guides our way of being.

But beneath this, just under the surface of our personality and ideas about who we are, there is our essence. Our essence is our crystalline energetic body that has been ours since before our conception, throughout all of our lifetimes and even when we're not in a body. Our essence is the part of us that is connected to all living things. It's our oneness. Completely untouched by our conditioning, our essence is always there, within us, waiting for us to embody it as who we really are. Before the world taught us how to be and before we collected evidence about relationships and power and worth and love, we were inherently connected with this deeper part of ourselves.

For me, it was at the age of 10 that the mask of my persona moved to the forefront of my awareness and I lost touch with my deeper wisdom and expansive witness mind. Children only know they exist because they're seen. Energetically we harden around our human experiences and lose sight of the vast, expansive softness of our essence when we're not seen for it. Since the people in my life lauded my accommodating and easy persona, I willingly worked to be a "good object." I ignored my pain and my darkness in order to earn love and approval, abandoning my subjective inner world. No one was attuned to my deeper emotional interior or my powerful True Self. Subsequently, I fell asleep to my essence and started living from my small, conditioned self.

My identity became unified with my false self, and I believed that I needed to follow the impulses of my conditioning to navigate this world with success. Before this time, I was in touch with a deeper part of myself that others didn't seem to notice. Although I didn't have language for it, I was in touch with the core of my being, with my True Self. I had a connection with a part of me that was more expansive, truer, and wiser than my chameleon-like persona. Since it seemed as though the people around me were all in agreement that we would measure one's worth on appearance, status, and likeability, I was unsure if this spiritual self and consciousness was valid. I started to doubt if this deeper part of me was real.

Witnessing the craziness of my life, my conscious awareness could see the players acting out patterns and engaging with one another in a false and distorted way. I was in touch with my wisdom of spiritual and psychological dynamics, but I wasn't sure why nobody else was talking about this. To me, it was the most obvious part of being alive.

In my life, falling asleep to my essence was the cause of much destruction and suffering. Something that I was so connected to at birth began to fade. In my transition into womanhood at the age of 10, my personality became my identity and I completely lost touch with the essence of who I was. I lost touch with my alignment with the Source that beats my heart—with my connection to God. I forgot that I was big and expansive, and I played small in order to earn connection, safety, and love.

When we loop in a cycle of feeling small and powerless in the world, we are identified with our conditioned self. Our conditioned self is our learned values, behaviors, and misbeliefs about who we are. From the lens of our conditioning, we can feel wounded, separate, and broken. This is our source of illness, pain, and suffering. When we identify with this small part of us and think we are our conditioning, we try to either exert power over others (be better, right, or more in some way) or we collapse around our will (making others more important than us). When we can see that this is simply the way we think we need to navigate the world to earn safety and connection, we can see that there are more options available for us than living from this small place.

In order to align with the essence of who we are, we need to take our power back from our shaping and differentiate from our wounds. We need to stop identifying with our distortion in order to live in alignment with the True Self. By claiming our shadow, pain, and darkness, we also claim our light, wisdom, and power. This brings us closer to the core of our being, the rod of strength and solidity that lives down the midline of our body. Aligning vertically with Source, anchoring that to the core of the earth, we can embody our true nature with the flow of the universe.

2
SEARCHING FOR THE LIGHT

"Hope is being able to see that there is light despite the darkness."
— Bishop Desmond Tutu

CONDITIONED VICTIMIZATION

In elementary school, I never quite fit in. Not only did I start school a year early and was younger than all of my peers, my light blonde hair and blue eyes set me apart as different in the private Jewish school I attended. Wanting to protect me from the public school system—which was not great in our neighborhood—my parents thought this was the best choice for my education. However, since my mom wasn't Jewish, I was constantly reminded that I wasn't actually Jewish and that I didn't really belong there. I was already marginalized for being only half Jewish (and the wrong half at that), and my appearance set me apart in a different, more confusing way.

I first learned about the Holocaust in first grade through the eyes of Anne Frank. As my class read her story, the genocide and the spreading of evil scared me to my core, especially since young children weren't immune to the killings.

As we talked about the story, Ms. Carrie, my history teacher, told us that many people were killed in gas chambers.

"They would gather all of the families and people who were staying in the camps, and they would tell everyone that they were going to take a shower. People would line up for their shower, but when they got inside, gas would come out instead of water," she explained matter-of-factly.

I was terrified. At the age of 6, I was just beginning to develop a relationship with time as a linear concept. On the level of spirit, time is not linear. There is simply spacious oneness in the spirit realm, and since children are new to this dimension they haven't yet learned this navigational tool. Developmentally, I didn't fully understand linear time, so I thought the Nazis were still actively trying to eradicate all Jews. At home, I became desperately afraid of taking a shower, fearful that gas would come out of my water pipes and kill me.

When I told Ms. Carrie that I was scared, she assured me that I would not have been killed.

"They didn't kill the Jews with blond hair and blue eyes," she said to me.

At first I felt relieved, and then I asked, "What would they have done with me?"

"Well, the men would have kept you to have you cook for them and to be their wife."

Terrified by the idea of being forced to be the wife of a Nazi, I froze as fear jolted through my young body. Unconsciously I reasoned that my safety with men came from their attraction to me. If men desired me, I would live. If I opposed a man's attraction, certain death would ensue.

The patriarchal view of male and female dynamics that lives in the collective unconscious has been passed down to all of us in one way or another. Although changing quickly and dramatically, the old paradigm of men as superior and women as the weaker sex has been so pervasive that sometimes it's hard to recognize its presence in the media, our world view, or our sense of self. When there is a history in the family lineage of a man abusing his position of power, the impact goes on throughout the generations. Both women and men in the family react to this abuse by either identifying with the perpetrator to find a sense of power or collapsing around their will to find a sense of safety.

Learning about the Nazis imposed the threat of the unhealthy masculine to my young mind. In that moment, I made an unconscious decision to embody the unhealthy feminine. I was conditioned to play submissive and seductive to try to earn safety with men because I felt inherently unsafe. I realize now that this is not a dynamic of "perpetrator and victim," where men are bad and women need to be rescued. This is a dynamic of wounding and conditioning and pain for all genders.

The unhealthy masculine has been conditioned just as the unhealthy feminine has. When we heal and grow and evolve beyond our wounds and conditioning, we embody our healthy expression of masculine and feminine energies. We all have both masculine and feminine energy within us, and cultivating an integration, balance, respect, and honor for both of these energies within us is what cultivates the balance of these energies in the world.

It's a masculine trait to want something and to take initiative to go and get it. It's a feminine trait to be open and receptive to holding what's present.

As a feminine woman, much of my work has been about learning how to claim my desire and take initiative to go after what I want. This practice helps me to cultivate a healthier expression of my femininity. Masculine men need to work on being more receptive and expanding their capacity to "be with" what is present. This creates in internal balance that allows them to come into a healthy masculine expression.

At 6, I was conditioned to embody my unhealthy feminine expression. I was submissive, demure, and manipulative. I disowned my power, my voice, and my desire. I wanted men to find me attractive, and I wasn't sure why.

In the same year I learned about the Holocaust, I started having sleepovers with my best friend from school, Sarah. Sarah would spend a lot of time at my house, since that was her preference. But every once in a while, I would stay at her house. I liked Sarah's mom, but her stepdad, Shane, had an energy about him that scared me. He was always very interested in us, and he would play a game where he would try to grab my toes. Even when I pleaded with him to stop, he kept playing the game because my struggle clearly amused him.

One evening at Sarah's, Shane offered to give us a bubble bath. I felt uncomfortable and didn't want to take a bath at her house. I tried to voice my resistance, but Shane encouraged me by saying that we could play "find the bar of soap" under the bubbles and Sarah assured me that it would be fun.

As I stood in the bathroom naked waiting for the tub to be filled, Shane looked at me with desire. My body recoiled in embarrassment, but then he reached over and touched my vulva. I looked over at Sarah and she smiled. At that quick brush of his hand, fear pulsed through my body. Violated, I shrank with fear and shame, feeling as if my body wasn't mine. Resigned to being powerless to Shane's shadow, I stepped into the bath.

Shane dropped a bar of soap into the bathtub, and he put both of his hands into the water pretending that he was trying to find the soap while he groped us. Even though we were all laughing, I was frightened and tried to avoid his hands at all costs. I never told anybody about that incident, and since our families were friends, I spent a lot time with Shane.

Although I have no memories of him touching me inappropriately again, terror rushed through my body every time I was in his presence. On time in the backyard of my home, Shane was trimming one of our trees while Sarah and I played. As we were goofing around, I jumped on a branch, and that branch accidentally jabbed Shane's leg, giving him a gaping wound. Enraged, he shouted that he was going to beat me. The shouting continued as I raced across the half-acre of our yard with him close behind.

Luckily, my mom saw me from inside the kitchen and ran out to me. I was panting as I hugged her, and he went back to his tree trimming.

After that incident I never went back to Sarah's house. And a few short years later, we got news that Shane had locked himself in the trunk of his car and shot himself with a gun. He had been sexually abusing Sarah throughout her entire life, and once she told her mom about the abuse he apparently couldn't live with himself any longer. Through his being conditioned to act as a perpetrator, I imagine that Shane endured tremendous early trauma that kept him from embodying his true nature.

Heartbroken for Sarah, I felt shame that I hadn't said anything about how he had violated me. I wish I would have helped to protect her. The culture we were living in was seeped with sexual shadow and it was hard to decipher right from wrong. There's a photo of Sarah, me, and our friend, Erica, gathered around Shane in my backyard. He was completely naked, and we were in our bathing suits as he sprayed us with a water hose. With his penis right at the level of our eyes, he was laughing as we tried to not get wet. Our mom's should have protected us from him. But they didn't. They were too conditioned to be in their unhealthy feminine expression, giving power over to the men in their lives.

Given my mom's history of sexual abuse and her work with clients, it seems that she would have been more diligent about protecting me. However, her wound distorted her relationship to sexuality and boundaries. Even though she was afraid that I would endure the same hardship as she had, she didn't seem to take preventative measures to keep me safe. Instead of feeling protected, I felt powerless and subservient to men with no understanding of clear boundaries.

As fear was growing in my young mind, my mom was distracted with her work and social life. She would throw big parties where people were naked in our hot tub and as they walked around our house. At these parties, I felt invisible to her. I was scared of the men at the parties, especially when I couldn't find my mom to cling to her leg. I would try to evade them, but more than once, I was certain I was being cornered by a man who wanted to violate me. I never stayed near them long enough to find out, because the fear in my body caused me to run.

"If you ever think something bad is going to happen, trust that intuition," my mom had said to me on many occasions. This gave me permission to run, but it didn't quite give me permission to own my "No." It also didn't give me permission to tell her about all of the ways I felt unsafe in the world. Although I didn't know it at the time, my mom was projecting "victim" onto me, and I wore that projection around for a long time unconsciously believing it was true.

When we're learning about who we are in the world, we're being conditioned by our experiences. But what may be less obvious is that we are also being conditioned by other people's projections. My mom had a construct for young girls in her mind based on her experience with sexual abuse. Because she was victimized as a young girl and hadn't fully healed that wound when she had me, this wound was projected onto me. Energetically I could sense her projections of me and on some level I took on her belief that I was a victim. Simultaneously, my experiences with her conditioned me to abandon myself and make others more important than me, which reinforced my victim-like behavior.

Never owning my "No" and setting clear boundaries, I played the role of victim because that was all I knew. I couldn't even see that there were more options for me to explore. Playing along with men's desire, viewing my body as an object for their pleasure, hiding my pain and silencing my voice were the only ways I knew how to navigate relationships. I didn't even know where I acquired these destructive thoughts and behaviors, I simply followed them around as if they were truth.

"No" can be the most powerful and important word we ever speak. Knowing what we're available for, we are responsible for setting our own boundary. Standing solid in ourselves, we know that our own wants and needs are important even if someone is upset with us. Having agency of choice around our actions is a great act of dignity and honoring of self. When we leave it up to someone else to treat us with respect and then resent them for not doing so, we set ourselves up for victimization. This pattern of self-betrayal is a manipulative tactic to earn safety. It keeps us from having interactions with the world that are in integrity with the core of our being. As we undertake the process of maturing into a wise and powerful being who is self-possessed and sovereign, "No" can be the very word that guides us to the next level of our evolution.

A GLIMMER OF HOPE

"I'd like to bring you someplace special," my mom said to me when I was 6 years old. "It's a place where they teach you how to meditate. Would you like to learn?"

I wasn't sure what meditation was, but my mom assured me that I'd like it so I willingly agreed to go to this special place.

Anticipation and fear pulsed through my body as we pulled up to a small home in my mom's forest green Volvo station wagon. The old Victorian-style house did look special, and when we walked in the front door I could feel a high level of energy, almost like a vibration.

"This is my daughter, Harmony," my mom said with pride as she introduced me to the teacher. Keeping my gaze down and one arm around my mom's leg, I reached out to shake his hand.

"I'm so happy you're here," the teacher said. "Come with me into this room and I'll give you your mantra."

This lineage of meditation was called transcendental meditation and this teacher was my guru. Although he seemed nice enough, he was a man and I was terrified of him. I didn't have the will or the voice to express that I didn't want to be alone with him, so I bypassed what I was feeling and followed him into his sanctuary.

With many cushions arranged on the floor, the cool room felt peaceful. Sitting down on a cushion that seemed like a safe distance from my guru, I felt my body tighten as he scooched toward me. As he commenced teaching me about meditation, I was relieved that he legitimately seemed to want to teach me meditation.

After he told me my mantra, I closed my eyes and repeated the mantra aloud. He then instructed me to never tell anyone what my mantra was, lest it lose its power.

Being the disciplined Capricorn child that I was, I would sit daily in meditation, even reminding my mom that it was time for my practice. This was just one way that I self-parented. My mom was too distracted to understand that I had even basic needs like a consistent bedtime or healthy food, so she certainly wouldn't bother to track my meditation time.

Every day I would go to my room alone, close my eyes, and repeat my secret mantra.

One day as I was meditating, from the core of my being I heard a deep, resounding voice. The voice sounded masculine and quite unlike my 6-year-old one, but when I heard it I felt comforted, like I was getting reacquainted with an old friend.

"*All of this pain has a purpose,*" the voice stated.

I felt deep relief. Hearing this masculine voice speaking this simple truth gave me reassurance that I didn't even know I needed. As I continued with my meditation, an image of the world appeared in my mind's eye. I saw all of the people of the world as characters in a game. All of these characters had lessons to learn, and they were being moved around in certain directions in order for the player of the game, presumably God, to win. I was being shown how everything we experience is in service of the greater good, even when that experience is painful.

The voice then said, *"You chose this. You agreed to this. This is your path to walk."* In that moment an image of me and my parents came into my awareness. I could see that I had wanted these lessons, that in some way my pain and fear were in service of evolution and goodness to bring healing to the planet.

Since children are new to this dimension, they have access to more spiritual wisdom and wholeness than the adults around them. Being given simple tools to turn toward this deeper aspect of their humanity, children can touch places that most adults crave. However, when the adults in their lives are identified with their bodies, roles, personas, and wounding, children are not nurtured to embody the full range of their humanity. Later in life, their personal development becomes about returning to the place within that was so accessible early in their existence.

Although my mom failed me in many ways, she was in touch with her spirituality and wanted to pass this gift on to me. She was able to embody this part of her with her clients, and they could all see the powerful goddess and magical healer that she was. However, she wasn't able to embody her True Self with me, so all I could see was the unhealthy feminine who had been wounded by the men and women in her life. I saw her pain and anger and collapse. Even so, she pointed me toward my True Self, which gave me an anchor to come back to over the course of my life.

After this experience, I knew that I wanted to be a healer. When my mom's friends or clients would come over to our house, I started noticing dark energy that looked like vaporous muck covering their hearts. I could see their subtle energy, and I wanted to help them move that stored pain out of their bodies.

With my innocent concern for others, at 6 years old I started instructing my mom's friends and clients to lie down on the couch. I would choose a crystal from my collection to place on their sternum, and then I would instruct them to breathe into their heart. After indulging me, they would get up and I could see that there was still energetic pain stored there. This bothered me deeply and I wanted to know how to create a deeper shift.

When our unhealed wounds live in our energetic body, they harden in our energetic system. For those who can see subtle energy, this can look like energetic pollution or darkness in the energetic field. The physical experience of these hardened places can feel like tension in our chest, throat, face, or stomach. It can feel like pain or blocked energy. It can feel like we're leaking energy out the head or sacrum. It can feel like an imbalance from the right and left side. Or it can feel like armor or a shell around the body.

Over time, we become accustom to these hardened energy constructs. We start to identify with them and see the world through the lens of our energetic pollution and old wounds. These hardened places are waiting to melt back into the wholeness of our energetic body. Like a vast ocean, the True Self is inherently whole and soft and fluid. Old wounds are like ice that has hardened in the ocean of our energetic field. The process of healing is about melting these hardened places, cleansing the energetic field of acquired misbeliefs, and bringing the whole system back into a state of balance. From here, we can embody the original state of health, power, and bliss that is our birthright.

THE SAVIOR

I had a recurring dream during this time in my childhood where my entire family was in the back yard of our house.

Our family home in Sacramento was a cute 1940s farm house on a large plot of land. The house was of red brick, with blue-painted wood and a low roof. Laid out in an L, the backyard was large and private. In my dream, a group of bad guys would break in and try to get us. As I ran to the back yard I realized that I had the power to fly away. However, in order for my family to be safe, each person needed to touch me so they could fly with me. I desperately wanted my powers to propel my family into flight. I gave it all I had, and at the end I saved everybody.

Unable to protect me, my parents needed me to rescue them. Even though I also needed to be rescued, I couldn't turn to them for help so I cultivated the power to do it for all of us.

FIREWALKER

My house was busy with excitement as my mom, her new husband, Jim, and her friends and assistants prepared for a workshop to take place in our back yard. Jim was a nerdy man who was eager to please his new wife. He adored my mom, and aside from when he walked around my house naked, Jim didn't bother me.

Our yard was big, with beautiful landscaping, a laughing Buddha statue, water fountains, a greenhouse, and a hot tub. All of this landscaping made our yard very private, and my mom frequently hosted workshops and parties on our property. Sometimes I would be at my dad's when these workshops happened, but when I heard that there was going to be a firewalk at our house I begged to attend. I was 7 years old and I desperately wanted to see people walk on fire.

"You can be here for the firewalk," my mom said to me, "But if you feel afraid, the coals will burn you. So you can only walk across the coals if your mind is free from fear."

Being so young, I wasn't 100% certain that I could suppress and ignore my own fear, but I said what I needed to say to get the clearance to walk on fire.

Nervous with excitement, I watched Jim set up the patch in our yard for the walk. He prepared the coals over the course of several hours, and he put great care into the formation of the patch. I was fascinated and eager to participate, but as all of the people began to arrive I retreated to my bedroom.

I had been playing Barbies in my room for the entirety of the workshop. I could hear the chatter of the workshop participants who filled our living room. Mom came to fetch me when it was time to hear the instructions for walking over the coals.

I listened to the guidelines about taking mindful, even steps. If you ran across the coals, one could get caught in your toe. Also, your mind needed to be clear of fear, for if you were afraid, you would likely get burned. Simple enough.

In the darkness of the summer night, I followed the crowd to our back yard where I had watched the coal patch be prepared earlier that day. All of the adults started chanting "Om," and I could feel the warmth of the burning hot coals on my face. I stood back by my mom, clinging to her leg, as I watched the participants walk barefoot over fire. I stared at the burning embers wondering why people weren't in agony. Jim was on the other side of the coals holding a hose, rinsing each person's feet after they walked to ensure no embers had gotten stuck on their skin.

Hollering with elation and joy when they came across the other side without pain, everyone seemed empowered after their walk. As excitement was building within me, I was certain that if they could overcome their fear, I could also do this successfully.

Right before it was my turn, a woman who had just crossed got burned by an ember stuck in her toe.

"She was afraid," my mom said. "It was her mind that made it happen. If she had trusted the process she wouldn't have gotten hurt."

This was New Age guilt: if she were only more enlightened then she wouldn't have gotten hurt walking over hot coals. "Fear is just False Evidence Appearing Real," my mom taught me and all of the participants at her workshop.

Uncertain about my relationship to my own fear, I wondered how this connected to my terror around men. Was that false evidence appearing real? Or was that intuition, like she had said? In hindsight, I can see that fear is normal. I now understand that all of our emotions are valid, including fear. The thoughts that our emotions ignite are not always valid, but the emotions are. When we loop in a thought pattern that we believe is real, we get pulled off-center and become further away from the core of our being. If we resist the experience of being afraid (or angry, sad, etc.), we disown an essential part of ourselves and cast it out in the shadow, giving it more power.

Welcoming everything we find within us, we are able to attune to our emotional body, honor what our feelings are trying to communicate, and validate the full range of our humanity. Even when there is an immediate threat to our safety needs and the mind becomes hijacked by fear, welcoming the fear gives us mastery to use it for our self-preservation. When fear becomes chronic, it can be challenging to expand our capacity to welcome it. However, the same principle of "welcome everything; push nothing away" applies here.

Emotions are very feminine, and they have been deemed as weak or bad by a society that sees the masculine as superior. Even philosophies of mindfulness and spirituality encourage people to bypass their emotions, saying that if we were truly present we'd be free of this human experience. However, emotions are an important part of our humanity. We have emotions for reason. Anger is the great boundary setter and change maker. Fear allows us to assess our safety and keep us alive. Grief gives us an outlet for loss of love, life, and potential. When we suppress or deny our emotions, they come out in their unhealthy form. Anger becomes rage or depression. Fear becomes chronic anxiety, obsession, or post-traumatic stress. Grief becomes collapse or deep depression. Even joy suppressed becomes mania, and love suppressed becomes obsession.

Having a healthy relationship with our own emotions is important for our mental health. When we are attuned to what we are feeling, we can get curious about what that feeling is asking us for. We can turn toward ourselves, breathe into our emotions, and support them in moving through us to completion. This act, in itself, can stop us from looping in unhealthy mental patterns.

I was 7 years old and about to walk over hot coals. I should have been afraid. I felt totally responsible for being enlightened enough to not be afraid, so I pushed my fear down with all of my might, something I became quite skilled at to my detriment over the years.

Once all of the other participants had gone, my sister went and she made it across without getting burned. In awe of her, I took a deep breath, told myself to just do it, and proceeded across the hot coals.

Everyone cheered. My mom picked me up and hugged me tight, and Jim rinsed my feet off with the hose. I sat down by the light of the moon and examined my feet, totally amazed that I had no burns.

I felt powerful, and I was quite certain I never wanted to do that again. I just wanted to go back to my room and play with Barbies.

Meditate. Overcome fear. Trust my intuition. Move forward with trust.

These were all concepts my mom, in her clumsy and often painful ways, taught me throughout my life. I was encouraged to align with a deeper part of myself, but the neglect and harm that I encountered under her care was never acknowledged or owned. My complex feelings toward my mom were made all the more mystifying by how her clients adored her. I was dependent on her for my life, but her neglectful and self-absorbed way of mothering kept me feeling unworthy. The way she repeatedly told me how amazing I was added another layer to the perplexity of our dynamic. I was constantly trying to find safety in our connection, and so I tried to be what I thought she wanted me to be: easy, accommodating, and quiet.

SCREAMING OUT IN PAIN

Two years after the firewalk, my mom left Jim to be with Kristin. She beamed with joy as she sat in our living room telling her best friend Jane how this was the first time she truly felt loved. Of course, I was mortified and appalled. Now 9 years old, I just wanted a normal life.

Kristin moved in with us and joined our family. As any step-parent would do, she picked us up from school, joked around with us, and came on family vacations. In private I liked her, but I was mortified of being seen in public with her because I didn't want to be outed as having a gay mother.

On a family trip down to Laguna Beach to visit my grandmother, we all got ready to go out to dinner after a long day at the beach. I was excited to wear a new outfit my mom had bought for me at a fancy boutique earlier that day. The outfit was made of stretchy jersey fabric with navy blue and peach stripes. It was the shortest, sexiest skirt I had ever owned, and I thought the matching shirt was especially chic.

I came outside to where my mom and Kristin were sitting on the terrace to get validation of how hip and sophisticated I looked. "What do you think?" I asked.

Without regard to my feelings or my humanity, my mom reached out with her hand, touching my pubic bone, and said while laughing, "Your pussy is showing."

41

Fear jolted through my body, and shame washed over my soul. Deflated and humiliated, I stood there in silence as I started to collapse. Hiding my pain, I went inside and changed my clothes.

I felt like I didn't belong anywhere. I didn't belong in my body, I didn't belong at school, I didn't belong in my family, and I didn't belong on this earth. Desperately wanting to escape my existence, I felt trapped in a nightmare.

And where was my dad? He was off the hook because he wasn't around and because he was financially generous. He was a kind and caring doctor, and when he was present we had an easy relationship. But his womanizing ways had me feeling as much as a victim of him as my mom felt. Watching him give all of his attention to his new wife and son (whom I barely knew at this point), I never felt like I mattered to him. I felt unlovable and unworthy of his attention. And because he wasn't comfortable with emotions, when I spent time with him I tried to be what I thought he wanted. I tried to fit in a tight box of my expression, obsess about my appearance, and quiet my emotional pain in order to have some sort of connection with him.

In some ways I felt orphaned. There was so much that I needed that I wasn't getting. I needed attention, safety, stability, care, concern for my well-being, attunement to my emotions, and room to voice my opinion and truth. But I didn't know how to ask for that, and I didn't even know if I deserved it. So instead, my body started screaming out in pain.

I was in fourth grade when I started getting chronic urinary tract infections (UTIs), a clear physical sign that I was suppressing and holding in my anger. The pain of the UTIs was so intense that I would regularly miss school. I had gained weight; for the first time in my life I was heavier than what was healthy for my frame. I was diagnosed with scoliosis when I was in sixth grade, because my spine had an abnormal curvature. I started feeling strange pains in my joints and I was having a hard time holding a pencil or fork.

My dad diligently worked at trying to help me get better. This was the first time in my entire life that I remember having his undivided attention. I felt his care when I was ill. I knew I was important to him when he worked to get me healthy. Otherwise I felt invisible to him.

Strange illnesses continued to plague me throughout childhood, often times without any diagnosis to help me understand my symptoms. I woke up the last day of sixth grade and couldn't stand. My legs hurt so badly that I just collapsed. I was taken to several specialists, but they could find no cause. Each step I tried caused excruciating pain, so I spent that summer in bed. This happened many times throughout my young life, where I simply couldn't stand on my own two feet or hold a pencil to write. I had chronic headaches and my back was in constant pain.

I felt victimized by my body, blaming it for my pain. But what I couldn't yet see was that this pain was a reflection of my deeper psychological and emotional state that I could neither understand nor give voice to. Stuck within me, unfinished, the experiences of my young life were living inside of me, causing my whole system to stay in a state of illness. I wasn't even aware of the experiences that were affecting me. I wasn't even aware of the thought pattern that I was looping through that kept me stuck in my distortion. And I wasn't even aware that I felt fragmented from my alignment with Source, and that this fractured connection was keeping me in a state of chronic pain.

My inherent health before the events of my life happened came from my alignment with Source. As the vital source of life, the True Self is the energy that animates us all. When we fully embody the True Self, our vitality is strong and life force energy pulsates through our entire system. When we interact with the world from our line of distortion, we keep ourselves small and out of alignment with Source. We behave in ways that aren't life affirming and true to the core of our being from our distortion, and this is a breeding ground for illness and pain.

I was so disconnected from the vital source of life that my body suffered as deeply as my spirit. The aches were real. The pain was real. The infections were real. The curvature in my spine was real. And even though some of my symptoms were caused by physical experiences, they endured and worsened because of my fragmented inner state.

I resisted my pain. I resisted being in a body. Unconsciously I wanted to die or disappear. Not knowing whether my existence mattered, I hid my emotional pain and my needs. Desperately wanting my physical pain to go away, I felt powerless to it and hopeless that I would ever feel okay again. As I resisted my experience of my pain, it continued to worsen. Decidedly, being in a body was to be in pain, and I went into a deep internal collapse around my will to get better.

One day when I was lying in bed, alone and in agony, I had an epiphany. I was staring out my window, longing to be outside and feeling good when I thought to myself, "*I don't want to suffer to get my dad's attention.*"

After this revolutionary thought crossed my mind, I could understand that my body was speaking on my behalf when I wasn't able. Although it took me years to learn how to ask for attention and give voice to my desire, this epiphany was the beginning of my deciding to be well.

The pain we experience (either emotional or physical) matters little in comparison to our relationship to the pain. It's a natural response to resist pain and to contract around the sensation. However, in the resistance to pain we hold it in place. We give our pain power when we contract around it because we're meeting it from our small self.

It's counterintuitive to turn toward our pain with curiosity and compassion. However, this degree of openness and trust in our ability to heal is what it takes to cultivate deep healing. Simply closing our eyes and looking at our pain with curiosity shifts our relationship to it. Welcoming the pain, we can choose to breathe life and love to it. Just as we would for a dear friend who is suffering, we can meet our pain with compassion and unconditional love. This allows our physical, emotional, and energetic bodies to soften. And when we soften in the presence of our pain, we are able to align with Source and bring in more God consciousness, which is the energy needed to integrate and heal.

Learning to honor my body's communication and welcome my physical pain empowered me to stay expansive regardless of what was present within me. With the mindset of curiosity, I learned how to use my inner eye to see my pain and to see the way my body was processing my inner state. Appreciating my body for all that it was holding—and loving the pain with my conscious awareness and breath—I developed an identity with the watcher of the pain, not the pain itself. Empowered with my witness mind, I eventually came back to my wise, expansive self.

Inseparable from our mind and spirit, at its core the body is a messenger for anything off in the entire system. Ignoring or suppressing the body's symptoms with distractions, medications, or surgeries may seem like the best option. However, no matter how much we treat the symptoms, the source of the imbalance is still present.

Physical interventions that are in service of bringing the whole system back to a state of balance are more effective than interventions designed to suppress the symptoms. The combination of mind, body, and spirit healing is in service of deep transformation rather than simple Band-Aids covering up pain. With a gentle nudge, our bodies can heal. Our bodies want to feel good and be free of pain. But until we look at the content of our mind and the state of our emotional and energetic bodies, the physical body will continue to communicate to us in the only way it knows how—by screaming out in pain.

3
LAPSE IN POWER

"Here's to strong women. May we know them; may we raise them; may we be them."—Author Unknown

FAMILY VALUES

I stood in the kitchen of our 1940s cottage-style farmhouse serving myself ice cream. It was a small, outdated kitchen that had brown finishings from the 1970s. With brown tile, outdated cabinets, and drab walls, this sad kitchen reflected the truth that we didn't eat much fresh produce or many home-cooked meals. We had a junk drawer, where I could get unlimited candy. My mom kept it well stocked and at my level for easy access. We had plenty of cereal and chips. And we ate out most nights.

To many people, the food we had in our home seemed fine. This was the late 1980s, before the science of good nutrition and balanced eating had a presence in the media, so there was nothing abnormal about having highly processed food in the house. What was disturbing was the portion sizes and gluttony that abounded in my family.

My mom didn't know how to stop eating when she was full. Watching her shove food into her mouth disturbed me deeply. It seemed as if she was totally disconnected from her body. As she heaved forkful upon spoonful upon handful past her lips, repeatedly, without stopping, bite after bite, I couldn't tell if she was enjoying the food or even if she was aware that she was eating. With the TV on, she seemed totally checked out.

When we're identified with our wounds, we feel a sense of relief when we disconnect from our bodies. Overating, undereating, alcohol, drugs, and so on keep us disembodied. The relief we feel from disconnecting from our experience of our wounds is temporary, and the implications of our actions keep us feeling powerless and hold us in the cycle of pain.

Food, in particular, is a way to try to get nurturance when we a younger part of us feels neglected and lonely. Turning to food for comfort, we temporarily feel nurtured. However, the fleeting nature of the experience keeps us looking to food for nurturing. Subsequently, we keep turning away from the source of our pain, which is the wounding from neglect.

With me having no clue that I was feeling neglected or wanting attention, my mom's habits became my habits. I ate to the point of pain almost daily, and I was becoming excessively overweight. I tried to ignore how ashamed I was of my size, but I thought about it constantly.

As I stood alone in the kitchen, serving myself ice cream, I filled the bowl with a portion size fit for four teenage boys. I was trying to gauge an appropriate portion size while also being driven by my love for ice cream. Even still, as I put each additional scoop into the bowl I thought to myself, "*This is way too much. I should put some back.*"

I wasn't sure if it was okay to put it back after I had served it, so I decided to keep my bowl filled as it was and I walked back to my room to continue watching television by myself.

On the way back to my room, my aunt Dallas, who had been watching TV with my mom in the living room and wore size 0 jeans, saw my bowl and was horrified by the abundance of my sweet treat.

"Harmony! That is way too much ice cream. You should really put some back," Dallas encouraged.

"You're right," I agreed and started back for the kitchen.

"Don't tell her what to do!" my mom snapped. "If she wants to eat that, then she can eat that."

"No, Mom. She's right. It's too much," I admitted.

"No! You served that because you wanted it. You go eat it," my mom demanded.

And so I did. I sat in my room alone, watching TV and eating enough ice cream to satisfy a team of growing boys. The nurturing I was longing for never came through that bowl of ice cream, and I felt lonelier and more depressed than I did before.

It was as if she wanted me to be fat. And I was. The loneliness of my neglect had caught up with me and I consistently turned to food for comfort and nurturing. We were all fat in my house; even my cat, Romeo, was obese. I felt so uncomfortable in my body. I was 12 years old and I wanted to be able to feel free to run and do cartwheels and wear whatever style of clothes I wanted. But I couldn't. I was clumsy in my body and I squeezed into the biggest size of pants that they sold at the Gap.

I was humiliated by my appearance, just as I was humiliated by my mom's appearance. Her belly was so big that I would look at it and think that she could have something growing in there and she wouldn't even know it. I saw it once on Maury Povich, a woman who was obese and had a tumor with teeth and hair growing in her belly and she didn't even know it. That could have easily been my mom. I was scared for her. I was scared for me.

We dieted a lot. At 300 pounds, my mom desperately wanted to lose weight. I was 7 when we went on Jenny Craig, 9 when we went on Nutri System, and 13 when we went on Weight Watchers. I hated the diet food these weight loss plans sold, so I would starve myself and lose weight quickly. Once we got off the diet, slowly my weight would come back. Vacillating between gluttony and starvation caused me to develop an unhealthy relationship to food and my body.

Even though my mom wanted to be thin, she was also afraid to simply be. Because of her abuse and trauma history, she didn't feel safe in her body, which had me feeling unsafe in mine. Some part of her wanted me to be obese too, so that my large body would make me unattractive to potential pedophiles. Of course this was unconscious, but I asked her about it when I was in my twenties and she admitted to thinking that if I was overweight, then I would be protected from men. Unwanted and unpursued.

While her fear of men was passed on to me, I was also taught that it was important that men were attracted to me. Even though she had a lesbian lover and was obese, my mom thrived on attention from men. She wore low-cut tops that showed her cleavage. Her style was eccentric and glamourous, and her blonde curly hair was radiant. She had a powerful glow about her that everyone seemed to be attracted to.

When I was 13, I started high school. With my December birthday and easy personality, my mom had enrolled me in kindergarten at the age of 4. I always felt behind and unintelligent, like I was out of my league. This really hit me in high school when I was the youngest one in my class with the most mature appearance. Having started my menstrual cycle so early, I was fully developed and looked like I was 17 when I entered my freshman year.

We had just had a summer of Weight Watchers, so I was slim and ready to be socially accepted. My social status was the most important aspect of my education to my mom. My dad understood the value of an education, but I saw him so infrequently that his influence didn't make its way into my schooling. My mom would buy me clothes, put me on diets, and ask me about who I hung out with. She never asked me about my assignments and what I was learning or even about how I was feeling.

It seemed really important to her that boys in my class be interested in me, but the attention I got was from older boys. Even though I was attracted to the shy boys my age, 17- and 18-year-old boys seemed to have the confidence to pursue me, and I looked old enough for them.

I was growing up fast, so fast, in fact, that I couldn't keep up with all of the sexual advances and offers of drugs.

The first time I smoked pot, it was the second month of my freshman year. My friend Amy brought it to school because she had recently gotten high for the first time and wanted to share the experience with me. After school, we gathered in a park by my house with some older boys, and I acted as if I had done it before. I had seen people smoke throughout my entire life, and I had numerous contact highs before (even eating a pot brownie when I was 6!), so the actual smoking part didn't seem like a big deal. We found a wall to hide behind and I was given the pipe first, to show the others how to do it. Even though Amy had smoked before, my friends all looked to me as the one in the know, and I willingly played into that role.

I took a hit off of the wooden pipe. It tasted disgusting, and I passed it to Dave. After a couple of rounds, we were all laughing so hard. It was as if there were no walls between us. No boxes for us to fit into. We could just be goofy and say stupid things that we'd otherwise censor.

Part of me was scared of getting in trouble, but my parents didn't condemn marijuana. "Don't be an alkie," my mom said to me once, encouraging me not to drink too much. But when I told my sister that I had smoked, she invited me to get stoned with her, my mom, and my grandma.

My sister was a senior in high school when I was a freshman. It was her seventeenth birthday and we were getting ready to go see the musical "Les Misérables." I had on a black cashmere shoulder-baring sweater and tight jeans. My frame was bigger than most girls, which caused me to feel insecure. But in this moment I was fairly lean and was admiring my curvy body and sexy outfit in the mirror when Grace came in to invite me to puff with them. I was nervous. I thought I should be getting in trouble. In reality, I should have been getting in trouble for being 13 and smoking weed in the park with my friends. But instead of being offered a lesson in responsibility and brain functioning, my mom gleamed with pride as she watched me take a hit from her bong. I had never seen her proud like this before. I knew instantly that she felt connected to me in this moment.

This was the beginning of me smoking in the house daily, before and after school, which lasted for the entirety of my high school career. I was disassociated from my body and disconnected from reality on a regular basis. This disassociation may have seemed cool and fun at the time, but that was only because I couldn't see that what I really needed was to get embodied. I needed to feel and move and experience my body. I needed to attune to myself and explore the range of my humanness. However, my capacity for such exploration was low and disassociating was a welcome break from my chronic emotional and physical pain.

I had no real motivation for anything other than smoking weed and hanging out with my friends. And the sad thing was that this is what I was lauded for. My dad also supported my pot use, and smoking became a family affair. Although he was more discreet about it than my mom, he was also an old hippie and thought marijuana was harmless. I was going along with the family values and simultaneously stunting my own emotional and cognitive development.

In each moment, we're either turning toward the light of awareness or turning away from it. In an attempt to turn down the noise of our conditioned mind, we turn away from ourselves and ignore our deeper experience. Alcohol, drugs, nicotine, medication, food, social media, television, porn, and so on, are attempts to suppress our pain, which in turn suppresses our light. We can't pick and choose what we suppress.

Disassociation and suppression create a lack of continuity between our thoughts, surroundings, actions, identity, and memories. In many ways we're all culturally encouraged to disassociate and turn away from our light of awareness. People make money off of our reliance on such unhealthy diversions. However, when we indulge these behaviors, we never fully embody the essence of who we are. Our baseline becomes our distortion and dissociation, which then has us further away from accessing the light of conscious awareness that we long to connect with.

LOST INNOCENCE

At 14, I was checked out by being stoned every day; I was insecure about my body because a part of me always felt fat even when I wasn't; I didn't have a voice because I suppressed it for acceptance; I was curvy and mature looking because I had started my period so early; and I desperately wanted to feel loved. Clearly, I was ready to start dating!

I had a large group of friends, many of whom were boys and many of whom had made sexual advances toward me. Just like no one had talked to me about not doing drugs, no one had talked to me about sex in any sort of appropriate way. My mom was a very sexual woman who talked openly about her sexuality. There was a sexual energy in our house all of the time. Aside from her lovers and wild parties, we had the famous books *Where Did I Come From?* and *The Joy of Sex* on our coffee table for viewing pleasure. And although my dad was more conservative, I sensed his womanizing and addiction to porn.

In spite of all of this, no one actually talked to me about sex. How old should I be to consider having sex? What about consent? Pleasure? Safety? None of this was in my field of awareness.

The summer going into my sophomore year, I was at the park one evening with my best friend, Mark, and a bunch of his friends. We had been smoking pot, and there was an older boy there, Joe, who was 22. When Joe started to pay attention to me I was excited and surprised. He was so handsome, and I couldn't believe he was interested in me.

As we all sat around the picnic table in the dark, Joe sat close to me and touched my leg. I felt worthy in the presence of his attention, like I was enough for a man to desire.

At the end of the night, Joe offered to give me a ride home. Mark seemed tense and concerned, as he and I had an unspoken crush on each other. It was only a matter of time until we'd become high school sweethearts.

I got in Joe's black Jetta, and I felt so grown up for a 14-year-old.

When we arrived at my house, Joe asked if he could come in. I didn't know if I wanted him to come in or not. I wasn't practiced in knowing what I needed or wanted, but clearly, he wanted to come in. And I desperately wanted to feel worthy and loved, so I said "Sure."

It was late. My mom was already asleep. I never had a curfew or any rules about riding in cars with boys. So I didn't think that what I was doing was dangerous in any way. It didn't even occur to me that Joe had an agenda.

Our house was long, with many additions. And in the farthest end of the house my mom had a large space with its own entrance that she used as a home office. I didn't want to wake my mom, so I took Joe back there.

We walked in and I turned on all the lights.

I felt tense and nervous. I didn't know what was going to happen.

Joe looked at me with his piercing eyes. He grabbed me and started kissing me. Fear surged through my body. I had kissed other boys before, and several 18-year-old boys had tried to get me to have sex with them before, but Joe wasn't a boy. He was a man and he was confident and well versed in taking a woman. But I wasn't a woman. I was a girl, and he was going to have his way with me.

I was surprised by the intense energy coming from him. It all happened so fast and I didn't know that I could stop him. I didn't know that I had agreed to this. I wanted him to stop and leave but I didn't know that I could even say "No." So instead, I deferred to him and followed his lead.

He laid me down on the carpet.

I was terrified.

He took my pants off.

My body contracted in fear.

I was so scared. So confused. Was this happening?

He asked me if I had ever had sex before. I lied. I wanted him to think I knew what I was doing. I wanted to be seen as a woman. I didn't want him to not have sex with me. I thought my inexperience made me unworthy of him, even though the truth was I had never had sex and I wasn't even sure that I wanted this.

Without a condom and without regard for my pleasure, Joe put his penis inside of me and started penetrating me fiercely. I burned and felt split in two. My heart broke every time he pushed himself into me. But I took it. I didn't let on how much I wanted him to stop. I tried to act like I knew what I was doing and that I liked what he was doing. Wasn't that my job here? To give him what he wanted?

When he pulled out and came on my stomach there was blood on his penis.

"I thought you weren't a virgin," he frowned.

"I must have started my period," I blurted.

But this blood was different. It wasn't period blood. It was the blood of lost innocence and purity. This blood was spilled without any care to the child lost that night. This blood shattered my heart. But I didn't let on. No way. I didn't want anyone to know about my pain. Ever. I was really good at that, so that's what I did. I hid my pain and pretended like it was fun. Even when bruises started to appear on my inner thighs from how rough he had been with me, I laughed it off like it was nothing.

I didn't know until decades later how this fear lived in me. My body would freeze every time a man wanted to have sex with me, but I got so skilled at bypassing my fear that I didn't even recognize it. I didn't know that this was an important and valid part of my experience that I should honor.

A few days later my friends and I were at an outdoor rave that took place during the day at a water park. We were high on ecstasy when I told them that I had had sex with Joe.

"Oh my God! You need to go get an AIDS test," one of my friends warned.

"What if I get pregnant?" I sobbed.

"We're here for you," they all assured me.

As an adult, Joe was totally responsible for his shadowy sexuality and every action he took with me. If he were in his healthy masculine expression, he would have never violated me in the ways that he did. Similarly, had I been in my healthy feminine expression, I would have never abandoned myself in his presence. By following the impulse of my conditioned self I subversively made myself the victim of my own sexuality. I was shaped for self-abandonment, and my shadow colluded with his.

This is the cost of self-betrayal. We feel victimized by others when we collapse around our will. Empowered with conscious choice, we have agency over our decisions and actions. We can honor ourselves, our desires, and our dignity when we stay true to ourselves. Learning to give voice to our truest truth and knowing that our truth is important gives our relationships the opportunity to be healthy. It's so easy to see someone else's unkind behavior and wonder why they would treat us harshly. It's another thing to see all of the ways we enable that behavior by being unkind to ourselves and disregarding our own truth.

Given my level of development and identification with my wounds, I didn't have the capacity to say "No" and set a boundary. I didn't have the capability of holding myself in the complexity of this experience. It would have been wonderful if Joe had been a healthy masculine for me to practice being empowered with, but I couldn't even see the ways I had disempowered myself.

Eventually I told Grace about Joe because I wanted to know more about my risk of pregnancy and disease. My sister was concerned for me, so she told our mom.

When my mom walked in my room just one week after I had sex with Joe, I didn't know she knew. When she sat on my bed, I hadn't a clue what she wanted to talk with me about. Her voice was calm and her demeanor was seductive, almost like she was trying to be cool.

"What did it feel like to have sex with someone you're not in love with?" she asked.

If I had been mature enough to know I had been raped, I would have been indignant. But that was her job. She was supposed to protect me and tell me that I had been violated by an older man. But as she sat there she didn't seem mad, and she clearly wasn't disciplining me. I assumed she was proud of me, like she had been when she found out I was getting stoned.

Women have been fed confusing lies about sex and femininity for centuries: "Be sexy but don't be easy." "Please your man so he doesn't stray." "The male orgasm is more important." "The female orgasm is complicated." "The purpose of the female body is to attract a man." "Have sex with your man even if you don't want to so his needs are met." "Be naughty and seductive so he'll want you." "Let him be rough with you so he feels in control." And somewhere in there, very subversively, we have been taught that we don't matter. That our "No" doesn't matter, that our pleasure doesn't matter, and that our desire doesn't matter.

To feel deeply honored as sexual beings, we need to feel safe to receive a man. Receptivity is the quality of the female genitalia, and women feel available to receive in the presence of man who is a protector of boundaries, not a violator. The dignity of our receptivity is taken from us when men insert themselves into us without our consent, pleasure, or desire being considered. Whether sexually, emotionally, professionally, or domestically, when a man asserts himself over a woman it can be traumatizing, even if we've never been sexually assaulted. This dynamic calls on the feminine to become ever clearer with our power and our voice, never betraying ourselves to get connection.

After my mom asked me about my first sexual experience, I felt even dirtier and more shame-filled than I had after Joe raped me. I was offended and wanted to squirm away and hide from her. Then I felt awful and was annoyed by her lack of concern for me. I wanted to surrender into her arms and weep, but she wasn't a safe person for me to do that with. I couldn't believe that this was the best she could come up with when she found out that her 14-year-old daughter had sex with a 22-year-old man. I couldn't even dignify this absurd question with an answer, so I got up and walked away.

She couldn't teach me about healthy sexuality because she was still too entangled and identified with her own sexual wounding. She believed the painful stories about her body and sexuality that she had learned from being victimized, and I think it pained her that she was passing them down to me. I believe that, deep down, she wanted me to feel empowered in my sexuality, just like she wanted to feel empowered in hers. But she failed me when I needed her most, and this was one more time I felt completely abandoned by her.

After I stormed out of the room, we never spoke of it again. That was it. Nothing else. Nothing about statutory rape. Nothing about condoms. Nothing about whether I felt like I was ready for sex at 14. Nothing about my own pleasure or agency in the decision.

Had I felt that she cared about my sadness, had I felt safe talking with her, I would have told her that I was traumatized. That it was painful and he was rough with me and I wish I had never done it. I would have told her that my heart hurt and I lost an important part of myself that night and I was afraid I would never get it back. I would have told her that I did it to feel loved because I believed I was totally unlovable. But that I felt even less loved and less lovable than before, that I felt broken.

We all experience varying degrees of trauma in our lives, and when we're unable to fully move through the experience to completion it gets stuck in our psychological, emotional, physical, and energetic bodies as unfinished business. On the continuum of trauma, sexual assault is a high degree of shock to the entire system and can leave us feeling broken and wounded. All trauma has us feel split from our alignment with Source, and the way we organize ourselves around the fragmentation becomes our patterned way of engaging with the world. Differentiating from this pattern and realigning with Source, we're able to heal and embody the part of us that is untouched by these painful experiences and stand solid in our wholeness.

SEARCHING FOR LOVE

Unable to acknowledge to myself that I had been raped and having no one around me affirming the distortion of this sexual experience, I couldn't put words to my own pain around what had happened. Driven by shame, I presented a face to the world as if I were okay. I hid my suffering behind a mask of happiness.

Joe knocked on my bedroom window in the middle of the night a few times, trying to get me to let him in. I hung out with him on a couple of occasions, but I never had sex with him again. I didn't tell him how badly he hurt me, but I put up an energetic wall when I was with him. Afraid to actually say "No," I misled him with a confusing "Yes, maybe." Unable to give voice to the boundary that I wanted, I played a game in order to feel a sense of safety and power.

I desperately wanted someone to validate my existence. I was searching for evidence of my worth and value, trying to find that from boys. But I didn't feel safe wanting anybody. I had been in love with Mark since I began high school, but I didn't express this desire because I was deathly afraid of rejection.

Mark was disappointed when he found out that I had sex with Joe. When I told him, he dropped his gaze and didn't respond. I could tell he was sad, and I felt even worse for hurting my best friend. I believed Mark would never love me after this, so a few months later I had sex with two of our other mutual friends, John and Sean.

Once sophomore year began, I had more freedom because many of my friends could drive. We'd sneak out and go to raves, dancing all night high on ecstasy. While dancing, I would make out with strangers—or rather they would kiss me and grope me while my eyes were closed and I never stopped them. I never even bothered to find out their names. I'd go to Grateful Dead shows and take mushrooms and acid all weekend. My mom was a Deadhead, too, so she was at the shows with her friends and sometimes we'd see one another. I also smoked pot daily, before, during and after school, which my mom didn't seem to mind.

One week after I turned 16, a big group of my friends and I were getting ready for a New Year's Eve party at our friend Phillip's house. The plan was to drop acid and spend the night there, but on the way we decided to caravan to my house to pick up some weed. Three Volkswagen buses pulled up to my house with fifteen of my closest friends. Eager to start the party, we all decided to drop acid at my house so that we would already be feeling it by the time we got to Phil's, which was a twenty-minute drive.

Before we left my house, the LSD started kicking in and we knew we weren't going to make it to the party. My sister was at our house getting ready to go out dancing and she suggested that we hang out in her room, which was a large, attached apartment in the back of our house. I felt her care and appreciated her opening her room to a large group of us. In my psychedelic haze I decided to write my mom a note telling her that we were in Grace's room and we'd see her in the morning, hoping she would leave us alone.

Right when my mom got home from dinner she came back to the apartment and called me to the kitchen.

"Harmony, what's going on?" she said with suspicion.

"We're high," I replied, fidgety with fear.

"What does that mean? High on what?" she asked.

"Trippin'. On acid," I said, scared of her reply.

"Everyone back there is high on acid?" she asked.

"Yes, we were going to go to Phil's but it kicked in too quickly," I explained.

"Okay, let's go back there. I need everyone's keys. No one is driving tonight," she said.

I followed my mom down the long hallway to the apartment, and I was stunned as I watched her collect the keys from all of my friends.

"You all are spending the night here," she declared. "Have fun. Be safe. Let me know if you need anything."

She then proceeded to give all of us Rescue Remedy, which is a flower essence for shock. She said that it would help us stay grounded and embodied.

I was in awe. My friends were elated. We had total permission to be in our trip in a safe home base. And considering that this was the most potent LSD I had ever experienced, I needed the space to go into it fully.

Mark and I were super cuddly all night, rarely leaving each other's side. After soaking in the hot tub, we lay outside under the stars on the cold winter night, holding each other fiercely. He cried. I cried. We snuggled up and it seemed like our love was growing in the most beautiful way. As we lay there, I hoped with all my heart that I would be enough for him, but I couldn't understand why he didn't kiss me.

The next morning, after an intense night of hallucinations for all of us, my mom invited us to the dining room for breakfast. When we walked into the dining room, the table was covered with nourishing food. Eggs, toast, fruit, potatoes, orange juice, and so much more. All fifteen of us crammed around the table and feasted on this glorious breakfast.

"So," my mom said out of nowhere, "Who's going to call your parents and tell them about last night, you or me?"

We all looked around at each other in complete shock. We thought she was totally cool with all of this, but apparently she was mad that her New Year's Eve plans had been thwarted by a group of teenagers on acid. Many of my friends cried, some knew their parents wouldn't care, but one by one they all made the call. In some cases my mom was sitting right there next to them, and in other cases my mom was the one explaining to the parent what had happened.

When everybody left, my mom told me that I was grounded from my new car for a month. I had just gotten a new convertible Geo Tracker for my birthday, so I was devastated.

The only exceptions to my restriction of my car was driving to school, running errands for my mom, or seeing Mark. This didn't really feel like a punishment to me, especially given what I had done. Instead of hanging out with my larger group of friends, I now spent all of my free time with Mark.

The following week, Mark and I were sitting in my car parked in front of his house, listening to "Sugar Magnolia" by the Grateful Dead.

"I want to kiss you," he said before moving in for the long-awaited first kiss. I had wanted this moment for over two years, and now it was happening.

Under the guise of "best friends," Mark and I had been snuggling and kissing each other on the cheek whenever we hung out. We saw each other daily, and our affection felt natural and easy. In this moment, as Mark moved in to kiss me, my heart opened. It was the first time I felt loved by a man, and I loved him, too.

We all long for deep intimacy yet the vulnerability it takes to cultivate it can seem insurmountable. To speak our truth in such a way that leaves us open to rejection or humiliation is a courageous act of dignity and self-love. Disowning our desires may protect us from rejection, but it leaves us feeling insignificant, powerless, and alone. The invigorating feeling that comes from being in total integrity with our truth lights us up in a way that nothing else can.

"I want us to be together," Mark courageously professed. "I want to be your boyfriend."

"That's all I've ever wanted," I smiled as I moved in for another sweet kiss.

After we made out, Mark looked at me with a sparkle in his eye and started bopping to the music with excitement. We said goodnight and then Mark ran over to his neighbor's house to tell his childhood friend, Matt, we were finally together. They whooped with excitement and I giggled from my car.

"I love you!" Mark screamed from Matt's house.

"I love you!" I screamed back from my car.

I was floating on a cloud as I drove home that night. Everything felt right in the world. We were finally together. I felt worthy and less broken having this relationship. Even though boys pursued me daily, I never thought I would have the boy that I wanted. Having him want me, too, gave me the validation that I had been craving. Without him, I felt worthless. With him, I felt like I mattered and like I belonged.

Now that I had my very first boyfriend, I felt more comfortable letting my friends know that my mom was gay. My mom had a new girlfriend, Tracy, who I wasn't that fond of. But Mark and Tracy would smoke cigarettes together in my backyard and we all smoked pot together. Somehow, my mom being gay became cool, even, and many of my high school friends who were gay came out to her. They all considered her a life saver during their own confusion and search for courage.

Mark and I were a good couple. Everybody seemed to think so. Two hippies who shared a passion for classic rock, good weed, and parties with friends, we were made for each other. We both had long hair; mine, thick and blonde, passed my waist and his, wavy and brown, below his shoulders. We went to endless concerts together; we would hang out at the river and swim and inner tube; we would play football in the park with friends; we'd host parties together at my house; and we'd camp by the beach in Bodega Bay. We smoked a lot of pot, took some psychedelics, and had a lot of sex.

Everywhere we went we would make love. We were young and in love, so we needed to get creative about where we could be together. In my car, at the bank of the river, or in our rooms with our parents home, we wanted to be as close as possible as often as possible. Sometimes we got caught by the police or security guard or even our own parents, but those were only temporary inconveniences.

We cared deeply about each other, so for the first time in my life sex was a wonderful exploration of mutual respect, pleasure, and love.

One day, quite by accident, I had my very first orgasm. Mark was sitting in a chair and I was on top of him. While we were making love, my clitoris rubbed against him in such a way that I experienced deep pleasure for the first time in my entire life. As I climaxed, everything seemed surreal. The world seemed to moving faster and slower at the same time, and I was more in my body but out of my body than I had ever been. I was completely surprised by the intensity of this experience that seemed to last ten minutes or more.

I had no idea that this was possible. My sister had given me a vibrator for my thirteenth birthday that I tried to use once but couldn't figure out. I knew something was supposed to feel good about my clitoris, but I didn't spend much time exploring my own genitalia.

Mark and I were both utterly blown away by this experience. From that day forward, we went on a mission to figure out how this happy accident had occurred so we could make sure it happened again.

Considering that I had had sex with three of his friends before we got together, Mark was insecure about our relationship. Just like my mom, in a deep unconscious way, Mark wanted to find a way to keep other men away from me. Aside from spending all of our time together, Mark would encourage me to eat past the point of satisfaction.

"I'm full," I said as we finished our macaroni and cheese.

"You don't need to be hungry to eat ice cream," he replied while feeding me a spoonful.

It was in this relationship that I really started to gain weight to the point of verging on obesity. Before this I had been chubby alternating with average weight, depending on where I was in the cycle of yo-yo diets. But now my body grew to the point where shopping for clothes was not easy.

But still, there was something about Mark and me that people loved. Our parents loved us together as did our peers. We were portrayed as "El Camino High School's Jim and Pamela Morrison" at a rally during our senior year, and there was an 8×10 picture of us hugging in our yearbook as the page introducing the seniors. We weren't in the popular crowd or the high-achieving crowd or the athletic crowd—we were hippies. And everyone loved us as a couple. It was as if my significance came from this relationship. I needed his love to be okay in the world. And I would have done anything for him, even sabotage my own body.

My grades in high school were so low that I was afraid that I wouldn't graduate. No one had ever asked me about my school work, and I got by doing as little as possible. I also was never asked about what I wanted to do after graduation, so I never took the SAT or toured colleges or thought about working.

I somehow managed to get my grades to a place where I could walk at graduation, and Mark and I decided to walk together, hand in hand.

After we graduated high school, we started attending the community college together. A few weeks into our first semester, Mark started acting strangely, staying up all night and sleeping all day. He was restless and fidgety when he was awake, and when he slept he was out to the world, unmovable. He seemed to stop wanting to spend time with me, and when I asked, he denied that anything had changed.

We started growing apart, and I was puzzled and sad. I tried to be okay with everything, hoping that our love would last. I would talk to him about how he seemed different, and he would promise that he would be around more. But every time we hung out, he would pass out and sleep for hours.

Eventually, I couldn't take the pain of being neglected in our connection, and after three and a half years of being together I broke up with him. The pain was unbearable, but I ignored my own heartbreak and started spending time with other boys. I misused my sexuality while partying, and I had many threesomes and orgies to escape my own heartbreak. The love of my life wasn't by my side anymore, and I felt lost and lonely without him. In turn, I went to something that I thought would soothe my pain—or at least distract me from it.

When Mark found out about my sexual escapades, he was heartbroken. In his pain he finally admitted that he had been using meth. While I looked in his eyes as he told me, he seemed vacant and dark, unlike the boy I fell in love with. We tried to get back together, and we went to Narcotics Anonymous together to try to get him clean. I stopped smoking pot to support him, but he didn't take his sobriety seriously. After a few months of trying to clean up, we eventually broke up for good. Still entangled in a mutual friend group, it was painful to see him with other women so eventually I split up from my friends, too.

Lonely, without my best friend or our friend group, I felt totally and completely lost. I had no drive for a career and I had no propensity for the academic world. I thought that no one would ever love me again. At fifty-five pounds overweight, I had low self-esteem and I became depressed. Marijuana was the only constant companion I had, so I smoked all day every day. Worthless and hopeless, I always had pot to keep me company.

When we think our validation comes from our romantic relationship, we engage in a variety of contortions to try to keep that relationship intact. Ignoring our own pain and desire, we leave ourselves to try to keep connection, yet no connection is fulfilling from this place. There are certain relational skills necessary to have healthy relationships, and so few of us are taught how to show up for intimacy with the level of skill needed to have a clean and clear connection. Revealing our truth, staying curious about our partner's subjective truth, and doing the dance of connection with autonomy takes practice and skill.

Once we're able to recognize the deep truth that our relationships are not here to make us happy or whole, we can begin to see that anything off in our relationships is a reflection of our own shadow and disowned parts. Every relationship we have is designed to help us see ourselves more clearly, integrate, and nudge us to grow. Cultivating the deep level of self-awareness required for a mutually empowering, healthy relationship, we can become available to the level of connection that we long for.

4
SELF-LOATHING

"You yourself, as much as anybody in the entire universe, deserve your love and affection."—Buddha

DESPERATE FOR LOVE

There were two junior colleges in town. One was located in the suburbs of Sacramento and the other in the more diverse midtown area. Since Mark went to the one in the suburbs, I went to the one in midtown. To prepare myself for the experience of not knowing anybody at school, I went on the Atkins diet, working hard to lose weight.

Far from all of my old high school friends, I entered a cultural milieu that was equally intimidating and exciting. The varied styles evident on this midtown campus opened my mind to the beauty of different self-expression, ancestry, and walks of life. Even with the wild parties, San Francisco excursions, and unconventional lifestyle in my upbringing, I was still fairly sheltered from diversity.

I had never learned to be a good student during high school, and I had never developed a good work ethic. Since my dad showed his love through money, I was fairly entitled and never considered the idea of needing to take care of myself. Vacations to Hawaii, high-end clothes, a nice house, and a convertible car on my sixteenth birthday had me unconsciously thinking that I'd always be taken care of.

I still lived at home for junior college, so this was my first entry point into "real life" where people struggle to earn their way into a life that they want to create. I could see how my relationship to money was very different from the population here, and that jolted my naiveté. With all of the emotional and physical neglect in my life, I had always had more than enough material comfort. Money was never a point of need in my life. Here, on the other hand, money seemed to be the thing driving people to make their life livable.

I was sitting in a political science class during my first semester, and I noticed a classmate looking at me with interest. He was two seats ahead of me and one aisle over. He had light brown skin, big red curly hair, and seductive brown eyes. I had never seen a black man with red hair before, and he seemed very comfortable with his exotic look, which surprised me since I didn't find him attractive.

"I like your boots," he mouthed to me during class.

"*Why is he complimenting my footwear?*" I thought to myself. "*He must be gay.*"

I looked down at my boots and smiled back, as if to say "*Thank you.*"

No longer a hippie, I was wearing a black velvet button-front shirt, tight jeans, and black boots. My thick blonde hair was shoulder length and it was styled with a 1950s flip. When I looked in the mirror I thought I looked great. I wore size 10 pants, which was a healthy size for my frame. But I wanted to lose more weight because I still thought of myself as obese. Even though I could see in the mirror that I was attractive, when I walked away from my reflection my mind held a constant stream of thoughts telling me that I was too fat to be loved. I felt like I weighed 300 pounds and that I would never be worthy of sexual attraction.

Listening to the boring lecture on politics, I was distracted by this intriguing new man slipping me a note. It read, "Hi. I'm Troy. Can I have your number?" I wasn't even sure if I wanted to give it to him because I wasn't attracted to him. But since he was interested, I saw no harm in sharing it with him.

When Troy called me the next day, I was elated. Someone was interested in me! I felt great excitement and relief that my worth was being validated by a near stranger. I wasn't even sure if I was interested in him, but that didn't matter to me one bit because I didn't even know that this was a question to ponder.

When Troy invited me over to his apartment, I eagerly hopped in my car and drove to the ghetto.

Troy was 25 and had two kids from a previous relationship. He lived in a one-bedroom apartment that felt uninhabitable to me. Really, no one, especially children, should have been living there.

Housed behind a small home where his children lived with their mother, Troy's small apartment seemed to have been built by someone who didn't understand construction. Rickety and unfinished, the building should have been condemned. Surprisingly, Troy seemed proud of where he lived.

"I have bunk beds for my boys in here," Troy said, showing me how his kids' beds were in his one and only bedroom.

I tried not to be judgmental. I tried to be okay with the squalor. But internally I was horrified. I tried to appear relaxed about everything as I sat on his couch.

Troy sat next to me, looking at me with a huge smile. He seemed happy to have me as his guest, and his large, brown piercing eyes were telling me he wanted me.

"Can I kiss you?" he asked.

I felt the familiar discomfort in my body of wanting to say "No" but bypassing that desire. Since he wanted me, I decided to defer to his desire.

I looked at him seductively as he moved closer. The kiss quickly turned into him on top of me. Making out like crazy, he invited me to his bedroom. We took our clothes off, and he put a condom on. I was relieved that I didn't have to ask him about protection, because I wouldn't have had the courage or dignity to make the request.

"What are you doing to me?" I asked while he moved me around in several uncomfortable positions. He was being rough with me and I wasn't enjoying myself. However, I wasn't sure how to ask for what I was wanting.

"I'm trying to show you the moves I've got," he replied with a smile, as if he were proud of himself.

I had very little pleasure from this sexual encounter, and in hindsight this might have been a good time to end whatever it was that was happening between us and count my losses. But after jumping into bed with Troy, I jumped right into a relationship with him.

I tried to be okay with his dilapidated apartment and aggressive sex. I would have put up with anything to have something that remotely felt like love, and so I did.

Whenever we take action that feels out of alignment with the core of our being, we can always feel it and recognize that it's happening. However, when we are identified with our conditioned self, it's easy to follow the impulse of the familiar action to try to find safety. Although painful and disempowering, the instincts of the conditioned self are habitual. We know how to do the conditioned thing, and trying something new takes tremendous awareness and courage.

Troy was a deeply emotional and feminine man who had been raised in a tough neighborhood. With his eccentric looks and love of art, Troy had a rough childhood where he was bullied by gang members. His dad was a harsh man who was a descendant of slaves, and his mom was a red-headed Irish woman who suffered from bipolar disorder and post-traumatic stress from a lifetime of abuse.

Troy had four siblings and had grown up in a motel where prostitutes worked. He stayed connected to his soft side through drawing and art, but his art was always sexual and perverse. He had volumes of drawings he had made where naked men dominated naked women. I recoiled at these drawings but quickly bypassed any concern by pretending not to notice the thematic elements and only commenting on his skill. He had talent.

I plunged right into Troy's life and tried to help out the best I could. When he had his kids I would care for them as if they were my own; when Troy had no money I would buy them food; and when Troy wanted to have sex I would participate in any number of deviant sexual acts to please him. Many nights I would wake up to him having sex with me in the middle of the night. He would hold me tight and tell me he just needed to feel closer to me. He forced himself onto me while he penetrated me hard, and I was in a fog of sleep that I didn't even think to tell him to stop. I didn't even know this was rape.

I was so desperate for love and felt so undeserving of a safe lover that when he asked me to have sex with his friends it seemed like no big deal. No stranger to group sex, I had participated in threesomes before and I had started an orgy with several of my friends after high school. I had already given my body over to Troy without regard to my needs or desires, so I was perfectly capable of doing that with his friends, too.

"We'll ravish you," Troy convinced me. "You'll feel so desired and we'll all be making sure you come."

But that's not what happened. I would lay in his bed and Troy would sit across the room and watch me navigate five black cocks. I pretended to like it, because that's what I thought I was supposed to do. Some of the experiences were pleasurable, but my action was coming from deep self-loathing and microscopic self-esteem. I performed for them all and bypassed my fear and insecurities, objectifying myself and pretending that I liked being objectified.

Once Troy was sufficiently turned on, he would tell them to get out of his way and he would have me for himself. I was his sex slave, and I'm certain this wasn't the first lifetime I was his object of use in this way. Many years later I had a past life memory of Troy being my master and I his black slave. In this life, I was born the entitled one, yet the same pattern of oppression was karmically played out.

Karmic relationships can be painful, but they are here to teach us something important about ourselves. The pattern is replaying itself so that we can transcend the old way. Learning to stay in alignment with Source, we're given the opportunity to stay solid in ourselves even in the presence of ancient trauma. The universe conspires to help us learn these important lessons so that we can heal and feel empowered. Sometimes the work is simply about getting through the experience— we don't need to anything enlightened or brilliant other than survive the experience. Other times, the work is about doing the different, truer thing in each moment. Either way, the experience is not here merely to cause us suffering. Empowered with conscious awareness, the experience is here to illuminate the wounds that have been driving us so we no longer identify with them.

TRAPPED BY MY OWN FEAR

When I met Troy, I had my own apartment attached to my mom's house—the same one my sister used to live in. In order to isolate me and have me for his own, Troy convinced me to get my own apartment. He didn't want my mom coming between us. She didn't like Troy, and he didn't want her influencing our relationship.

Alone in my apartment, Troy's anger became more explosive. I was terrified of him. Our dynamic reminded me of my relationship with my sister, where I tried to please him and be perfect for him, and I believed his blame and criticism when he told me that everything was my fault. And similar as with my sister, I felt confused by the conflicting emotions of loving him and fearing him. I wanted him to be happy, and I felt wholly responsible for his state of being.

My sense of self and sense of worth came from what he was feeling. If he was happy and turned on by me, I was good. If he was upset and dissatisfied with me, I was bad. Orienting toward him, I wasn't anchored in myself enough to notice how I felt, what I wanted, or what my state of being was as a separate individual from him.

Every time that I tried to end this volatile relationship, Troy would vigilantly stalk me. I would be sitting in class listening to a lecture, and when I glanced at the window I would see him staring at me with longing in his eyes. I would be walking across campus, and I'd catch him staring at me from across the quad. I would be driving down the street and glance in my rearview mirror, frightened when I'd see him following me in his car. Sleeping in bed, he would knock on my window. He would leave signs of his presence randomly on my doorstep, like a Q-Tip or condom. I felt scared and powerless against him. So each and every time, I would let him back in and give him what he wanted.

Lost and deflated, I turned to Jane, my mom's business partner and best friend. I had taken some workshops with my mom and her, and she had given me a couple breathing sessions over the years. When I told her how badly I was suffering and I described my sexual relationship with Troy, Jane was horrified.

"Are you going to keep letting him rape you?" she asked bluntly with a fierceness in her voice.

With a stunned look on my face, I sat in silence. Staring at her in disbelief that she would call my sex life rape, I wasn't sure what to say.

"He's not raping me if I'm letting him do it," I defended.

"It's like the way you play the abused wife with your sister," she explained. "That's not who you really are. You're more powerful than that."

But I couldn't see it. I couldn't see the pattern of self-betrayal that Jane was trying to illuminate. In being blind to the dynamic I was protecting myself from the harsh truth that I was choosing to be victimized. If I admitted that I was being raped by my boyfriend, then I would be admitting to my utter lack of self-worth. I didn't have the strength or courage to do that. Had I known the full spectrum of consent, I would have understood that Mark was the only partner I had ever had consensual sex with.

"Let's breathe," Jane offered when she realized I was clearly at an impasse. I trusted her more than anyone, so I lay down on the floor to breathe in this unique rhythmic pattern I'd only experienced a few times prior.

Soon after we began, my lips started tingling as did my fingers.

"Just keep breathing. You're doing great," Jane encouraged.

Breathing in and out my mouth, I continued to stay with the breath pattern as my body began to surrender to the process. A few moments later, the scene of my parent's divorce flashed through my mind:

It was two days after I had turned 4 when my dad came to my room to tell me that he was leaving.

"I'm not going to be around as much, but we'll still see each other. I love you," was all he said. Then he gave me a hug and left.

After the door shut, my mom started crying hysterically, "I can't believe he would leave us like this!"

Then my sister ran up to me and yelled, "It's all your fault! He left because of you!"

As I continued to breathe, I watched this scene play through my mind as if I were watching a movie of my life. Tears started streaming down my face as I saw my younger self hunched over and heavy with shame. Believing my sister, 4-year-old me thought Dad left because of me. I thought that I caused all of this pain and fracture in our family. I could feel the shock that had rushed through my body at the time beginning to move as I continued to breathe and cry and scream.

I saw myself alone, sitting in my room, full of confusion. I was playing by myself, putting puzzles together and keeping my head down and my pain locked away in my body. I never cried. I never told anybody that this was excruciating or hard for me. And no one seemed curious about the impact on me. Even if they did ask, I know I wouldn't have been honest. I was already a master at hiding my truth. With nobody attuned to me, it was easy to hide, and I unconsciously believed that this was the only way to get the approval I longed for.

Since nobody was there to help me process this traumatic life event, this belief pattern got locked in place and lived in me as truth: *Dad left because of me. I'm not enough. I'm totally unlovable.*

My life was a painful disaster. My mom went into a deep depression. My sister became full of anger at the world. My mom had always said that Grace was born angry, but now her rage became intense and mostly directed at me, blaming me for all that was wrong with our family. In Dad's absence, she became the masculine energy that I was conditioned by, fearing her volatility and trying to please her. If she was happy, then I would be okay, but when she was upset I felt totally unsafe. She would hit me, yell at me, and instinctively play off of my fear and shame. I wanted desperately to earn her love. I looked up to her, after all, and she hated me. I tried to find a way to get her to love me, but everything I did made her mad.

Once I was done breathing, I slowly sat up and drank a cup of water in silence.

In shock at this revelation, I could see for the first time how I'd been affected by my parents' divorce. Just like the brain stores prototypes of objects to use for ease of navigating the world, the brain also uses schema of past relationship interactions to easily navigate relational dynamics. For example, when we see a chair, we know that we can sit in it. We don't need to figure out each and every time that this object is a chair and it is here for us to sit in comfort. Similarly, we store schema of past relationship experiences and project these experiences onto current relationships to easily navigate the zone of social engagement. When the schema are created during painful, frightening, or otherwise dysfunctional relational dynamics, we use them in an attempt to garner a sense of safety. Relational schema can be formed in childhood and projected onto current relationships, or they can be formed recently. People often treat their partner as if they are a former version of themselves while missing who they have become or who they are in the present moment.

Unconsciously, I used my schema of relationships that I formed with my sister and to navigate my relationship with Troy. Playing small, as if I was a young child dependent on Troy for safety, I wasn't standing in my dignity as an individual. Jane was right—I played the role of the abused wife to my sister and to my intimate partners.

Troy was not my sister, and I was not the young one who felt enslaved by her. I was looping through this old disempowering pattern, and I couldn't see my way out. I was gripped by an inner conflict of wanting Troy to leave me alone and wanting to feel connected to him. I didn't know that I could be angry at Troy for the way he treated me, and what I wasn't unable to express in words my body expressed for me. I started becoming very ill, with excruciating pain in my gall bladder and my back, and I began rapidly gaining weight again.

All of the fighting and powerlessness and anger and fear kept me in a state of illness for over a year. I dropped out of college because I became unable to focus on school work, and I tried to numb my pain with muscle relaxers and alcohol.

Troy didn't want me drinking alcohol or using drugs. Under his control and trying to please him, I agreed that I wouldn't. Because I thought his will was "the will," I hid my drug use from him and never told him that I wasn't willing to stop. I still smoked pot daily, and I was paranoid that he would find out. I would have panic attacks when my pager went off. He would frequently page me with a "911" and I'd feel the pressure to drop everything and come to him. It was never an emergency; it was just him keeping a tight leash on me.

On the rare occasion I would go to a bar with my friends, Troy would track me down and find me. He would scour the town until he saw my car, and the moment he walked in, my heart would sink and I would pretend to be sober. I was never free of him; he had infiltrated my life and my mind. In some sick and twisted way, I felt like possession was love. I thought he loved me so deeply that he couldn't be without me, but I had no idea what real love actually was. I felt imprisoned by his desire for me, scared to set him off.

Eventually my friends didn't know me anymore. The people I had known for years didn't want to hang out with me. I didn't know myself, either. I wasn't myself. I was Troy's sex slave. No opinion. No choice. No gumption.

Unconsciously I believed that love was painful. I had never felt unconditionally loved, and in my desperation to feel some semblance of love I would endured any pain. Thinking that love was synonymous with possession, I didn't know that real love empowers and uplifts. Had I known this, had I known that I was deserving of real love and that I deserved a safe lover, I would have gotten a restraining order. Instead, I got pregnant.

We had just gotten back together again, and Troy was so happy to be with me. It was like I was his drug and having sex with me was his fix. We were having sex at my apartment when he looked at me and smiled as he climaxed inside of me. We hadn't been using condoms for a long time, but I felt confident that I wouldn't get pregnant with the pull-out method. But since he didn't pull out, I knew instantly that I would conceive.

When my home pregnancy test came back positive, I sat Troy down on his couch at his ramshackle apartment and said, "I'm pregnant." Troy smiled hugely. Now I would be his forever. He was already a dad so having another child didn't freak him out at all. I, on the other hand, was completely terrified.

I didn't like being with Troy. There was nothing enjoyable, loving, or sustainable about our relationship. He wasn't a capable partner, and at that time, neither was I. Unsure about what to do, I turned to my mom and sister for advice.

I stood in the sad, brown kitchen of my childhood home with my mom and my sister, and I told them I was pregnant.

"You're going to have an abortion, right?" my sister asked.

"I'm not sure," I hesitated.

"You cannot have a baby with Troy," my mom said.

My neglectful mother, who was more of a disengaged friend, finally had an opinion about a choice I was making. It wasn't even a demand so much as it was her own terror of us never getting rid of Troy. He was dodgy and didn't fit into the hippie culture of our family. My mom must have been worried about me, but she never vulnerably shared that. I needed a loving role model for a healthy feminine woman, and without that my mother-wound was growing. Without a map, I wasn't sure what direction my life would take.

When my dad found out about my pregnancy and dark emotional state, he set up an intervention. He invited two of my closest friends and a few family members to talk with me about getting help. While they were trying to convince me that I was clinically depressed, my dad was overtly flirting with one of my closest friends. My heart sank as the young one in me felt totally underserving of his love and attention, even when I was at my lowest.

FINDING MY WILL

In the days that followed, I became suicidal. I felt depressed and powerless in this dysfunctional and abusive dynamic. The thought of having a baby with Troy made me realize that I would be connected to him forever. This led to me thinking that the only way out was to kill myself.

As I drove my car down the street, I had intrusive images of driving into a big rig. The only reason I didn't was because I didn't want to injure the other driver. I hoped daily that some freak accident would kill me. I thought of drowning myself. On a few occasions, I drove after drinking large amounts of alcohol and combining it with muscle relaxers, disappointed when I woke up the next morning in my own bed.

One night I was alone at my apartment and I decided to take a knife and lie down in the bathtub. I lay in the empty bathtub of my apartment and sobbed. Troy's energetic cords were so entwined with mine that I truly felt like the only way to get him out of my system was to die. I was carrying his baby in my womb, so my choice was to either keep the baby and stay connected to him forever, or kill the baby, which would kill a part of me. Either way, I couldn't get rid of him by my effort alone, so suicide seemed like the best possible choice.

Still in my clothes, I turned on the faucet in the bathtub and plugged the drain. As the water filled up the tub, I held the knife to my wrist. I contemplated what would hurt less: drowning or slitting my wrists? I stared at the knife pressing into my skin. I sank deeper into the water, wanting to escape into oblivion. When the water reached the top of the tub, I turned off the faucet. I examined my wrist with the knife still pressed against it, trying to muster up the courage to puncture my skin and draw blood.

I was in so much pain, yet the idea of causing myself more pain scared me. I took a deep breath and decided I was too afraid of hurting myself without a guarantee of ending my suffering. I sobbed. I had no will to live and no will to kill myself. I lay there until the water turned cold, and with deep resignation I unplugged the drain.

Sitting in the tub with soaking wet clothes, I hunched over as I cried harder than I ever had and watched the water drain out of the tub.

I set the knife at the edge of the tub and I stood up with complete resolve to have an abortion. Killing myself would have killed my baby anyway. I was already suffering, and I realized that I would be trapped in pain eternally if I had Troy's baby. I needed a way out, and an abortion seemed like my only option besides suicide.

When I told Troy that I was going to terminate the pregnancy, he was surprisingly supportive. I think deep down he knew that he could never trap me to the degree that he wanted, and he was scared of supporting another child when he couldn't afford the two he already had.

The first time Troy and I went to the abortion clinic, there were about twenty protesters holding signs with pictures of aborted fetuses. Their stares ignited deep shame and grief within me. Through tears of overwhelming sadness, I asked Troy to keep driving. I couldn't face hordes of people shaming me further.

I found a clinic that didn't have protesters and made an appointment for the following week. Each day seemed like an eternity while still carrying this unwanted fetus in my body.

Once again, Troy drove me.

As I talked to the nurses I felt numb. Troy seemed uncomfortable and guarded, like he was anticipating being shamed by the professionals there. As I remember it, everyone was very kind and gentle with me, but I felt vacant and absent from my experiences as I was led to the room where I prepared for the procedure. The anesthesiologist did a wonderful job putting me out, because after I counted back from ten I remember nothing other than waking up with Troy by my side. He looked so ugly to me. I was relieved to be done with him.

"This isn't who I am," I thought to myself as we drove back to my apartment. *"I don't know who I am, but life has to be more than all of this suffering."*

After I terminated the pregnancy, I knew I had to get Troy out of my life. When he dropped me off at my apartment I told him that I didn't want to see him anymore. Seemingly sympathetic to my fragile state, Troy agreed to leave me alone, but this was an agreement he didn't keep.

For the next eight years, Troy, continued to sporadically stalk me. I would be driving down the street and look in my rearview mirror to see him following me. I would try to lose him by driving all around Sacramento, but when he stayed on my tail I would drive to my mom's or to a public place.

One time I went to go for a swim at my dad's and he was there in the pool waiting for me. While shopping at the mall, sitting in a class, or hanging out with my family, I would glance up and Troy would be staring at me with an intensity that gripped me deep inside. He would leave flowers on my car and send his friends over to talk with me. I moved to a different part of town so he couldn't find me, and for years I couldn't walk down the street without looking over my shoulder to ensure he wasn't following me.

Broken and filled with grief, I had no idea how to heal the deep wounds I carried. I thought this pain would be my burden for the rest of my life, and so I went into deep self-loathing. I hated everything about myself: the way I looked, the actions I had taken, the thoughts I had, and the wasted space I took up for existing.

Within us, we all have both a life urge and a death urge. In our death urge, we feel small and powerless. We think that we can't create the life we want and that we're here to endure suffering. When we're in our death urge, we try to fit into a tight box that is acceptable, killing parts of ourselves in the search for safety and connection. Dimming our light with television, social media, alcohol, drugs, etc. is all part of our death urge. Unconsciously we think that we need to die in order to get back to God, which drives the unconscious impulse of our death urge. Similarly, we think that others might kill us if we're fully in our life urge, so hiding our full expression is an attempt at self-protection.

Our life urge is the will to live our life's purpose and follow our Soul's urge. When we're in our life urge, we know that we belong here on this planet and in this body. We do life-affirming things to build our vitality and expand our powerful life force. We speak our truth, live our dreams, and honor ourselves, which is all an expression of our life urge. The full expression of our life urge can be seen in the degree to which we embody Source. Here in this dimension, claiming how powerful, wise, and capable we are is the courageous act of living in our life urge. Standing our sacred ground with dignity, treating our body lovingly, and meeting the world from our wholeness is the essence of embodying our life urge.

Our life urge is our source of healing and evolution, and it is also the source of healing on the planet. When we can get our life urge to be higher than our death urge (even just 51% to 49%), then we begin to heal. And once we get more people on the planet living in their life urge than in their death urge, then the planet begins to heal. We simply do not engage in destructive behavior when we're in our life urge.

COMPULSION TO CHANGE

Feeling like I had control over nothing in my life, I decided to take charge of the one thing I could: food. As I made my way out of deep depression, an abusive relationship, and the grief of aborting my unborn child, I began starving myself. At the age of 22, I started exercising for the very first time in my life, and I tried to eat as few calories as humanly possible.

After taking a few semesters off from school because of the physical pain caused by my deep emotional suffering, I eventually became a full-time student at California State University of Sacramento. The only subject I was interested in studying was psychology, but I minored in English because I wanted to hone my writing skills to support my success in the field of psychology.

Partying took a back seat, except for the occasional night out dancing with friends. Since I viewed alcohol as empty calories, I didn't drink. And since cannabis gave me the munchies, I didn't smoke.

In my obsession with my appearance, I found cocaine, an appetite suppressant that kept me social and skinny. I had tried cocaine before, but I didn't like it very much. It hurt my nose and kept me awake for too long. I had a sensitive system, so when my friends would snort huge lines I would only take a small bump. I reasoned that I had control over my substance use.

I entered my first year of university as a junior. It had been four years since graduating high school, and having a few good teachers at community college gave me the motivation and assurance in myself to develop the skills to be a good student. I was surprised to find that with a little bit of focus and motivation, I was a very good writer and quite capable in math. Wanting to find a healthier way to exist in the world, I put all of my focus on getting good grades, exercising, and eating healthful food.

With my newfound motivation for education, I quickly excelled. From the outside, I looked like a great success. I made my way into the psychological honor society; I became a research assistant for abnormal psychology and earned authorship on a research study; I was a teaching assistant in social psychology; and I tutored psychology students in the writing center. Studying a topic I loved in service of doing something positive with my life changed my relationship to school. The intrinsic value I obtained from studying psychology and contributing to the psychology department gave me the drive I needed to bring out my inherent intellectual self that hadn't been nurtured before this time.

Scholastic achievement came naturally to me, and while accomplishing all of that I looked amazing. No longer a chubby child or obese adolescent, I took control over my physical appearance. I was running several miles a day, clumsily navigating the weights section at the gym, and eating healthy food. Afraid that if I took one day off that I'd gain back all of my weight, I never skipped a workout. Every day, seven days a week, I trained. And every day I tracked every single calorie I consumed with detailed precision, measuring everything I ate and writing it down.

Soon, the intensity of my effort turned into thinking "If low calorie is good, lower calorie is better" and "If low fat is good, no fat is better." I would play a game with myself to see just how little I could eat in a day and still have energy to accomplish my school work and physical exercise. I would drink coffee instead of eating when I was hungry, and if my mind went to eating sweets I would get up and go for a walk.

My family and friends were so proud of me. I developed a sophisticated style and put tremendous energy into my appearance. My hair was layered just below my shoulders. I bought expensive clothes that were unique yet understated——nothing too flashy. I couldn't leave the house without someone telling me that I looked like Nicole Kidman, and everywhere I went men were falling all over me, asking me out and telling me how beautiful I was. But it was never enough; I never believed them. In my mind, I was still fat and ugly. Even though objectively I could look in a mirror and see my thin physique, the moment I walked away my perception of myself turned into that of a 300-pound person who no one would ever be attracted to—an internalized image of my mom, from being enmeshed with her and taking on her appearance and identity as mine.

My mom and dad were extremely relieved to see me doing so well after my suicidal ideation and traumatic relationship. To my mind, school and appearance were the things I needed to be well, so I worked endlessly on being perfect in these two domains.

But I wasn't well. I was dark and heavy inside. I was trying to find my life urge after being so depressed, but my death urge was always just beneath the surface. I didn't feel deserving of life; the pain felt insurmountable. I worked so hard at presenting a happy, beautiful face to the world that no one would have guessed how deeply I was suffering. This was the cost of caring more about the way things looked than the way things actually were: people believed the lie I presented. I was too prideful to let them know the truth. This was part of my distortion from my conditioning, where I hid my shadow while presenting my light to the world.

As I was looping in my distortion, my work ethic and my food consumption turned compulsive. Eating six almonds for breakfast, a child-size frozen yogurt for lunch, and a giant plate of broccoli for dinner while running 45 minutes a day may have looked great on the outside, but it wreaked havoc on my inside. My hormones were out of whack and eventually I stopped menstruating.

Binging on cocaine and muscle relaxers each weekend didn't help much, either.

Wanting to feel empowered with men, I stopped jumping into relationships—but that didn't stop me from jumping into bed. Searching for validation and confirmation of my worth, I used men but never opened my heart to them. I had decided that I didn't like the men who approached me at a club or bar; they were sleazy and full of themselves. I had been groped and touched inappropriately so much in my life that I didn't trust men at all. In order to feel safe, I looked for the shy guys, the ones who were the designated drivers or too insecure to come up and introduce themselves to me.

"Hey, what's up?" was all I needed to say to get a guy to start talking to me.

The look of excitement I knew would appear on his face was all I needed to encourage me to go up to any guy and start talking to him.

My old friends were surprised by this newfound confidence, especially after it had been oppressed for so long in my relationship with Troy. I felt empowered by choosing men rather than waiting around to be chosen, and I wasn't shy about wanting to have sex with them, either.

"Do you have a condom?" I would ask before going back to their place at the end of the night, high on cocaine.

"Yep," they would say eagerly.

Then I would have sex with them, making sure I came first, frequently without them climaxing at all. Sometimes they would go down on me and then I would leave. More often than not, the man was hopeful that we would start dating and see more of each other, but I was too guarded to even consider such a thing. They would leave my house in tears, and I hardened my heart with each experience. I was so out of touch with my heart and emotional vulnerability that I pitied the men who were interested in me. I couldn't see that these men weren't the ones who hurt me. The way I projected my pain onto them made it so I couldn't see who they actually were. I had expected them to be like Joe or Troy, but they weren't. At the time, there was no way for me to make sense of this, and so I decided they were pathetic.

This was my attempt at reclaiming of my power after being disempowered for so long. As destructive as it was, it felt way better than being a man's possession. And I couldn't see a third option.

I was desperately trying to find a sense of my own worth and authority because my thoughts were consumed by self-loathing. Day in and day out I lived an experience of myself that was oppressive and mean. I tried to bypass or ignore these feelings by staying busy and distracted, but my anxiety grew to such proportions that I started having panic attacks. My chest felt heavy, I couldn't get a full breath, and I was full of fear about my inadequacies. These were all signs of my death urge trying to reveal itself, but at the time I couldn't understand why I couldn't inhale deeply.

I was miserable when I was fat and I was miserable when I was thin, so I eventually started to see that my body was not the source of my misery. I still wasn't sure what was causing me so much suffering, but it seemed clear that my size, appearance, and accomplishments had nothing to do with it. If being a good object was all it took to be happy, then I should have been full of joy. I had no idea why I thought that I wasn't enough in and of myself. Discovering how wrong I was about this misbelief was the most incredible moment of my life.

Any time that we loop through oppressive thoughts, engage in distorted behavior, or feel powerless in the world, we are identified with our wound. The outer world is essentially a hologram of our inner world. When we see the world through the lens of our wounding, we project that out onto the world. It's as if all we can see is the pain when we are identified with our wounds, and we feel powerless in our effort to cultivate the experience of life that we long for.

The work of healing is about inviting our wounds back into the vast ocean of our wholeness and embodying the True Self. The True Self is the crystalline energy that we originally came from. Before we were in a body, we were pure energy connected to universal bliss. We have experiences in this body and in this life that cause us to harden around our humanity. Healing those hardened places allows us to create an inner world that is fluid and harmonized. When we reflect this inner fluidity and harmony out onto the world, life is a joyous expression of our inner state. Life feels easy and satisfying when we reflect our True Self out onto the world. Embodying our wholeness, our relationships, community, work, home, and physical body reflect the beauty of our true nature.

5
A GLIMMER OF LIGHT

"The mind is its own place, and in itself can make a heaven of hell, a
hell of heaven."
—John Milton, Paradise Lost, 1667

ELEVATING AWARENESS

With my newfound passion (read: addiction) for exercise, my uncle
suggested that I go to his girlfriend's new yoga and fitness studio.

Rose had offered me a free class, and I was really nervous to try. With
my perfectionistic tendencies, I was scared that I would be bad at yoga.
Rose showed me around her quaint midtown studio located in an old
Victorian house on J Street. As this was my very first class, she loaned
me a yoga mat. I was wearing an oversized cotton T-shirt and running
shorts, and I felt terribly out of place at this boutique studio.

"You look great!" Rose said enthusiastically. It was the first she'd seen
me since I lost so much weight.

No longer obese and awkward, my slim body received a lot of
attention, yet when people talked about the way I looked, I felt
complete embarrassment. Compliments seemed to tug on my
insecurities and feed into my eating disorder. I wanted to disappear and
not be noticed at all.

"Thanks," I said hesitantly.

The class began and the instructor, Julia, led us in a short meditation.

My mind was full of chatter, as I observed how much nonsense occupied my awareness. Incessant thinking all on the theme of how I wasn't enough circulated throughout my mind. It seemed to me that I had absolutely no control over my own thoughts. I fruitlessly tried to rein them in.

"I have no business being here. I'm so fat. There is no way I can do this. I have no idea what I'm doing. Look at Julia. She is so perfect. Why can't I be like her? I bet she has an adoring boyfriend. Nobody will ever love me. I have nothing to offer. I'm too fat to be loved. I'm too fat to be here. Get up and leave. No. They will think I'm crazy if I leave. I want them to like me. What if I can't do yoga and they laugh at me. What if no one here wants me to be here? I should go ..."

"And take three deep breaths," Julia's sweet voice instructed.

Ahhhhhhhhh.

Class began with cat and cow, which was easy enough.

"I've got this. I'm so good at this. I fit right in." My superiority complex popped in.

Next was downward facing dog.

"Oh my God. I can't hold this posture for three more breaths. She must be crazy. I can't do this. What am I doing here?" My inferiority complex chimed in.

Throughout each posture, my mind evaluated my worth based on my ability. All the while, sweet Julia encouraged us not to compare ourselves to anybody else, reminding us to listen to our bodies with compassion.

The real beauty of yoga for me was moving into places of my body that I had completely disconnected from. I had a deep curvature in my spine that had worsened throughout my life. Having a sedentary childhood where I was overweight and held in my voice caused my scoliosis to worsen. When I was with Troy, the pain in my back became excruciating from the constant tension and stress of our abusive dynamic.

My right shoulder was lower and collapsed forward quite a bit, causing me to endure a lifetime of chronic back pain while also being lopsided and hunchbacked. I was deformed, and the rotation in my back made it so my muscles were very tight and weak. It had been suggested to me that corrective surgery where rods would be placed in my spine would be the only way to heal my curvature. I had declined the surgery, yet I had never considered that there was anything I could do to heal my misshapen spine. As it turned out, yoga was the beginning of a long healing journey, and a new understanding of how I stored my emotional pain in my body.

The entire yoga class was excruciating. I sweated. I trembled. I groaned. I struggled. I hurt. I felt parts of my body I didn't even know I could feel. I felt defeated. I was humbled.

This was just what I needed. Being with my resistance, my pain, my edges, and my inadequacies while using my breath and my mind to accept them was revolutionary to me.

As I moved throughout the class, my body began to open in ways it had never been allowed or encouraged to before.

The next day I could barely move. Sitting down on the toilet was painful because my leg muscles were so sore. I probably overdid it, I definitely hated every moment of it, and I wanted more. Because I wasn't naturally good at it, my perfectionism decided that I had to work hard to become an exceptional yogini.

Rose offered me a job working the front desk at the studio, and I could take as many classes as I wanted. Being around all of these fit, gorgeous women was hard for me. Even though I was thin, there was still a fat little girl in me that compared my body to everybody else's and could not see the reality of my physique. I criticized my body daily, and I desperately tried to find the right amount of food each day that would give me energy to exercise while also maintaining or losing weight.

Every day I would go to school for my morning classes and then head straight over to the studio. It was my home away from home. I studied there. I worked out there. I worked there. And I fell in love with yoga there.

Seeing my enthusiasm for the practice, Rose offered to comp my yoga certification if I worked the front desk during the training. At the age of 22, I eagerly took her up on her generous offer, and before long I was teaching there.

I practiced teaching incessantly before I led my first class. My family and friends were willing students, and I worked every day on improving the flow of my class and precision of my instruction.

During the hour leading up to my first paid class as an instructor, I had constant diarrhea from nervousness. I trembled with fear of being not enough and tried to calm myself down with full belly breathing. With a few minutes to spare, I went to the bathroom one last time. When I walked into the yoga room, I saw my best friend, Lindsey, setting her mat next to mine. The room was packed with barely any space for me to walk around all of the mats. I welcomed everyone and thanked them for coming to my first class. At my statement that I was brand new to this I sensed some hesitation from some of the participants, but I invited them to close their eyes for meditation.

With everyone's eyes closed, I felt my system settle and I could breathe again. I encouraged everyone to set aside their expectations and comparisons and to honor their body's needs. The class was beautiful and effortless, and flowed with ease. My diligent practice made it so that it seemed as if I was a seasoned instructor, and when our practice was complete I heard one of the hesitant woman say emphatically, "I can't believe that was the first class she taught."

For the first time in my life, I felt embodied in a room full of people. Leading in this way felt natural and right to me, and I felt more aligned within myself for having done it.

Yoga became my new compulsion.

I stopped using drugs. I gave my television away. And I started eating healthy food in normal amounts. Rose was a nutritionist and she helped me to see that if I was going to build muscle, I needed to consume enough of the right foods to keep my system nourished. She gave me some guidelines of how many calories to consume and my dad introduced me to *Eat Right 4 Your Type*, also known as The Blood Type Diet. I only ate foods compatible with my blood type, and Rose reviewed my caloric intake weekly. I was still compulsive about how much I ate, but I ate reasonable amounts because I wanted my body to be able to sustain my yoga practice.

Mindfulness meditation was key for me during this time. This is the practice of differentiating from our thoughts and our conditioned self. Stopping the stream of thought and putting our attention on our breath gives us space from our mind. Where typically we identify with our thoughts, believing that truth and reality live in our mind, meditation is the practice of developing the watcher mind. No longer a passive agent to our thinking, we elevate our consciousness by creating more spaciousness around our thoughts.

People commonly believe that they cannot meditate because when they sit in silence it seems impossible to stop the stream of thought looping through their mind. But this is what the mind does—the mind thinks. In mindfulness meditation, the work is about noticing that, stopping the stream, and choosing where you want to focus your attention. Even if it's for a split second, focusing on the breath for one instant before the mind starts up again elevates consciousness. This space is necessary to differentiate from the false self. In the space that we nurture away from our thinking, we are able to access the part of us that is bigger than our conditioning.

REALIGNING

I lived alone in a sweet little treehouse apartment in East Sacramento, right in between Sac State's campus and the yoga studio. My life consisted of school, homework, shopping at the natural food co-op, meditating, exercising, practicing yoga, and teaching yoga.

When my mom saw the way I lived, she commented that she used to think I did life like her, but now she could see that I did life like my dad: orderly, clean, and healthy. From this place, my mom didn't know how to relate to me. Where our family time had always consisted of smoking pot and gluttony, I was no longer engaging in either. There was a shift in family dynamics based on my choice to take a different path.

I had a crush on a guy who came to my class regularly, and even though he seemed to like me I was convinced I wasn't enough for him. I felt too vulnerable to pursue any connection with him outside of the studio, even though I talked about him constantly to the women I worked with. If he had been a random guy at the bar, I would have had no problem approaching him. But here, in my home away from home, I couldn't fathom the idea of rejection. When I was closed off to men,

I felt powerful. I didn't trust men and I had a thick veil over my heart, so the idea of opening up and being vulnerable felt like death to me. Although I appeared to have a strong sense of confidence, deep within I felt worthless. My warped self-perception caused me to have body dysmorphia (an intrusive preoccupation with the perceived imperfections of your body); I still viewed my body as fat and undesirable.

Since using men the way I had been didn't feel right to me anymore, and since I was too scared to open up to men, at 23 I decided to be celibate for the first time since I was 14. I decided to say "No" to any sexual advances from men and to turn my focus inward.

I had been trying diligently to create an experience of life that would have me feeling better on the inside. My external focus, though, didn't have the transformative impact I needed in order to alleviate my internal suffering. My thoughts were still consumed by being not enough, and I felt tremendous shame about who I was. There was never a moment in my existence that I wasn't consumed by my lack of self-worth—either wallowing in it or desperately trying to find my way out of it by compulsively and obsessively doing everything I thought I needed to do in order to be worthy.

Not knowing how to make a shift, I called Jane one day to talk to her about how I was feeling. She had been a constant guide and mentor for me throughout my life, and she was the only person I could think to talk to about this.

"For one full week, write down every single negative thought you have," she said.

I didn't understand the purpose. My thoughts were disempowering. I wanted them to go away. It didn't make sense to me that she would have me write them down. It seemed like putting them to paper would give them more power. But I trusted Jane, so I decided to give it a try.

The next day, I started the practice of writing down my negative thoughts. When I awoke, the self-loathing was there immediately: *"You look terrible. Don't wear that. It makes you look fat."*

I wrote this down and then I changed my clothes eight times before my mind was semi-satisfied. *"You can't leave the house in that. Everyone is going to judge you. You just shouldn't leave the house at all."*

With my heart racing from anxiety, I wrote this down and then I continued to get ready for the day. *"If that's the best you can do, fine. It will work. But that skirt makes you look fat."*

Frustrated with my own anxious and fearful thoughts, I walked away from the mirror to prepare my food for the day. *"Don't put that much peanut butter on your toast. Put some back. No. Put more back. Do you even need peanut butter?"*

After eating, I drove to campus in my red convertible Toyota Celica. *"Look at those guys checking me out. If they saw me naked they'd never like me."*

I parked, wrote this all down, and then walked to my first class. That's when it hit me. I realized that I was doing this to myself! I was suffering because of my own thoughts! No one was telling me that I was unworthy or fat or ugly but me. Me! This was an incredibly empowering and exciting moment for me.

I had only been tracking my thoughts for one morning, but somewhere along the way, meditation had given me the ability to be the watcher of my thoughts. I had just never been as conscious about tracking negative ones as I was that morning. I had never brought the mindfulness practice off of my meditation cushion and into real life. Writing down these thoughts gave me enough distance from my thinking to realize that they were only in my mind. They were not reality. They were simply constructs of my mind.

I felt slightly manic with this revelation; however, I still wasn't sure what to do about the negative state of my mind. While part of me felt empowered by this newfound awareness, I still felt powerless to cultivate a different experience of myself.

A few weeks later, I taught a yoga class during the June 21, 2001 summer solstice solar eclipse. The class was unremarkable even though I could feel the heaviness of depression lurking in my body. The strange light felt ominous. I felt somewhat zombie-like throughout the class, which was rare for me. Typically I was an enthusiastic yoga and meditation teacher, but my sadness was surfacing in a new way and I couldn't deny, ignore, or suppress it anymore.

After the class ended and the participants left, I was alone in the studio. It was just me in the dark room with a diffused light outside. I felt empty and sad and defeated. I had been trying so hard to change and transform, but here I was, still disempowered and full of self-judgment.

Resigned in my misery, I lay on the wood floor of the yoga room and sobbed.

I cried from the depths of my soul. My body undulated with my moans of deep emotional agony, and the tears flowed profusely.

"Why?" I screamed. "Why am I so miserable? Why do I hurt so badly? When will this pain ever go away?"

I wailed and bawled more intensely than I ever had before. I let myself cry until there was nothing left. After an hour of deep emotional release, I peeled myself up off the ground, locked up the studio, and drove home.

Since I had no drugs, television, or junk food to tune out with, I decided to sit in meditation. I lit some candles and sat with my pain. Typically in meditation I focused on stopping my thoughts and staying anchored in my breath. This time, I focused on my pain in a way I had never experienced before. I looked at my pain courageously, with deep curiosity and appreciation. I became intimately familiar with it. From the vantage point of my inner eye, I could see the way I held my pain in my body. I could see its shape. I could see its color. I breathed around it with total and complete acceptance. No part of me resisted this pain in this moment. I even came to a place where I felt grateful for it.

My mind was totally silent. In being with myself from a place of gentle curiosity and sweet surrender, I slipped into the most peaceful silence I had ever experienced.

And that's when I saw it.

Light. Inside of me. And it was bright.

Mesmerized and in awe, I spent what felt like hours exploring this light. Tears streamed down my face in deep gratitude for the gift of this light. I had been in so much pain for what felt like an eternity, that seeing something else within me that was so different moved me in an incredibly profound way. I was surprised that this light was just beneath my pain, and the more I stayed with it the more it held my pain in love, dissolving it into the wholeness of my being.

I felt purified and liberated. Like getting reacquainted with an old friend, I felt comforted and trusting of the process of life. I had been asleep to this vital part of myself for so long, yet the recognition I felt when seeing it was totally undeniable. This part of me is who I really am. This is my truest self, beyond conditioning and beliefs, and bigger than my thoughts or my body.

Awake, for the first time in a long time, I felt alive.

Pure joy and vast, unconditional love illuminated every cell of my being.

Where I once felt like a passive agent to my thoughts and conditioning, I now felt empowered in my alignment with essence. This experience woke me up to the part of me that is divinely connected to all beings. I could see that separation only exists in the perception of the ego. In this moment, I was in a state of oneness, connected to the Source of all life.

On the level of spirit, there is no separation. When we're identified with our conditioned self, we feel separate and small and lonely. In accessing our spiritual body, we can see that at the deepest level there is no "other." Otherizing occurs when we identify with our wounds because when we experience trauma we split from our alignment with Source. And when we split from Source we feel fragmented and broken. Reflecting this out onto the world, we can no longer see other people's wholeness and spiritual essence. When we awaken, we access oneness. On this dimension, in human form, we are different. But on the higher dimensions, in spiritual form, we are one.

It was late at night and finally fatigue set in. I reluctantly went to bed, hoping this light would still be accessible to me when I arose the following morning.

As soon as my eyes opened the next day, I sat in meditation to reconnect with my essence. And the moment I dropped into myself, I started crying. My light was still there, and with it was a clear voice with a message of wisdom and hope.

"As you are, in this moment, you are enough," I heard the deep masculine voice say.

I wept. I needed to hear this, and receiving this message from within, without need for validation or acceptance from outside of myself was humbling.

"Your life has meaning. All of this pain has purpose," the voice continued.

I cried even harder. I wanted to believe this. I wanted to embody this truth. Hearing this felt disorienting and I decided to respond with a question.

"Why, then? Why do I feel so worthless?" I asked.

"You have so much to offer. Stop masking your light."

I cried some more. "I feel powerless," I said.

"If not you, who? If not now, when?" the voice stated. *"Individual self-love and acceptance is the path to world peace. Stop masking your light."*

This landed in my system in a deep way, and I felt open to the possibility that I might have something of value to offer the world. I grabbed my journal and started writing fervently.

Once the pen was in my hand, the message continued to flow with ease. Truth and wisdom poured from the depths of my soul, and I gratefully and enthusiastically took notes.

With this newly accessed wisdom, I got dressed and drove to campus for my morning classes. I was taking summer classes to get ahead on my credits for graduation the next semester, and on this hot June day I felt like I was walking on a cloud. I floated from class to class with joy. The last time I had been on this campus, I had been full of self-loathing and judgment, wanting validation from everyone else. Today, I was full of inner joy, self-love, and love of humanity. Being this way felt replenishing, like the endless well of this light could sustain as I generously spread love everywhere I went.

After my last class of the day, I drove over to my grandmother's condo to let her know I loved her. She had tightened around her misery in her old age, saying mean things and complaining about the past. She sat on the couch and I sat on the floor at her feet, holding her hand and reminding her of her light.

"You are so much more than your mind can conceive," I said. "You are brighter and more powerful than you could ever imagine. I want you to remember that. Please."

Tears streamed from her face as she looked at me. "You're glowing," she said. "You look like an angel."

"You see my light," I acknowledged. "You have this same light within you. You've just forgotten."

She thanked me for seeing that in her, then she went on to tell me how her dad, who she later learned was actually her stepdad, used to put his penis in her mouth when she was a child. She would choke and couldn't breathe, and the way she chronically coughed was her unconscious trying to get him out of her. She could see that her life had been so painful that she had hardened. She regretted the way she mothered her children, passing on her pain to them. She also regretted her choices with men, but at the time she felt like she had no other choice. She was in pain, and instead of going within, she tuned out with alcohol and television.

After I left my grandmother's, I went to see my dad.

I told my dad about what happened, and he looked at me in total amazement.

"You're glowing," he said. "Look at you. You are shining so bright. You are going to do amazing things with your life."

He seemed proud as he honored my essence, and I felt so supported by him. I had been afraid that people would think I was crazy, like admitting I had heard a deep voice from within would land me in the psych ward. But instead, the people I had told up to that point could actually see it, which helped me to trust it even more.

When I told my mom, on the other hand, she seemed distant and cold, and I assumed she was jealous of me or scared that I had surpassed her. She had been such a pioneer healer in our community, but she had stopped working on herself and she was still overweight and depressed.

"I had an awakening," I said to her. "I'm in touch with my inner light, and I can hear sweet messages from within that feel empowering and reassuring to me. I've never been happier."

Seeing me express joy and embodying my sparkling light, she said "Cool. I'm happy for you," in a tone that wasn't congruent with her words. The look on her face made me question whether she believed me or whether she was envious. I knew she loved me and wanted good things for me, but she felt stuck in her life. Longing to feel loved but never satisfied with the love that was there, she was lonely and deeply identified with her depression.

I kept my distance from her for a while after that, and once the summer session of classes was over I spent the summer traveling and writing. Wisdom flowed through me easily. Out in nature, up in the mountains of Lake Tahoe and the Napali coast of Kauai, I allowed myself to be guided by Spirit and life felt magical. In touch with my own rhythm, I was intrinsically motivated for the first time in my life. Doing what felt good to me, I would write for hours a day, walk alone in the forest, and easily make friends with people I encountered. Without my fear of being not enough guiding my actions, my warmth attracted people everywhere I went.

Awakening happens by accident, and conscious awareness is available to all beings. We all have deep wisdom and expansive power within us. By doing life-affirming things, such as breathing deeply, eating well, being sober, exercising, and meditating, we help our life urge ignite our alignment with Source. And once we see this in ourselves, we see this same Light in everyone else. It's undeniable: the True Self is our true nature.

WIDESPREAD PANIC

With access to vast wisdom, I started writing a book. I was only 22 years old, so my message was still unclear and immature. However, this was when my dream to write came into my sight. The more I wrote, the more it became clear to me that we all have access to the same source of wisdom. The Master teachers who offer truth to the world in profound ways have beautifully embodied this Source, and we all have the potential to embody this message, too. Even though we have fallen asleep to this part of us, it's still there. And it's never going away. It awaits quietly for us to turn toward it in recognition of our powerful, expansive True Self.

As I enjoyed this new connection to Source, I continued with my education and my teaching. However, everything I did was done with more presence and joy and truth. I found that when I went to the grocery store to buy food, I no longer worried endlessly about my caloric intake. I consumed food that supported my vitality, and I happily nourished my body. When I exercised, I did so because it felt good to move my body, and I felt grateful for the body I had. Judgment and comparison were replaced with deep acceptance and gratitude. I got dressed in the morning with ease; I enjoyed being with friends; and I wasn't the least bit concerned with getting attention from men. I trusted in my ability with school, and I was in flow with the unfolding of life.

I wanted to bottle up this joy and love and ease, but every time I tried to cling to it I noticed it get dimmer and less potent. So instead, I stayed with the practices that got me there: meditating for about two hours a day, practicing yoga for my own development, teaching yoga, eating healthfully, listening to music that uplifted me, like Kirtan (Sanskrit chants of sacred spiritual ideals), and eschewing drugs, alcohol, and casual hookups. All of these choices helped me to embody my own presence.

Three months passed, and I was still deeply in touch with my inner light. One morning I was getting ready to drive to campus so I could tutor in the writing center, and I needed to print off an essay I had written. My printer was broken, so I called my aunt Dallas, who was the resident techie in my family. She quickly picked up the phone.

"Hey, Dallas. I have an essay to print before I leave for school, but my printer isn't working. Can you help?"

Her voice was full of fear as she responded: "Harmony! What are you talking about? Have you seen what's happened? Turn on the TV. It's on every channel!!"

"I don't have a TV. What's going on?" I asked.

"Some airplanes just flew into the World Trade Center. They're saying it's a terrorist attack! I've got to go. Go find a TV and watch the news." Click.

Clearly, something big was happening by the fear I could hear in Dallas's voice, but I didn't get the weight of the situation in this moment. Since I didn't want to be late for my first tutoring student of the day, I decided to print my essay at school. I packed up my school supplies, and drove to campus.

When I arrived on campus, it was uncharacteristically empty. Once I arrived in the writing center, everyone was talking about what had just happened, wondering if we were going to be sent home.

"Did you hear about what happened?" a wide-eyed tutor asked me.

"A little. What's going on?"

She explained how al-Qaeda terrorists took over two airplanes, crashing them into both of the Twin Towers and killing thousands of innocent people. The damage was still unknown, and my coworkers seemed to be worried about what was next and whether any other planes would be hijacked.

The situation was so grave that school administrators decided to close down campus and send us all home. I was starting to grasp the enormity of this situation, and sadness for those lives lost felt heavy in my body as I walked back to my car.

Once I got to the parking lot, it was clear that all of the students who had shown up that day were leaving at the same time. The traffic jam was so big that many of us sat by our cars talking about the terrorist attacks. I talked to one person who knew someone involved with al-Qaeda and another person who was afraid that a loved one had been in the towers when they were attacked.

I made my way out of the congested parking lot and drove straight to the yoga studio to be with my yoga community. As I walked in, everyone seemed to be shell-shocked. People were starting to tighten up and shut down around their fear. They were canceling travel plans and talking about what horrible people the terrorists were.

Where I had been driven by fear for so much of my life, in this moment I was in an expansive and trusting place. As I heard people give voice to their fear, it seemed to me that this was exactly what the terrorists wanted. Contracting around fear was the opposite of the solution. To me, the solution seemed to live in the way we meet our fear. The fear is there for self-preservation, but believing the stories of the mind that are driven by fear cause us to project more of the same fear out. In turn, we end up experiencing more of the very thing we don't want.

All of our feelings our valid. However, that does not mean that the stories in our mind that accompany those feelings are true. When we loop in a mental cycle, underneath that loop there is an emotion. The underlying emotion has validity. People were feeling afraid. That's inarguable. The stories that were engendered from the feeling of fear may not have been true. Thinking that it was now unsafe to travel, that the terrorists were monsters, or that all Muslims are terrorists are imaginations of the mind that are arguable statements.

The practice of turning toward our subjective experience when we're triggered brings us closer to our True Self. Owning that we are afraid and attuning to our fear gives us an access point to regulate and see objective reality more clearly. When we are regulated, we soften into our humanity and stay embodied. We can align in the presence of a trigger and become more solid for having experienced our emotion.

During the days that followed, I found myself wondering about the pain the terrorists might be in to cause such pain in the world. I thought about al-Qaeda children and how they might be raised to fear others. I had compassion for the way they seem to identify with their shadow. And from the depth of my heart, I sent them prayers of love and peace.

The way we meet others is the way we meet ourselves. If I disown my own shadow I want to disenfranchise people who embody theirs. If I treat myself as an object, ignoring my inner subjective world, it's easy to categorize the terrorists as "bad objects." Conversely, if I honor the full range of my humanity, including my fear and anger, then I can have curiosity about others. This does not mean that I collapse around my power and my boundaries. The opposite is true. When I claim my darkness and meet myself with depth and curiosity, I am better equipped to stand in sovereignty and take right action.

Every person in our lives, everything we see in the world, every idea we have about others is all a reflection of ourselves. There is no "other." *Radical self-love and self-compassion is the path to world peace.* This was the message that kept coming to me during this time, and this was my very first experience of seeing how when I am aligned with Source my experience of life (regardless of what is happening) is guided by deep unconditional love.

6
GROUNDLESSNESS

"Life is basically insecure. That's the intrinsic quality; it cannot be changed. Death is secure. The moment you choose security, unknowingly you have chosen death. The moment you choose life, unawares you have chosen insecurity."—Osho

FORGING A NEW PATH

After I graduated with my BA, I was still feeling empowered and inspired to write and travel in the aftermath of my awakening. I sold the majority of my belongings and decided to drive north up the Oregon coast because during one of my meditations, my inner voice said, "Go North." And so I did.

I packed the remainder of my belongings into my white Honda Civic and said goodbye to my friends and family.

Driving north without a plan seemed naive to my parents, but I didn't let that stop me. I had lived in Sacramento for the majority of my life, and I was ready to see what else was out there for me. My mom told me that I could call her friend Ellen once I got to Oregon if I needed a place to stay, but I didn't think that would be necessary.

As I drove up Highway 101, I was in complete awe of the beauty before me. The Pacific coast had never looked so majestic. The lush greenery and the gorgeous ocean soothed my soul. I wondered why nature was so often destroyed in the name of profit, and I felt reverence for Mother Ocean and Mother Earth. I stayed in a hotel in the coastal town of Coos Bay for a few nights, and I wrote and practiced yoga and ate healthful food.

After a week of being on my own, I realized that not having a plan, a job, or money wasn't sustainable, so I called Ellen to see if I could stay with her for a while.

"Of course, Harmony," she said in her thick Boston accent. "You're welcome to stay here as long as you need. Your mother has been such a godsend in my life, I'd do anything for her."

Relieved to have a connection and support outside of my hometown, I made my way to Ellen's large home in the picturesque town of Lake Oswego, just outside of Portland.

Ellen was an artist and a mother, and I trusted her because she was the only person who acknowledged the craziness of my childhood. She had been at the parties, she had taken the workshops, and she asserted many times that my upbringing had been dangerous. No one else spoke to this truth, and I felt surprised and comforted that Ellen would say this aloud. She always spoke her truth with clarity, and I admired her for that.

Ellen was a stay-at-home mom to an adolescent boy, and she and I spent a lot of time together in the year and a half that I ended up living with her. I felt so comforted by the normalcy of her household that I didn't want to leave. Ellen and I would cook healthy food together, sew costumes for her son, and exercise and shop together. I learned so much from her about practical living that I never learned from my mom.

Aside from her wholesome and safe routine, Ellen was also committed to her own growth and evolution. She had done tremendous healing with my mom when she lived in Sacramento, and now, here in Oregon, she was seeing a wonderful energy healer named Stacia. Ellen encouraged me to see Stacia for a session, and this was the first time in my life that I saw a healer who wasn't my mom or Jane. I had taken workshops with my mom and Jane, had several rebirthing sessions, and looked to Jane for guidance. But having an unbiased person witness me and hold space for me was an incredible experience.

In that vein, the first aspect of my healing to emerge was a need for energetic boundaries with my mom, as well as cutting energetic cords with the numerous boys and men who had violated me over the years. I had countless experiences of boys grabbing my pussy, putting my hand on their cock, and inserting their penis into me without explicit consent. I had pushed men off of me who tried to rape me, I had been roofied and I had even been stealthed, where men would put a condom on per my request and then remove it without my knowing so they could have unprotected sex with me.

I had played into countless encounters with men where I overlooked or denied the violation in order to get a sense of connection or safety. Afraid that they would hurt me if I spoke in opposition, I pretended that I wasn't hurt by their behavior. All of that pain was stored in my energetic system.

I worked with Stacia and other healers using a variety of modalities to support my healing: visceral manipulation, guided self-healing, body talk, and neuro-linguistic programming (NLP). With all of these processes, there is no self-analysis and very little talking. In each session, Stacia gently witnessed, held, and transformed the energetic holding pattern of my pain-body, which is the accumulation of painful life experiences that I was unable to move through in the moment they arose. I would leave feeling lighter, more whole, and fully supported to be my True Self in the world.

Since my conditioned self was not getting attention in these sessions (as it often does with traditional talk therapy), I began to develop a deeper awareness of my essence in the presence of healers. I was able to tune into my whole system during my sessions, and I was able to see myself more clearly than ever before.

Cleansing my energetic system, repatterning my thoughts, and setting energetic boundaries was deeply transformative. At the age of 24, I was starting to strip away layers of my conditioned self in service of living in alignment with Source. However, an underlying sense of urgency to work on what would eventually become this book kept propelling me into panic. I would work fervently on my writing, afraid that I would never get it to a place that was publishable, relatable, or impactful.

Looking for support and guidance, I submitted my first few chapters to a well-known publishing house, and the acquisitions editor said that she liked it.

"I don't think the world is ready for this yet," she said. "Are you planning on going to graduate school?"

"I'm not sure. I've been focused on writing this since I completed undergrad."

"I think you should get your graduate degree, then submit this once you're complete."

Since my mom was a healer without a college degree, I had contemplated skipping graduate school and going straight into private practice. However, my familiar drive to be normal and to fit in led me to listen to the editor's suggestion and I began the application process.

I attended a progressive private university in Seattle, Antioch. Antioch is known for its rich history in social justice and its forward-thinking approach to psychology. Coretta Scott King is an alum, and Antioch was the first university in the country to enroll black students and women on equal status with white men. Multiculturalism is embedded in every class, and alternative and progressive therapeutic techniques are integrated and taught by experts in the field.

I felt like I was home, like I had found my people. But there was still a part of me that felt like an outsider. Even though I was among community who got the deeper transformative effect of spirituality, energetics, and authenticity, there was a loud part of my mind that was conflicted, telling me that I wasn't enough, that I didn't fit in, and that I had to prove my worth. Similar to when I was an undergrad, my conditioned self was driven by shame and I projected that shame onto my classmates, believing that my inferiority complex was induced by them. Shame was such a pervasive part of my inner world that I couldn't even see how it drove me in all of my endeavors and interactions.

While I was living in the Pacific Northwest, my mom and I started developing a relationship that felt comforting to me. The work I did on setting energetic boundaries with her made it so I could see her as a separate person from me. From this vantage point, I began to develop a sense of self and I could see her as her own woman on her own journey, and I felt deep compassion for her pain.

"How can you just forgive her?" my sister asked me while on a short phone call. She and Mom hadn't talked for almost a year. Grace hadn't transcended or outgrown her volatile, explosive personality, and their relationship had become too conflict-ridden for them to maintain contact. When I was an undergraduate, I had stopped talking to Grace for over a year after she tore apart my room and threatened to cut my hair off in the middle of the night. She was in a fit of rage because I couldn't bring her the key to Dad's house when she wanted. No contact with Grace seemed to be the only way to set a boundary, which was confusing given how wise and tender she was at times.

"She's had a tough life," I responded. "Besides being our mom, she's her own woman with pain and suffering that she doesn't know how to navigate." I could forgive her for not meeting my needs as a child considering the pain she experienced in her childhood. In many ways, she had shifted her patterns with me and I could appreciate how far she'd come.

My mom and I would talk on the phone almost daily, and over time I felt closer to her. The complex experience of needing her for my survival in childhood but being failed by her in so many ways was painful, but it never inhibited my love for her. Even though I resisted being like her, we were a lot alike. We were both wise, fierce, magical, and insecure. I confided in her, and she confided in me. Our relationship still felt more like a friendship, where I was the mature friend keeping her grounded. But I enjoyed connecting with her as an adult.

I had tried to bring her to counseling on a visit to Sacramento, and although she had agreed to come, she was guarded and wore a mask of perfection throughout the session. Seeing her unwillingness to own her dysfunction and the impact she had on me, I could see that any wounds I was carrying from my childhood were mine alone to heal. I wanted to be free from my pain and my conditioned self, and rehashing things with her wasn't in service of that.

The distance of my move also brought me closer to my dad. We started talking on the phone every Sunday at 7:30 AM for thirty minutes, per his request.

"When I moved away from Michigan, I called my mom every Sunday. I want you to do that with me. Tell me what your life is like. Like, what do you do on a Tuesday up there?" he said.

My dad had gotten divorced from my step-mom many years prior to this. At this time, he dismissed monogamy and became an eternal bachelor. With many girlfriends (some of whom were my age) he and his womanizing ways made me uncomfortable. He would hit on my friends right in front of me, and in that act I felt unimportant.

I was shocked by his request to regularly talk on the phone. This was the first opportunity I ever had to talk with him without the distraction of other women. To receive his undivided attention weekly was a gift I had been craving for my entire life. In his asking for consistent connection with me, I felt his care and love deeply. I didn't need to be sick to get his attention as he willingly gave it to me. Talking on the phone afforded us the space to share things we normally wouldn't, and this is still a ritual we do weekly over fifteen years later.

"I've got to give it to you, Harmony. You're doing this whole graduate school thing without any help from your brain-dead parents," he said with pride one morning on the phone.

Since he was supporting me financially, I was surprised that he said this. To me I couldn't have done all of this without the support he had offered. However, he was pointing to the deeper way he had failed me, and I was in disbelief that he was owning his failure. I still couldn't see all of the ways he had failed me, and hearing this gave me permission to explore the impact of my childhood neglect.

When we are able to admit to the way our unconscious behavior has negatively impacted another, we karmically clean up our past interactions with the world. Acknowledging that we were living from our distortion is humbling, and it is the very act needed to stay in alignment with the True Self. Defensiveness and excuses for failure don't serve anyone. By amending all of the ways we have met others from our distortion, we begin to embody the True Self even more and our presence is innately healing. This atonement of the past makes it possible to have sovereign, clean relationships that are loving and honoring of Source.

MEETING "THE ONE"

I had been celibate for three years and was loving life. Without a boyfriend to trigger my codependent tendencies, I could handle the moderate fear I experienced at school. I felt healthy, and my lifestyle was built around maintaining that health. My life urge was winning, and I was ready for partnership.

One day before school began, I was waiting for a Pilates class to begin at the gym in Seattle's Westlake neighborhood. While I was warming up on my mat in the studio room, a man with dark brown hair and a gigantic smile walked in carrying his yoga mat. My whole spirit awoke to him. Everything inside of me felt attraction and desire. I was elated when he placed his yoga mat right next to mine.

He sat down and then turned to me and said, "Hello. How are you?"

I smiled and said, "Fine." Then I nonchalantly went back to my warm-ups.

When the teacher walked in, the man next to me greeted her warmly. I was slightly jealous that he knew her, but I would have never admitted that to myself. As class progressed, it became clear that the teacher wasn't skilled at articulating the nuances of this very intricate exercise, and the man next to me struggled to do simple movements. I felt compassion for him, and I was irritated by her when she encouraged him and told him he was doing great.

I had my teacher certification in Pilates at this point. I had been exposed to amazing teachers over the past seven years, and I had a deep understanding of this nuanced form of exercise. Along with energy work, Rolfing, and yoga, Pilates was one of the main elements in my healing of my scoliosis.

In order for the movements to have real value, one needs to move slowly and have an intimate relationship with the subtle connection of the smaller muscles. You achieve the elongation of the spine supported by the engagement of deep musculature by having a strong eye on the inside. Struggling and pushing through does not serve you in Pilates.

When the class was finally over, this man and I started talking. His name was Jason and had just moved here from San Diego at the same time I had moved from Lake Oswego. He had recently been in a bad car accident, and his physical therapist recommended Pilates. When I heard about his car accident, I told him that I used to teach Pilates and that I could help him with his roll-up (a standard Pilates movement). We exchanged numbers and made a date to exercise together.

For two months, Jason and I would do Pilates at my apartment and he would take me out to lunch. We were developing a close connection, and the attraction I felt started to turn into fantasy and obsession. It seemed like he was interested in me, but he still hadn't kissed me after two months of spending time together. I was accustomed to men moving fast, and I assumed he was only interested in a friendship, which was painful for me to consider. He was nine years older than me, and he was clean-cut and normal. He was a rock climber, he'd never done drugs, and he was close with his family. I was afraid that I wasn't good enough for him.

One day, after a Pilates session at my Queen Anne apartment overlooking Fremont, I stood in my kitchen preparing my lunch while Jason sat on the couch adjacent to my kitchen. I was preparing my lunch as I was getting ready to head to campus for my afternoon classes.

I didn't have many friends to hang out with, and I was explaining to Jason the mundane experience of my life. "I'm pretty boring," I said. "I don't go out anymore. My life is pretty simple with work, school, and going to the PCC." The PCC was the natural foods co-op.

"How can you say you're boring? You are the most amazing woman I have ever met," he proclaimed.

I felt a jolt of desire arise up the center of my body. I stopped what I was doing and looked at him. Slowly, I put down my utensils and I walked over to him and sat beside him on the couch.

Still in silence, I picked up my Osho Zen Tarot deck and asked him to pick a card.

"Comparison" was the card he picked, with its picture of a bamboo tree next to an oak tree. I read him the explanation of the card, which stated that you cannot compare bamboo to oak. The two are inherently different and beautiful in and of themselves.

I set the deck down on the table next to me. Then I extended my hand to the space between us and opened it as an invitation for him to put his hand in mine.

He accepted the silent invitation. I looked at him, and his gaze was cast down, looking at our hands. I waited in silence until he looked at me, and then he moved in to kiss me. It was the most beautiful moment I had ever experienced with a man. Slowly, purposefully, and mutually, we kissed.

Deciding to be in a romantic relationship with Jason felt natural, and our honeymoon phase intense. Craving closeness and shared experiences, life was in Technicolor and it seemed like all of Seattle was conspiring to help us fall deeper in love. Picnics on Lake Union, short trips to the mountains, hikes just minutes from the city, and delicious food at every turn. Everything was magical—except for the sex.

I couldn't quite figure out why with so much intensity and desire between us that Jason seemed cold and rigid in our physical intimacy. My expansive sexual boundaries were contrasted by Jason's rigid ones, and I kept trying to get him to be more open. I wanted him to be more sensual with the spirit of exploration, but he was more performance-oriented with a focus on penetration. I wanted touch and seduction and bliss. He wanted missionary, no foreplay, and traditional roles. Eventually I stopped asking for what I wanted and tried to make the best of it. Boring sex with a man I loved was better than what I had been experiencing pre-celibacy. I wanted connection with him, and if asking for what I wanted compromised that connection, I decided to stuff my desire.

"You bring out the best in me. I'm usually not this happy," he proclaimed. "I'm usually a curmudgeon."

I didn't believe him. I couldn't see how this sweet, genuine, loving man could be a curmudgeon. I brushed off his comments and enjoyed our connection. In hindsight, though, I just didn't want to believe that he had that side to him. There had been signs of it, where he complained a lot and criticized me in a joking manner. But my tendency to see the goodness in people, where people's shadow side was not obvious to me, was a pattern I was familiar with. This is why I stayed with Troy for so long; I was extremely skilled at convincing myself that I was responsible for making other people happy. I had been wanting to feel loved my whole life, and I was certain that any flaws Jason had couldn't be as bad as what I had endured in the past.

Just as the mind uses projections from experiences to navigate current relationships, early in relationships that mind projects fantasies of what we imagine our partner to be like. When we think it's our partner's job to make us happy, we choose relationships with people who we think can do that. Unable to see one another clearly, we project the image we have constructed in our mind of who we want the other person to be. Setting ourselves up for disappointment, we leave ourselves and believe the loop of projections rather than staying objective and sober.

It's also common in relationships to assign our feelings to the other person. Early in the relationship we assign our bliss, pleasure, and happiness to our new partner. Then later in the relationship, we assign our dissatisfaction, pain, and misery to them. Our feelings belong to us. They are ignited in connection with another person, but they are ours. Our pleasure, anger, hurt, and sadness is ours to experience and navigate. When we don't take full ownership of our feelings, we are victims to the people in our lives. When we recognize that no one else is responsible for our feelings, that our feelings live in us and belong to us, we cultivate agency of choice and self-responsibility. No longer being driven by the young one who wanted Mom and Dad to love us unconditionally and provide safety for us, we mature into a person who gives that to ourselves.

Six months into our relationship we planned a three-week adventure vacation to Costa Rica. When we arrived in this tropical paradise, I was finally able to see just how much of a curmudgeon Jason was. Complaining about the living conditions, criticizing the culture, and being stingy with money were just some of the reasons this was the most agonizing trip I had ever been on. He also put me down daily, whether it was about my luggage, my choice in food, or the way I dressed. My self-esteem was getting lower by the day. We fought about money, about where to travel, about what route to take, and about when and what to eat. It seemed like the only way to get through this vacation was to defer to him and have no opinion of my own.

I reasoned that the circumstances of our vacation must have brought out the worst in him. He didn't like sunshine or heat, and he didn't like the ocean or the sand. I was surprised that anybody could dislike the sun, ocean, and beach. But he said this is what made him grumpy, so I was as understanding as I could be.

Soon after we returned to Seattle, we attended a tantric retreat held at Breitenbush Hot Springs in Oregon. I had been wanting a transcendent sexual experience and Jason reluctantly agreed to give it a try. The workshop pushed both of our edges, but I felt at home with the sensual exploration while Jason felt like a fish out of water. During a guided tantric meditation, I felt my heart expand to the far reaches of the room. "*I love so big*," I thought to myself. Then just moments later I could feel Jason sitting next to me and his energy felt rigid and hard. "*I'm too much for him*," crossed my mind, and then I felt myself try to rein in my giant heart to make him feel comfortable. I decided that I needed to stay small to keep him comfortable, not seeing that this was my dysfunctional pattern with men—trying to fit into a box that they felt comfortable with.

Instead of the transcendent sexual experience I had hoped for, I left our tantric weekend with the awareness that I needed to squelch my giant heart in order to earn love and keep connection. Although I was aware of the impulses guiding me, I couldn't see that there was anything wrong with this.

I worked hard to be different for Jason, all the while wanting him to be different for me. We made this work fairly well, so I moved in with him. He owned a condo in Seattle's Eastlake neighborhood, and this was my first time living with a man. At the age of 25, I felt mature and happy about this step in our relationship, convinced that we would have the fantasy relationship I wanted.

The condo was newly renovated and had views of Lake Union. We lived right across the street from the Gates Foundation, and we could walk to happy hour at Sushi on the Lake or stroll up to the boat houses. We cooked together, decorated together, and snuggled together every night.

Of course, we argued sometimes and we did things that bothered each other, but all in all we were a match made in heaven.

Well, that's not exactly true. I wanted to believe it was. But since I was working hard to keep myself small, I was doing a good job of making it look like we were a perfect match. Ignoring how painful our relationship was for me, I walked on eggshells because I was scared to trigger him. Jason had a temper that was especially explosive when I didn't accommodate his controlling and dictatorial nature. If I had an opinion or a desire different from his, he would put me down and call me names; he even grabbed me a few times while in explosive rage.

He had been honest with me about being a curmudgeon; I just didn't know that this meant he would never be satisfied with me or anything else. No matter how hard I worked to be perfect for him, it was never enough. He was grumpy, rigid, and full of anxiety most of the time. Our sex life was rote, and he seemed to have a narrow idea of what was okay to do with one another. We tried to work on our relationship with a couples counselor but didn't seem to make any headway.

The inherent problem with traditional marriage counseling is that therapists typically work to keep the couple in the relationship. When we believe that the goal of couples counseling is to stay together, clients are working to change themselves and the other person to make one another happy and satisfied. When we try to fit our love into a box that the mind thinks will cultivate security, we meet love from our death urge. We kill parts of ourselves to try to fit the container we think love needs to survive and we end up killing it instead.

Love needs room in order to breathe. Love is expansive and uplifting and regenerative. When we approach relationships from a stance of honoring ourselves, we don't need our partner to change in order for us to be okay. We know what we're available for in our connection, and we trust ourselves to set boundaries and to walk away if that relationship isn't nourishing. We speak on behalf of our truest truth, which inherently is about us and not our partner. When we list all of the things that we want to change in our partner, we are dropping ourselves. When we speak on our own behalf, revealing our loneliness, our pain, and our desires, we vulnerably share ourselves with our partner. Then our partner gets to choose what they're available for and how they want to grow and evolve or not.

From here, we get to make conscious decisions about who we want to become. Rather than focusing on if we should stay or go, we focus on our growth and evolution. This is the sovereign act of dignity in relationship. Making the relationship more important than our own growth, evolution, or happiness is the codependent act of choosing from our wounds, not our wholeness.

SHAKEN TO THE CORE

After three years of being together, I was getting ready to graduate with my Master's in clinical psychology and I was contemplating breaking up with Jason. He had planned a trip to Nepal to celebrate my graduation. And although I didn't know it, he was planning on proposing to me there. Considering our trip to Costa Rica, I was deluded in my fantasy of what traveling to Nepal with him would be like. But I wasn't giving voice to my fear. I was more invested in what I thought our relationship could be like rather than being honest with myself about how our relationship actually was.

Two weeks before we were set to leave on our Nepalese adventure, my mom called me complaining about a pain in her abdomen. She had been in excruciating pain for over a month, and on this day it was at an all-time high. I panicked at the feebleness in her voice.

"Call Dad," I said to her.

My parents had remained very good friends over the course of my life, and I knew my dad would be there in an instant. Over the years, my mom made sure we did all of the major celebrations together; Hanukah, Christmas, birthdays and more were all spent as a family. My parents respected each other's work, and they would refer patients and clients to each other like colleagues. They were great friends and love remained at the core of their relationship even though it wasn't romantic love.

On this day, however, my mom refused to call my dad because she didn't want to bother him. Once we hung up, I called him and told him she had been in extreme pain for four weeks. He went right over there and told her to go to the ER.

Later that day she was diagnosed with uterine cancer.

Just six months prior, my mom had been flirty and alive with passion. We had taken a three-week excursion to Europe, exploring France, Spain, and Italy. On our trip, she had a zest for life even though her overweight body caused her pain. She had stopped dating women when I was in my early twenties, and on our trip, she made out with men all over Europe, annoyed that I declined male attention because of Jason. Despite her shortcomings, I loved her with my whole heart. As a child I had been afraid that she would have something growing in her stomach without knowing it, and now that fear had come true.

I flew down to Sacramento the very next day and drove her to the OB/GYN who had given her an annual just two months before. When she gave my mother a pelvic exam, she could see the cancer.

Because Mom's pain levels were so high, she was prescribed the highest level of morphine allowed in an outpatient situation, and that still wasn't enough. She moaned in agony all day and all night, and we had to wait two days before we could get in to see the oncologist. In those two days waiting for her appointment, fear overcame me. I developed intense insomnia and I was restless with anxiety. Since I couldn't control what was happening in her, I tried to control all of the circumstances that I could. The groundlessness I felt in the wake of this diagnosis shook me to the core. I was so afraid of losing her that I became vigilant about her caretaking. I managed her medication, set up her appointments, and made sure she had everything she wanted.

Overwhelmed and triggered with intense feelings of fear, my mind was looping in a thought pattern where I was trying to find safety in the presence of a threat. I couldn't regulate and I couldn't think clearly. When met with contraction and fear, death is something to resist and the world is something to control. When met with the light of consciousness, death can be beautiful and sacred. We can honor the impermanence of life and we can see that death is just as natural as birth. There was no part of me that was aligned with the sacred nature of life and death at this moment, and I navigated this experience from my small self.

At her appointment with the oncologist, we were told that she had a rare form of cancer caused by obesity. This type of cancer was aggressive and relentless in taking over the body. They wanted to start chemotherapy and radiation right away, but because she was in tremendous pain they were going to do surgery to remove the tumor before starting those treatments.

Ten days after my arrival in Sacramento, my mom was admitted to the hospital. My dad, my sister, and I waited in the hospital while she was in surgery, and when the doctor came out he looked as if he was bearing bad news.

"Is she dead?" I panicked.

"No," he assured me. "She's alive and in post-op, but I couldn't get the tumor out. The cancer is everywhere, and if I started to take this tumor out, I would have had to remove most of her intestine and she would have to wear a colostomy bag."

With that revelation, he told us he had closed up the large incision without removing any of the cancer.

"Can we start chemo?" I inquired eagerly.

"We can't start chemo until her incision is healed. It will be a few of weeks before we can schedule that."

With stage four cancer and an incision going the length of her abdomen, my mom was still suffering from the pain of the uterine tumor. In agony, she wept with fear hearing the news. Scared and in pain, she had a long, uncertain road ahead of her.

In the days following this devastating news, I spent every day with her in the hospital and nourished her with healthy food to support her recovery from surgery. Her friends and clients would visit often, my dad was there daily, and my sister spent the evenings and nights with her.

I was still frantic with fear, and Jason came down from Seattle to support me. He did chores around the house that would have otherwise fallen by the wayside, and he held me in love and support daily. We took care of my mom's Bichon Frise, Sashi, but she didn't seem to like Jason—or most people, for that matter. He put up with Sashi trying to bite him, and he was the most stable force in my life when I felt the most groundless.

Two days after my mom's surgery, I was in the hospital room with her and her brother, Gio. Gio was educated as an osteopathic physician, but he was on disability due to PTSD and hadn't practiced medicine for many years. Gio inquired with my mom's oncologist about why he wasn't giving her intravenous food, called total parenteral nutrition (TPN). He thought this would help her build her strength and heal from the surgery. The doctor explained that this would feed the cancer and that it was best to let her body heal in its own time.

Her wound was healing well, and I was giving her plenty of nourishment to build strength, bringing in healthy soups, shakes, and other easily digestible food.

The day after Gio inquired about feeding her intravenously, I was in the hospital room with her when the oncologist's nurse came in and said that she was going to hook my mom up to a TPN.

"I thought you said that would make the cancer grow," I said confused.

"We think it might help her to heal from the surgery," she replied.

Later that night, my mom's incision quickly went from healthy and healing to red and irritated. The wound was opening and looked infected, and her stomach became swollen and distended.

"I think I'm having an allergic reaction to the TPN," she said in a panic. "Get it out of me. My body feels horrible. I think I'm allergic to it!"

The oncologist came in and examined the wound. It was gaping open and spreading apart, and her stomach was bloated and growing bigger by the second. Earlier that day she had been healing normally, and now she was extremely uncomfortable and getting worse.

"I can feel the cancer growing. It's growing so fast! Please get the TPN out of me," she pleaded.

Scared that my mom would die in hours if we didn't remove the TPN, I pleaded with the doctor to take it out. After examining her, he quickly agreed that the TPN was harming her and making the cancer grow. The TPN was removed immediately, but it was too late. The cancer had been fed and she was dying, coughing up blood and losing strength.

As they prepared to move her to ICU, I called everybody and told them to come say goodbye. Certain of her impending death, I wanted everyone to have a chance to see her one last time. Her sisters, her brother, her nieces and nephews, her friends, her ex-husband, and Grace and I stood around her hospital bed and told her how loved she was. She was so high on morphine and so weak that she responded with slurred words of gratitude.

It was late when they transferred her, and I was exhausted. My sister went with her to ICU and said that she would call me if anything happened. I went home to sleep, but my insomnia wouldn't allow me. I took an Ambien and was still wide awake, so an hour later I took another.

My phone rang in the middle of the night. I picked it up, spoke, and after I hung up I passed out. It rang again. I picked it up again, and then passed out the second I hung up. Ambien amnesia is common, and this was the worst possible time for me to be knocked out on drugs.

When I awoke the next morning, I called my sister.

"Where are you? She's dead!"

"What? Why didn't you call me?" I asked.

"I called you twice. You said you were on your way. I kept her up for you as long as I could. She was spitting up blood and I suctioned it from her mouth all night long. I kept telling her to hold on, that you were on your way to say goodbye. What happened?"

"I was on Ambien. I don't remember any of that. I took two last night because I couldn't sleep. I'm so sorry. I'll be there as soon as I can."

I hung up the phone and called Jason right away. He had flown back to Seattle for work, and I needed him. He said that he'd be back in Sacramento that night, and when I hung up the phone I wailed. The deepest pain I have ever experienced permeated my heart, and I cried and cried and cried.

I threw on some clothes and drove to the hospital. Grace and I hugged and cried, and I thanked her for being with Mom as she passed. She said it was an indescribable experience, that she felt alone and traumatized. I so wish I had been there.

When I called my aunt to tell her that the TPN had killed my mom, she told me that Gio had threatened to sue the doctors if they didn't administer it. The degree to which I was infuriated was equal to the degree to which I loved my mom.

Red with anger, I called Gio and screamed, "You did this! You killed her. You killed my mom. You killed your own sister. You had no right to meddle in her treatment plan. You haven't practiced medicine in years. You know nothing about oncology. This is all your fault!"

"Harmony, I thought the doctors were too cheap to give her a TPN. I have a good friend who is an oncologist who told me that TPN was necessary to heal. I did it because I thought it would help her get better."

But I couldn't hear any of that. I couldn't even see that he hadn't caused the cancer. All I cared about was my loss.

Even though she had failed me as a mother, she gave me a sense of grounding on this earth. She was my anchor, and I loved her deeply. I could see how her pain made it hard for her to be the nurturing mother I needed, and I had forgiven her. She was my best friend. The closeness I felt with her was both comforting and empowering, and I couldn't imagine my life without her. She had believed in me in ways that embarrassed me to the core, but I had loved having her in my corner. I felt broken without her, like I was no longer whole.

Later that day I was lying in my mom's bed sobbing when I saw her spirit floating over me, an oval ball of white light. She was with two other spirits: one was her sister Cindy, who died before I was born and the other was her mentor, Brandon, who taught her how to be a healer in her own right.

"I'm okay now," she said. "I'm where I need to be."

"But I need you," I screamed. "I need you!"

"You'll be fine. Trust." That was all she said.

Seeing her like that brought me so much comfort. I stared, in awe of her beautiful spirit and overwhelmed with her love. I felt grateful that she was with two beings she had missed dearly throughout her life, and I could soften knowing that she was no longer in pain.

But that didn't fill the gaping hole of grief in my heart. No longer able to see her spirit, I spiraled back into complete collapse. Grief consumed me and I could not function in any way that made sense. When I snuggled Sashi I felt closer to my mom, and this brought me some degree of comfort.

We grieve as deeply as we love. The love in our heart that we feel for the person who passed gets entangled with grief. The grief merges with the love, and it can feel like a part of us died, too. At times, the pain can feel heavy, like it will take us down and swallow us up. We can become numb from such a big emotional experience, and it may seem like it will never end. To be with ourselves in the presence of deep grief honors the love, honors the connection, and honors the impermanence of our mortality. There's nothing to do about the grief, no way to fix it other than to be with it. Feeling every bit of it, we allow our hearts to break open in the presence of intense grief. We can become more expanded, more aligned, and more authentic when give ourselves permission to grieve uninhibitedly.

DROWNING IN GRIEF

The night my mother died, Jason arrived and held me tight. He assured me that he was there for me and that he loved me deeply. I hadn't eaten much over the twenty-two days since the diagnosis, nor had I slept without a sleeping aid. I was too skinny for my frame, and my system was depleted. Jason was the only thing anchoring me to this earth.

My friends, my mom's friends and clients, my family, and Jason fed me, loved on me, and honored my mom by telling stories of her. Over the next two weeks, I grieved uninhibitedly but I did not know how to truly meet the darkness from my expansive self. I was consumed by it, clinging to it as if that would keep me feeling close to my mom.

Two weeks after her death, in the backyard of my childhood home, we had a wonderful memorial honoring her life. Over 200 people showed up to honor her legacy of love, healing, and community. People I hadn't seen since my childhood days of firewalks and rebirther trainings showed up, along with my mom's ex-girlfriend, Tracy, her ex-husband, Jim, and my best friends from high school. We listened to music, shared stories of her irreverent personality, and cried deep tears of grief. We ate good food and drank good wine.

As I was talking with a group of people, my best friend, Lindsey, and my mom's best friend, Bonnie, ran up to me in a panic.

"What's going on?" I asked, unsure about what the urgency was.

They looked at each other trying to decide who would break the news to me.

"It's Sashi," said Bonnie. "She got out."

"What? When? How long has it been?" I panicked.

"Megan just called us. She opened the door when she got home and Sashi made a run for it." Megan had been watching Sashi so she wouldn't get out during the memorial with all of the people in our home. But apparently, Sashi was on a suicide mission to get to my mom.

"Let's go find her!" I exclaimed.

We grabbed Jason and my cousin, Ashley, and we left the memorial in a rush. It was dark out as we drove around the area slowly, looking for any sign of a small, white, fluffy dog. I called animal control and told them that my dog had escaped and to please call me if they found her. Just a moment after I hung up the phone, they called back and said they thought they located her but they weren't sure if she was alive.

We drove to the busy street of Watt Ave where they had found her, and when we pulled up it was clear that she was dead. I crumbled in pain. Devastated, I couldn't move.

Jason spoke to the men from animal control and identified Sashi as ours, and they placed her in a box for us to bring her home to bury. Lindsey asked me if I wanted everyone from the memorial to leave before we got back, and I agreed that this would be best. Bonnie cleared the house for me, and I returned to my mom's empty home overcome with more pain and sadness than I felt I could bear.

The next morning I woke up and told Jason that I needed to get a dog before he went back to Seattle. He needed to get back to work, and I knew that the soothing comfort of a canine companion would help me as I finalized the estate. We decided to go to the Humane Society to see if there was a dog we wanted to adopt, and when we arrived there were about twenty people waiting for the center to open. When the doors were unlocked, Jason grabbed my hand and pulled me to the front of the line in a desperate attempt to find a dog.

"Where are the small dogs?" he asked without stopping.

The woman at the front desk pointed to the back of the building, "In the back on the right."

We rushed back to the small dogs, and we split up to try to cover as much ground as possible before anybody else made it to the kennels.

I quickly looked at the dogs, feeling hopeless that there would be a fluffy one to replace Sashi. A few seconds later, Jason called out from around the corner, "How about this one?"

I ran over to where he was standing, and beside him was an employee holding the sweetest, most beautiful, grey fluffy dog I had ever seen. It was as if the Light of heaven shone down on this dog, and he was my angel.

"Yes! He's perfect," I said, feeling hopeful for the first time in several weeks.

I filled out some papers to go sit outside and get acquainted with this little dog, and I fell in love immediately. He was a 1-year-old puppy who weighed about twelve pounds, and they thought he was a Lhasa Apso-poodle mix.

Jason asked all of the practical questions, gathering data to make an informed decision. We had never talked about getting a dog together before, so this made sense to me that he had to think it through. But I wasn't in a rational place. I was heartbroken, and I needed this dog to help me through this time. I knew I wasn't leaving the Humane Society without him.

When we brought him home, Lindsey and Bonnie came over to meet him. They couldn't believe that I was smiling and happy given what had transpired the night before. Since "Sashi" was Sanskrit for "moon," we decided to name our dog "Ravi," which is Sanskrit for "sun."

After I had this glimpse of puppy sunshine, in quick succession my mom's two brothers died. One week later, her brother who had been living in Europe died of a heart attack, and three weeks after that, Gio died on a trip in Thailand.

Four deaths all within two months of each other.

As I navigated all of this, darkness and loneliness percolated under the surface of my bright smile and cheerful personality. Although I appeared to be handling everything with resilience and grace, I was resisting the heaviness of my pain and was constantly staving off a deep collapse.

As we sold off my mom's things, I learned that death can bring out the unsavory side of people. Everyone wanted something of hers to remember her by. Before I could even find my bearing, people were asking for things. Her sisters, her mother (who was still alive and had buried four of her eight children), her friends and clients all wanted dibs on something. They also wanted me to step into her role. Her sisters, mother, and nieces and nephews who had relied so heavily on her unconsciously elected me as the new matriarch, and her clients wanted me to take over her practice. The pressure added to the lurking heaviness within me, and a sense of groundlessness and overwhelm kept me turning to alcohol.

All I wanted was my mom, and it seemed like everyone else wanted her too, through me and through her things. I was in no state to be holding space for someone grieving my mom, and I was desperate to find someone to hold space for me. I tried to seek therapy during this time, but no amount of talk could help me shift this pain.

Without my family home or my mom, I wanted to run far away from Sacramento. There was an uncertain road ahead of me, but I rejected these invitations in favor of creating my own life. I eventually made my way back to gloomy, rainy Seattle and wallowed in deep depression. I had been overwhelmed with love for my mom throughout my life, and now I was overwhelmed with grief. I leaned on her for so much, and without her I felt lost.

One day, while we were walking Ravi, I turned to Jason and said, "I need a baby. If you don't want a baby, break up with me right now. If you do, marry me and let's get started."

I had always told Jason that I didn't want children, but in this moment the idea of bringing new life into the world was the only thing that gave me hope. There had been too much death, and I needed new life.

Confused by my urgency, Jason tried to speak rationally to me. But just like when we were picking out Ravi, I was not rational. I was too grief-stricken to be rational. Getting married and having a child seemed like my only way out of the pain I was drowning in.

Out of touch with the True Self, we try to find certainty on this dimension. Untethered and insecure as we are, old wounds of grief and trauma can have us feel split form Source. If we don't pause and come back into our alignment, all of our actions come from our distortion. When we are in an intense experience and make choices from our distortion, the impact is even more extreme than when we live from our distortion and life feels stable. Making decisions in the presence of urgency is an attempt to find safety and control in the presence of fear. And although counterintuitive, it's important to slow down, regulate, and move forward with both feet firmly planted on the earth.

In his deep love and care for me, Jason acknowledged that he had planned to propose in Nepal. We'd had to cancel that trip when my mom was admitted to the hospital. He wanted to marry me, but he never thought it would be under these circumstances. On my birthday, just two months after my mom passed, Jason proposed with the most beautiful platinum-set diamond ring I had ever seen. It was sophisticated and classy, with small diamonds giving it a vintage look.

I finally felt like I could breathe, like everything was going to be okay. I had a man who loved me, a sweet dog, and a life ahead of me that gave me hope.

What I didn't realize at the time was that by choosing security, I was thwarting my own growth. I couldn't bear being in the groundlessness of losing my mom and other family so close together. To make life bearable, I wanted something to be certain. The price I paid for that certainty was painful. I wanted to keep Jason, so I suppressed my truth about what the relationship was like for me and hid my authentic experience.

Even though he was amazing during my mom's sickness and death, I felt imprisoned in our relational dynamic. But what I couldn't see was that I was imprisoning myself by trying to be what I thought he needed me to be. I didn't know how to open the cage of my conditioning and be my authentic self, fully expressed and genuine.

Jason had a lot of rules to follow: there were rules about money, about sex, about work, about cleanliness, about socializing, about drugs, and about traveling. The way he tried to get me to fit into those rules felt like control to me. But what I couldn't see at the time was that I was trying to cram myself into his box and resenting him for it. I had no agency in myself. In choosing the security of this relationship, I stopped valuing my own voice and my own life force energy. I became dependent on him for my will to live.

What's more, I couldn't see that by trying to be perfect for him, by trying to make him happy, I was actually trying to control him. It was a subversive, manipulative type of control, but I wanted him to be different and I contorted to try to make that happen.

I was lost and I leaned way too heavily on him for a sense of feeling okay in the world. I abandoned any connection I had with myself and with Source, and I made Jason the God. I was so grateful that he wanted to do this with me, but trying to find my grounding in him prevented me from aligning with my own truth and desire. This was an old pattern of mine that I still couldn't see, and I couldn't see how I was projecting it onto him, either. I was blind to my True Self, and I didn't even know it.

Disconnected from our alignment with true Source, we make our primary relationship a substitute Source. Leaning heavily on our intimate partner, we leave ourselves and distort ourselves and manage our truth to try to keep our connection. Desperate to feel connected to Source, we put that longing onto our partner. The relationship cannot thrive in health and dignity from that place, because we're looking to our partner as our savior. Embodying the True Self and loving from our wholeness, we are the thing that we want. What we long for lives within us, and when we embody the bliss of the True Self we can meet our relationships from our sovereignty. This is where real connection and intimacy can thrive in health. No longer looking to our partner to complete us or make us happy, we meet our relationship from our wholeness.

7
DARKNESS IS PERSISTENT

"No one ever told me that grief felt so like fear."
—C.S. Lewis

NEW LIFE

The darkness of the Seattle winter continued to feed my depression. I wasn't working, and my dad and Jason were paying my living expenses. I didn't want to go outside in the wet and dreary weather, so I spent most of my time cuddled up on the couch with Ravi, watching television while Jason worked. One such morning, I was watching the Today Show and a guest was on giving tips on how to make extra money. She suggested that viewers with a Master's degree could teach online.

A light immediately went on inside me. I knew I couldn't sit with clients in my depressed state, but I could certainly teach online. This way, I would never have to leave Ravi alone and I could earn some income. Ravi had separation anxiety, and so did I. Leaving him to go to the grocery store was painful for me, so I felt relieved at the idea of contributing to our finances while using my degree and never leaving the house.

I secured a job teaching psychology for an online BA program, and Jason and I decided to leave Seattle. We both had a hard time with the lack of sunshine, and we set our sights on Boulder, Colorado.

Jason was able to transfer his job there, and once we arrived we planned a small wedding at the base of the foothills of the Front Range in the famous Chautauqua Park.

Boulder (often called "The Republic of Boulder") is a mecca for outdoor activities, farm-to-table restaurants, healing modalities, start-up companies, and people committed to their own growth and evolution. It's a bubble, unlike any other place I've ever been. Its people are mostly highly educated, successful, and liberal. With 360 days of sun each year, it was a welcome contrast from Seattle.

During the days leading up to our wedding, fear started to emerge. I was in disbelief that I was marrying Jason given the strain and struggle of our dynamic. In so many ways he was wonderful to me, but in the nuances of our relationship I didn't actually enjoy being with him. He was rigid, controlling, dismissive of my needs, and on top of that he was politically conservative. With my liberal, hippie background, we had completely different views of the world with no real tools to help us meet in the middle. I had been trying to change him into the man I wanted rather than actually loving him for the man he was. Simultaneously I was trying to fit into a box that he felt comfortable with so that he'd want to be in connection with me.

Part of me wanted to call off the ceremony, but another part of me wanted him more than anything. My ambivalence was painful for both of us. In a hysterical moment of fear the night before the wedding, I told him that I wasn't sure I wanted to marry him.

"I'm not even sure I like you," I said callously. "I'm not even sure we like each other. What are we doing?"

"Are you canceling the wedding?" he asked with fear in his voice.

"I don't know. I don't think so. I'm so confused. I'm so scared." I cried as he hugged me, trying to make this better.

He was desperately afraid that I wouldn't show up the following day, and I was still looping in grief. My mom had passed nine months before and I was still crying daily. In that time, we had moved to a new state; I had no friends in our new city; I had a new dog; we were buying a new house; I had started a new job; and although I didn't know it at the time, I was four weeks pregnant with our daughter.

Nothing in my life was familiar except for Jason. I reasoned that I was experiencing PMS with quintessential "cold feet" and everything would turn out for the best. Our friends and family were in town, so with the help of my two dearest friends, I calmed myself down with a few glasses of wine and prepared for the ceremony.

On that picture-perfect day, Jason and I promised to be partners in life and in love. We vowed to cherish one another, to transform together, and to nourish one another through the difficult and the easy. Ravi was our ring bearer, and I chose to walk down the aisle by myself, without my dad, because I didn't want to perpetuate the patriarchal "giving away" of one's daughter as if I were property. I wanted to believe I was independent, but two weeks later when I noticed that my dad stopped depositing money into my account as he had been for the past twelve years I realized how very wrong I was about that. In a sense, I *had* been given away.

The weeks after our wedding, I became acutely nauseated. We were at a movie theater watching the animated film "Wall-E" when it became unbearable. That's when Jason asked me if I had skipped a period. My period had been due to start on the day of our wedding, but in the stress of everything, I had completely overlooked that it hadn't.

We immediately drove to Target to buy a home pregnancy test, and when I checked the wand I saw a faint pink line, indicating positive for pregnancy. We had been trying to get pregnant, assuming it would take some time since we weren't tracking my cycles. But lo and behold, it took us no time at all. We had conceived on my mom's birthday, while I was in a state of total grief.

Morning sickness lasted around the clock for me. I couldn't bear the smell of Ravi, and I couldn't handle Jason cooking food with any sort of aroma. I barely ate, I vomited all day long, and I lost twelve pounds in six weeks. Jason told me that I looked terminally ill, and he was extremely concerned about my well-being. He would work all day and come straight home to take care of me. When friends from work invited him to go climbing or out for a hike or a beer, he always declined because he didn't want me to feel alone in my agony. He was unhappy, too, and he wanted to be the best husband he could be for his pregnant, grieving wife.

Even though there was so much love between us, we each brought in our own unconscious assumptions about marriage. And in those assumptions, we leaned heavily on one another. We were still working under the unconscious belief that our partner was supposed to bring us satisfaction and happiness. Because we were unhappy, we wanted the other person to change so that we could be satisfied. However, neither of us was getting our needs met in the relationship, so we engaged in a tit-for-tat dynamic where it seemed like we weren't on the same team. We were engaged in the game of love, not real love.

Unable to embody the sovereign sense of love and wholeness we longed for, we resented one another for not being that for us. Our attachment wounds, projections, and fears lurked in the shadows, coming out sideways in anger, resentment, blame, and fear. We were in counseling, and it was mildly helpful for gaining communication and listening tools. However, no therapist highlighted for us the way in which we were entangled in the unmet needs of our younger parts and meeting one another from the false self. No one taught us about meeting one another from our essence, as whole and sovereign beings. It was painful to perpetuate these old patterns by projecting them onto one another and then being completely dissatisfied with one another's inability to fix our old pain.

We continued to live our day-to-day lives with apparent normalcy, not facing our pain and resentment while doing our best to uphold traditional marriage values.

Along with my online teaching job, I accepted a position with Boulder County Public Health leading alcohol diversion groups for college kids who had gotten multiple tickets for underage drinking. We bought a brand-new home with gorgeous finishes, and we landscaped the yard with beautiful trees, flowers, and rocks. We put tremendous effort into making our life together look amazing, but the details of our relational interactions were not tended to with such care and attention.

We had a nice house, we had money in the bank, we took vacations and camped, we exercised, and we ate well. Life was stable. This was what I had wanted for myself as a child, but now that I was living it as an adult, I began to see how this stability didn't magically create a healthy relationship. Jason's frugal and controlling nature combined with my accommodating and manipulative conditioning created a dynamic where I needed to ask permission to spend money even on simple things, like food and clothes. Every purchase was a battle, and I grew tired of continual conflict around finances. Eventually, I started hiding my spending from Jason, thinking that I was keeping a sense of stability. In reality, I was colluding in a very dysfunctional dynamic that I blamed him for. I reasoned that if he were less rigid around money we'd be fine. Thinking of myself as the victim to him, I couldn't see the way I was continually abandoning myself and hiding my truth.

We each lacked the self-awareness necessary to overcome our chronic conflict and nurture a secure connection. I tried to manage the emotional abyss I was sinking in, but I wasn't very good at that. I was good at making it look like I had it all together, but I wasn't actually skilled at using my pain for my healing and growth. I tried to seek out good therapy, but I was continually disappointed by what felt like surfaced presence with no healing in sight. I wallowed in my sadness and frustration, crying daily and isolating myself by not letting anybody know the truth of how much I was hurting.

As my belly grew, so did the distance between us. I tried to create a shift in our dynamic, but my effort seemed ineffective.

My mom had requested that her ashes be spread in Maui because that was where she had felt most free and alive. My sister and I had stopped talking after my mom's estate was sold. Grace had said hurtful things about me, Jason, and Mom during the end of Mom's life, and after she died Grace blocked my communication with all of Mom's friends, colleagues, and clients.

"Can I have Mom's email password?" she texted me. Since I had been the one communicating with everyone and organizing the fundraisers and memorial, I had also been replying to inquiries about referrals and staying in communication with people through my mom's email.

"Sure. It's goddess50," I replied without hesitation.

The next time I went to log in to check the email, I couldn't gain access.

"Hey, did you change Mom's password? I can't log in to her email," I texted.

No response. Ever. I was angry, I felt powerless, and I had no desire to continue to resolve this. Given the history of our dynamic, I wanted to protect my unborn child from her. She wasn't a safe person to be close to, and I wanted to protect my baby from being hurt by her.

When our interactions with the world come from our distortion, any effort we put forth to create the change we want doesn't have the impact that we desire. *It's not about the action we take or the words we choose. It's about the place within us from which we make that choice.* When we try to change our relationship dynamics from the place of our distortion, we can easily become frustrated by the lack of progress given the amount of effort we put in. However, when we attempt to cultivate change in our relationships from our alignment with the True Self, miraculous shifts can happen.

From our alignment with Source, we feel differently when we take that action or state our truth. We feel more empowered speaking on our behalf. We feel more solid when interacting at work. We feel more regulation as we do the dishes or clean the house. We feel more joy when parenting or exercising. We can be doing the exact same thing we did when we were living from our distortion, but the felt experience and the results are completely different.

THE TRANSITION

Because of my pregnancy, urgency pushed me to spread half of my mom's ashes before my baby was born and send the other half to Grace. This was not the most enlightened response I could have had at this time; however, it was the safest. When I contemplated going to Hawaii with Grace, memories of our family trips to Hawaii where she would explode with intense anger flashed through my mind. If things weren't going exactly as she wanted, she would become volatile. Going without her, keeping a safe distance, seemed necessary for my well-being and that of my child.

While traveling with Jason to my favorite Hawaiian island, I was given a painful reminder of how different we were and how hard it was for us to be in sync together. He didn't want to spend money on eating out, he hated the sun and the sand, and he complained about the price of everything. We were staying with a family friend up on Kula, and my dad had given us air miles to fly first class. We were spending so little money for this amazing vacation to honor my mom, and my attention was pulled toward appeasing Jason and making him happy.

Unconsciously thinking that I was responsible for other people's frustration and angst, I also unconsciously thought that it was my job to make them feel better. I cooked in our tiny kitchen, told him that I didn't need to eat out, and didn't buy any souvenirs. However, now that I was pregnant, that façade was becoming harder to uphold. We had some sweet moments together, but I was beginning to see how I really didn't like being around him and I started getting snippy with him.

"Fine, we don't need to have any fun if that will make you happy," I said in a moment of sideways resentment.

What I couldn't see at the time was that I was collapsing around my desire and blaming him for it. We had differing ideas of life, and I submitted to his to make him happy. But the payoff was my own misery.

I was banking on this baby to be the bridge that united us and the being who helped me to feel whole and happy. That was a lot of pressure for an unborn child, and I think she felt it because she did not want to come out.

Two weeks after my due date, I still hadn't started labor.

I loved it when people asked me when I was due and I could reply, "Two weeks ago." My midwife didn't want me to go past two weeks because there was an increased risk of the baby having her meconium (an infant's first bowel movement that is tar-like and sticky) in the womb. If the meconium was passed while in utero, the baby could ingest it through the amniotic fluid, presenting a great health risk to the baby.

It was a rainy spring day when we drove to the hospital for my induction. We were quiet with anticipation, and my body was tense with anxiety. I wanted to wait for natural labor and I had tried everything to get labor started: acupuncture every other day, chiropractic, sex, spicy food, nipple stimulation, and bouncing on an exercise ball, all in an effort to start labor, but to no avail.

We were lucky enough to have the option of certified nurse midwives in the hospital who had OB/GYNs as backup. This was a gift of living in such a progressive and holistic-minded part of the country. I felt safe with my team of birth professionals, but the hole where my mom would have been was a hugely painful part of my experience. My mom loved babies. As she was dying in the hospital, I had promised her that I would make her a grandma if she got well. She had supported many of her clients as they gave birth, and she was known for her loving presence during labor and delivery of the babies of her sisters and friends. Now it was my turn, and she wasn't there.

My induction started at 10 AM. As the midwife slowly introduced the Pitocin to my body, she tried to mimic natural labor as best she could, following the cues of my contractions. Since my mom couldn't be with me, I had hired a doula. Ruth encouraged me and fed me broth and walked me around the hospital to keep me engaged in the process and to have as natural a delivery as possible.

As my contractions increased, fear gripped me. Unable to surrender to the process of giving birth, I tightened with resistance. I didn't trust my body to birth my baby, and I cried, saying I didn't want to do this. Uncertain how to help me, Jason fetched my midwife, Merrilynn. In a moment's time, she was right there rubbing my low back, confident in my innate ability and power to succeed at delivery. Somehow, her presence gave me the courage to trust this process and the opening of the birth canal.

At 7:16 PM, just nine hours and sixteen minutes after the Pitocin was first administered, I pushed out my baby with all my might. Never in my life had I felt the amazing strength and power of my vagina. Feeling my baby move out and through me was strange and pleasurable, like the most satisfying bowel movement ever. I tore quite a bit during the delivery, and parts of my vaginal wall needed to be removed, then cauterized. Somehow I still felt like I could run a marathon after birthing my daughter.

Merrilynn immediately placed my baby on my stomach. The baby was perfect. She was beautiful, strong, and whole. My heart opened with love the moment I saw her. My sweet child, so full of love and purity. New life, not at all shaped by pain and suffering. Only love. That's what I saw in that moment: the birth of Love.

I wept a lot in the next few days. Baby blues hit me hard, but I also saw so much beauty. Oxytocin pumped through my body because I was breastfeeding, and I was in awe of everything. All I wanted to do was look at this angelic being and breathe in her beauty and light. I was in love with my daughter, who we named Mylah. My heart was growing bigger as my emotions were starting to grow darker and more unstable by the day.

When we birth a child, our hearts open in such a way that all of our unhealed trauma from the past come to the surface. Rising from the deep unconscious, the mind is trying to protect this new being from experiencing the pain that we felt in life. When we're able to meet that pain and fear consciously, we are able to purify ourselves of it at a deeper level. When we don't know how to meet it, the thoughts and feelings grow to large proportions and we loop through postpartum depression and anxiety.

The first months of motherhood were harder than I ever could have anticipated. It wasn't only my emotions that were hard to navigate; figuring out how to nurse and sleep were torturous for me. My nipples were in so much pain; she woke every two hours to eat around the clock, and my brain was starting to lose its faculties from lack of sleep. Simultaneously, I couldn't close my eyes. I was consumed by the fear of her dying. I loved her so much, and my unconscious mind was diligently alert to ensure her survival, which meant total insomnia for me.

All night long I would try to rest and recover only to pop up the moment I was about to surrender into sleep and watch to make sure she was still breathing. We crafted a plan where Jason would stay with her after her middle-of-the-night feeding, but I begged him to promise that he wouldn't sleep. I could only rest if I knew she was being watched. When I walked in and saw him asleep a few nights into this plan, I knew I couldn't trust him to keep her safe.

Because I was totally irrational and unable to regulate my system, my resilience was low, as was my tolerance for anything remotely stressful. Jason kept wanting to fix it—to fix the problems and to fix me. In his masculine approach to my feminine, emotional state, I felt dropped by him. I needed him to be emotionally attuned and responsive. In his wanting to fix me I felt shamed and worn in our interactions. I felt dismissed, like he was minimizing my fears. All I needed was to know he cared and loved me and would help keep us safe. I longed for him to be responsive to my emotionality, and he longed for me to be emotionally stable.

I had fantasized about bringing my child into a utopian home, where she felt loved and safe and cared for in the healthiest way possible. Instead, fear and anger were being imprinted on her through my projections. My deep love for her brought to the surface all of the ways

I didn't feel safe in the world. I thought this was all about the loss of my mom, but over time I realized that it was about all of the ways I had felt unsafe in this world. All of my old traumas were triggered in my relationship with Jason because I felt unsafe with him. He wasn't a caring and attuned partner. This became most obvious when I became suspicious of Jason sexually abusing her, which he wasn't doing. My mind was working overtime to keep her safe from all potential threats.

In my fear, I was causing more harm than good and I was drowning in anxiety. To make matters worse, I learned at her four-week wellness check that I wasn't making enough milk. I felt like a failure as a mom, and my life became consumed with trying to increase my milk supply. I tried lactation consultants, homeopathy, herbal tinctures, hops, oats, and fennel. I tried pumping around the clock to increase my supply. The consultants, my doctor, everyone told me to rest. That was the one thing I was incapable of doing, which increased my feeling of inadequacy. My supply never increased, and we were forced to supplement her diet. Not agreeing with the ingredients in commercial options of formula, we made our own natural formula using goat's milk as the base.

When a new baby is brought home, all parents feel stressed with the introduction of having a new being to care for. Couples who are securely connected, communicate as if they're on the same team, and genuinely listen to one another are able to meet the stress of that transition with resilience. Couples who do not feel secure and loved in their connection, argue against one another. Genuinely not understanding where the other is coming from, they miss one another in their suffering. Even though they love one another, the inability to stay regulated during this stressful time can severely fracture their connection. This is one way we pass on our attachment wounds to our children.

When we choose our partner from our wounds, our relationship reflects that, and then our children are affected. This doesn't mean that we have harmed our children. It simply means that we need to make a choice about our own healing and evolution. Once we become parents, our healing becomes our children's healing. Differentiating from our own wounds makes it so we don't project those wounds onto our children. Healing into life with our children is a clumsy journey filled with dignity, power, and love.

Just as our intimate partners trigger our disowned parts, our children do as well. Because our connection with them is emotionally close and intimate, we are more likely to project our unmet needs from childhood onto our partner and our children. The constant needs of children can be draining and depleting when we're identified with our wounds. Caring for our children can become the most uplifting and rejuvenating journey when done from our wholeness and alignment with Source. Partnership and parenting as a spiritual practice can guide us to the next level of our evolution when we meet the stress with conscious awareness.

SUPPRESSION

When Mylah was 7 months old, my postpartum anxiety turned into a deep depression. It was the Tuesday before Thanksgiving and I had planned to take a Pilates reformer class. I was desperate to do something for myself, and it took all of my energy to get out of the house and to the studio on time. Mylah was fed, Jason was prepped, and no one was going to need me for two whole hours. To a new mom who was drowning in grief and anxiety, this small window of self-care felt like a life boat.

When I arrived at the studio, the class had been canceled. I crumbled. I felt defeated and unimportant and heavy with sadness. I drove home distraught and in tears, and when I arrived I crawled into bed and thought of suicide. While my suicidal ideation was triggered by the canceled class, it really had nothing to do with the class itself. My desire to be dead came from a deep belief that life would never be joyful or happy. Stuck in my death urge with no end of suffering in sight, I couldn't muster the strength to go on.

My marriage was full of conflict, I felt like a failure as a mother, I was scared all of the time, and there was no one on this earth (I reasoned) who truly loved me. For three days I lay in bed, eating next to nothing, and moving only to nurse my child.

For months leading up to this, Jason had begged me to get help. I saw a therapist who specialized in postpartum mood disorders, but I found no value in talking about my agony or hearing her advice about self-care. I was adamantly opposed to pharmaceuticals so I refused to see a doctor. I wanted to be able to do this on my own. I wanted to be an amazing mom, a loving wife, and a successful professional in my field, but I was rapidly sinking.

"I understand now why some women were institutionalized after having babies," Jason said to me, trying to get me to understand the impact my postpartum state had on him.

Hearing this, I realized he was right. I wanted to be institutionalized, so at thirteen months postpartum, I went to a psychiatrist. Having grown up with alternative medicine as the only medicine, I had never taken a mood stabilizer. But I was desperate. I did it for my daughter, and I felt so much shame driving to see Dr. Jones.

Dr. Jones specialized in postpartum mood disorders, and during my first session, she explained to me that there are three precursors: a history of disordered premenstrual moods; a history or family history of anxiety or depression; and a severed or strained relationship with one's mother, including a death. I later learned that there is also research supporting the idea that having an emotionally unresponsive partner and a strained marriage contributes to and exacerbates the symptoms.

I felt relieved knowing that I had all three of these precursors. It gave me a sort of permission for falling apart and coming undone. And when she prescribed me Zoloft for my depression and Clonazepam to help me sleep, I needed total reassurance from her that these were okay for a breastfeeding mom to take. She assured me that these medications were safe for my baby, and against my better judgment I filled the prescriptions, desperate to find some sense of emotional stability and resilience.

When we birth our children, everything unresolved within us comes up in order to be purified. This happens because we love our baby so much and we're being given the essential gift of transformation, which is seeing our darkness more clearly. The challenging part of this gift is that it comes at a time when we're navigating more stress than imaginable. Working on ourselves and investing in our healing can seem overwhelming and untimely, especially when we don't know where to turn and we don't have a network of women we can call on for support. However, self-development and healing is essential for a secure bond with our child(ren).

I had thought that with our financial security, new home, careers, and physical health, Jason and I would be solid parents. I had done good work on myself, we had been going to couples counseling for many years, and we loved each other. What I couldn't see at the time was that having a baby wasn't the solution to my pain; it was the wearing down of all of the walls I had built against it. When I birthed my child, I opened up in a way that I wasn't equipped to handle, and it seemed that suppressing my emotions was the only way to survive at the time.

When we're conditioned to ignore our shadow and to present a light face to the world, we give our shadow power over our interior. In the denial of our own pain, we become a slave to it. In the claiming and welcoming of our pain, we become the watcher of it. From this place, we can cultivate a relationship to our pain and darkness that is empowering. We can develop a mastery over how we meet our inner world, and when we do this we are meeting the shadow from our powerful and wise True Self.

Courageously walking through the swampland of our unconscious shadow, we are using our pain to reconnect with Source. The only way through it is through it. And once we walk through it, once we walk through the darkness of our shadow, we emerge more solid in our alignment with Source. The impulse to zip up the pain and stuff the darkness away can be strong, especially when we have been conditioned to be easy and accommodating for our parents. We received safety and connection by hiding our darkness. But that story is outdated. The young one within might be scared, but in the presence of our own wise and mature self, we can hold her in her fear, see her in her pain, and give back any and all acquired misbeliefs about how to be in the world. Staying small is not what we're here to do.

8
COMING UNDONE

"For a seed to achieve its greatest expression, it must come completely undone. The shell cracks, its insides come out and everything changes. To someone who doesn't understand growth, it would look like complete destruction."—Cynthia Occelli

IS THIS WORLD SAFE?

Under the sedation of suppressive medication, I was actually able to sleep for the first time in over a year. Mylah had been sleeping through the night for many months, and now I could enjoy a good night's slumber once again. Zoloft did an amazing job at suppressing my anxiety and grief, but it also suppressed my joy and appetite and ability to have an orgasm. I felt like a zombie, imitating the picture of a perfect life by bringing my daughter to art classes and story time but feeling dead inside.

My vanity loved that food repulsed me. I lost all of my baby weight plus some extra pounds. I became so skinny that my pants hung on my protruding hip bones. My eating disorder was activated, and my suppressed appetite turned into a game for me to see how long I could go without eating. I stopped preparing food for myself and I only ate the remnants of Mylah's meals.

Though I was living only on medication and scraps of food, Jason thought I was back to normal. I looked great and I wasn't hysterical with grief any more. I was going through the motions of life, and this was a vast improvement from the year we had just come out of. And since I was so skilled at appearing like I had it all together, I went back to hiding how deeply I was suffering on the inside, masking my pain with my bright smile and stylish outfits.

Somewhere in the stability of the following year, I decided that I wanted another baby. I felt the spirit of this baby who wanted to come through me, and I promised Jason that if I had postpartum anxiety again I would get on medication immediately. He agreed, and after I titrated off my medication I quickly got pregnant.

I was attending a prenatal yoga class with my friend Rebecca, and on our way back to my house she asked, "What do you think about the new info out about fracking?"

"I'm not sure. I haven't heard. What is it?" I asked.

Our home was situated just five hundred feet from a large drilling site; we could see it from our house. The oil and gas company was horizontally drilling underneath our home, but we hadn't researched the potential environmental concerns of living so close to an active drilling site.

Rebecca invited me to a free informational talk on the potential hazards of drilling hosted by Erie Rising, which was started by a group of concerned citizens. The next day I met Rebecca at the public library to listen to the concerns and view the documentary "Gasland."

With the little bit of information I gathered, I became terrified for our children's health and safety. I came home and told Jason about the potential risks of living so close to a well, and he started doing his own research. When he looked at a map of active wells in our area, we learned that within a one-mile radius of our house there were sixty-eight active wells with more under construction.

Since we'd moved into this house, Jason had been getting bloody noses, and I was having a hard time breathing. Nested in the foothills of the Rocky Mountain's Front Range, Boulder sits at 5,328 feet above sea level. We had thought our symptoms were a consequence of living at a higher altitude than we were accustom. But with the possibility that there was something more dangerous going on, we didn't want to risk our children's development and well-being by staying there.

We mutually decided to sell our house, and to our surprise it sold quickly. There was so much fracking on the Front Range—and the housing market was so hot—that buyers overlooked the field of wells in order to have affordable housing. Unfortunately, given the booming housing market at the time, we couldn't find another place to live. There weren't many houses in our price range on the market, and when we did find a house we liked in an area far from fracking wells, we were instantly outbid. To make matters worse, the rental market was affected by the housing boom and we couldn't find a long-term rental that we wanted to live in with our children, either.

My due date was quickly approaching, and we had to move out of our house so the new owners could move in. We found a moving service that included temporary housing for people relocating, we put all of our stuff in storage, and we moved into a small furnished apartment that we could rent monthly. Every day in this apartment seemed like purgatory to my pregnant body. The bed was uncomfortable, the walls smelled like an ashtray, and the cooking utensils were nearly impossible to use.

Desperate to be in our own place before our baby was born, I cried daily at the grim circumstances of our life. I was horrified at the thought of bringing my new baby home to this apartment that smelled like cigarettes, with no crib, car seat, or nursing pillow. I tried to make this a fun adventure for Mylah, taking her swimming and to the playground every day. But I was hysterical with fear. I was gripped with anxiety as I searched online for homes, and I turned to food in the stress of it all, gaining over 80 pounds.

The day Jason came home to let me know that he found a beautiful home on a creek path for us to rent, I was both relieved and terrified. The house seemed beautiful in the pictures, but it was situated on a well-used walking path. I was afraid that Mylah would either get out of the yard or someone walking on the path would kidnap her. I made Jason agree that he would watch her diligently, and we decided to move into this rental.

The contents of our storage unit arrived as I was picking my aunt Dallas up from the airport, who was coming out to help us unpack. The next day as we were getting the kitchen set up, I stood up from sitting in a chair and my underwear were wet.

"Oh no! I think I just peed!" I said to Dallas as I looked at the floor.

"Quick, go to the bathroom!" she said.

We both started laughing, and more fluid kept leaking out of me.

"Maybe that's not pee ..." I mused.

"That looks clear, like your water broke!" she said.

I went to the bathroom, and sure enough I was not peeing my pants. It was two weeks before my due date, and I had been convinced that this baby would be late like my first. Having just moved into our new home the day before, we'd barely had time to unpack the car seat and crib. With such a small friend group and no family living close by, I was beyond relieved to have my aunt in town to finish unpacking and watch Mylah while I drove myself to the hospital, having Jason meet me there.

Even though this labor started on its own, my contractions were so far apart that I still needed Pitocin to move me along. My state of being was completely different throughout this delivery than from my first. Where I was scared and tense giving birth the first time, now I was jovial and receptive to care. I trusted my body's ability to birth this baby, and I was able to receive care and support from Jason. I had never spent the night away from Mylah, and I cried because I missed her. Throughout this labor and delivery, I felt softer and more open than I had in my entire life.

Seventeen hours after my water broke, at 5:26 AM, I was holding my son, Tobin, in my arms.

It was a hot summer day when he was born, and a few hours after his birth, lightning struck fire on the Flatiron mountain range. The hospital's ventilation system pulled air in from the outside, so right when we were getting ready to go to sleep our room reeked of smoke. Jason and I were scared of our beautiful new baby boy breathing in fire smoke, so we requested to be discharged. Since Tobin had had a healthy vaginal birth and I was a second-time mom, we were able to get discharged on the same day he was born. And because my aunt had been working so hard on moving us into our new home, I was able to crawl into my bed at 10 PM and sleep with my sweet boy on my chest.

All of the angst of potential environmental health hazards from the previous months had me on edge, and my anxiety was at an all-time high. I immediately went to Dr. Jones and started taking the same medications as before; however, this time they didn't seem as effective. Dr. Jones increased the dosage of both of my medications, and I still could barely sleep and was extremely restless and fearful.

Doing my best to take care of a toddler and an infant meant I rarely got out of the house. Desperate for adult connection and surroundings that were anything other than our home, I packed our bags for the three minute drive to the Farmer's Market. I was proud that I had managed to get all three of us in the car, and I felt like I could breathe again once I heard the chatter and the music from the market.

As we were strolling down the busy aisle looking at the fresh produce, I saw my colleague Joy from Boulder County Public Health, where I was still leading alcohol diversion groups. I was on maternity leave and wasn't sure that I wanted to return, because I had hopes of starting a private practice.

When Joy asked how I was doing, I told her how I was struggling to make enough milk for Tobin and that I was back on medication.

Without any other questions, Joy said, "This is all old grief," pointing to my breasts. "This is about your mom."

Stunned that she knew this so instantly, I said, "I know, but I don't know what to do about it."

"You need to see my homeopath. She can help you. Let me give you her number."

"If homeopathy could help me my dad would have given me a remedy by now," I replied.

"No, this is different. He can't see you because you're too close to him. You need to see my homeopath."

Because she was so insistent, I agreed to see her homeopath but balked at the price. Afraid that Jason wouldn't want me spending money on a homeopath when we had insurance that could cover my medical care, I was hesitant to follow through. However, being tired of appeasing

Jason's frugal nature at the cost of my own well-being, I was desperate to feel better so I made an appointment.

When I drove up the long driveway of Aspen Farm to see Deborah, the homeopath, for the first time, I assumed I was there to talk about my milk supply. Yet when I sat down on Deborah's sofa in her living room with my newborn baby on my lap, I felt like she could see right through me. I instantly became squirmy, trying to hide my pain from her. I wanted her to think I had it all together, the same way I wanted to convince everyone else of this fallacy. But Deborah was different. She listened with a clarity and discernment unlike any possessed by any other person I had ever encountered. Beyond my words, Deborah was tracking my whole system and she seemed to understand me in the deepest way possible.

As I told Deborah about the tragic death of my mom, I could feel my darkness and pain fighting to be seen. It was as if all of the suppressive medication and all of my suppressive techniques of denial and hiding were insufficient and my pain was struggling to get to the surface. Even though this was extremely uncomfortable, I could sense in a deeper way that this moment was pivotal for my growth and evolution.

Deborah was leaving for Nepal the following day, and she gave me four remedies to take in the month that she would be gone: one for old grief, one for fear of contamination, one for my milk supply, and one because my mom died from cancer, which helps us heal the way we give our will over to others and then resent them for it.

Deborah seemed to understand the way in which I felt unsafe in the world better than myself or any of the therapists I had seen.

"You need to feel really safe in life to sink into a nice sweet sleep," she said to me when I told her of my chronic insomnia.

She pointed out my fear of contamination and distrust in the world in connection to the fracking wells, the smoke of the Flatiron fires, and consuming food that wasn't organic. When I told her of my childhood, she could highlight the ways in which I didn't feel safe in the world due to the parties at my mother's house, my sister's anger, and my feeling blamed for the divorce. It had never occurred to me before this moment that my early childhood experiences were having me feel unsafe in the world now.

All of my experiences felt seen, validated, and welcomed in Deborah's presence, and her words landed in me like a soothing balm to my soul. I had been so entangled in my fear that I couldn't make any sense of it. Speaking to Deborah, for the first time since before my mom died I felt totally and completely trusting of the process of life.

When I left Deborah's I went straight to Joy's house to get advice on how to take the remedies. Joy encouraged me to start with the remedy for grief, and the moment the pellets touched my tongue I instantly felt more like myself, like I was aligning with Source.

From this place, I could see how suppressive medication is a Band-Aid that doesn't actually serve deeper healing. The grief remedy helped my mind open to the possibility that all of my pain had a purpose: that my mom's death, the conflict with Jason, and my fears about keeping my babies safe from harm were all in service of something greater that I couldn't fully comprehend.

I suddenly felt deeply accepting of all of my pain and I could see that my suffering was ignited so that I could go deeper into my healing. I had no resistance inside me anymore, only deep surrender to the unfolding of my journey.

When I told my dad about the powerful effect of these remedies, he immediately sent me copies of some pages from *Homeopathic Psychology* by Phillip M. Bailey (1995). In the section about the grief remedy, Bailey described a patient with a very similar past to mine and with similar behavior to mine, such as emotional outbursts, silent brooding, high expectations, and other contradictory states. I was astounded to see myself reflected in these descriptions. What's more, I was completely taken aback that Deborah could see these characteristics in me when I hadn't told her about my emotional instability.

Deborah's remedies worked with different aspects of my emotional dysregulation, and as I took them I could feel my system coming back into a state of balance. The anxiety remedy in particular was extremely helpful in easing my restlessness and fear of contamination. I had been cleaning nonstop, which Jason liked, but I was doing it from a place of fear. With the remedy in my system, I could still clean, but from a place of presence rather than anxiety, where I was more solid in myself.

Because there has been conflicting research on homeopathy, many people do not trust in its curative ability. However, it's an energetic medicine. It's designed to bring one's energetic system back into a state of balance, to clear delusions that have been acquired, and to align the Soul with Source. It uses diluted elements from nature to match the symptoms of a person. When the right remedy is given at the right time and in the right dose, it's magical. Science often dismisses and misses magic.

CULTIVATING MAGIC

With the right remedies in my system, I began to slowly wean off of the Zoloft and Clonazepam. And when Deborah returned from Nepal I was eager to continue working with her.

"Nothing else has been able to help me feel better. I want to learn how you do what you do," I said enthusiastically at my second session.

"I'd love to have you join my next class, which is starting next week. One thing you need to remember, Harmony, is that most people don't move as fast as you. Because you eat healthy and have had so little suppressive medication in your life, your vital force responds really well to remedies."

I passionately threw myself into my healing process and my study of homeopathic psychology. The study of homeopathy came naturally to me. I had been taking remedies since I was 8, and I had studied some of the philosophy in the past. In college I had given a speech on homeopathy and knew about the principles of like cures like and Herring's law where healing happens from the inside out, from the top down, and from the newest to the oldest symptom. The thing that I learned from Deborah that had eluded me before was that homeopathy is considered "God's medicine." It works with a person's vital force to bring them back into alignment with Source and gently nudge out any way they are holding old experiences.

As I was prescribed more remedies, over time my whole system—mind, body, and spirit—felt heathier and more aligned for having used homeopathy. Sometimes I could feel the remedies undoing the impact of the past on me. Literally, I felt like I was moving back in time through the experiences, stripping away the layers of the pain that had created my misbeliefs and mistuned energy.

When Deborah worked with a client, she cleared a person's miasmatic predisposition. This means that she cleared and cured current patterns of pain along with ancestral patterns of trauma in layers, like peeling away layers of an onion. Sometimes my experience of having my miasm cleared felt more like unwinding barbed wire from around my soul because the pain and agony of moving through my old trauma and my ancestral trauma was not necessarily blissful and easy. But I was so trusting of this powerful medicine that I continued to move through the process. My relationship with Deborah was essential to being able to see myself more clearly through her reflections, and the degree to which I trusted her had me trusting the healing process all the more.

Deborah was an angel in my life when I was most desperate, and the deeper I went into my healing with her, the more I began to touch old traumas that I had forgotten. I had always run a script in my head that told me I had never been molested or assaulted. I believed this with everything inside of me, but the remedies helped me to uncover the ways in which I hid my pain and pretended that everything was okay. In that uncovering, I remembered Shane touching my vulva, Joe assaulting me, Troy raping me while I slept, and many guys penetrating me without consent.

Along with remedies and talk therapy, Deborah used a technique called trauma resilience model (TRM) where I was guided to regulate and move through old trauma while staying embodied and grounded. In these session, I was able to be with younger parts of myself in loving and healing ways. I could access the part of me that had a felt sense and an intrinsic memory of past traumas, and I could see how all of my traumas had me split from my alignment with Source. Using the pain as the doorway to the Light, I would bring in a higher consciousness to the part of me that felt wounded and small and powerless. Just like with remedies, each TRM session had me feeling more differentiated from my wounds. I felt more whole, more expansive, and more like myself with each session.

THE FALL

Throughout my entire life I had been seeing the world through the lens of a wound I didn't fully recognize or understand. This ubiquitous and obscure wound caused me to loathe myself and believe I was ugly and unlovable. I couldn't see how I was identified with my wound until I started to differentiate from it while I was working with Deborah. I wore this wound as who I was, but I was so deep in it I hadn't a clue that my identity was wrapped up in it.

"I think you should know that I have an old head trauma," I told Deborah one day when I realized that she could treat symptoms that other people deemed unhealable.

Deborah had a look of astonishment on her face as I told her the story: "When I was 5 months old, my dad put me on the top bunk of a bed so I could sleep while we were at a friend's house. When I woke up I tried to reach for him and I fell on the hard floor."

Although I had no conscious memory of this fall, this was the story I had always been told. Hearing about the fall, Deborah prescribed a homeopathic protocol for old head traumas. Over the next eight weeks, I took my remedies as prescribed. With each dose, I started seeing my stored pain in my head more clearly and I started realizing the emotional impact of the fall.

In several TRM sessions with Deborah, along with deep work with other healers over the next few years, the story and the impact of the fall became clearer:

Five months after my birth, in the summer of 1977, my family went to a party at a friend's house. After nursing, I fell asleep and my dad took me from my mom to try and find a place to put me to bed. He tucked me into the top bunk of a bunkbed and proceeded to go party with his friends. There was a lot of weed and alcohol in the atmosphere, and that haze lived in my system as well.

When I awoke, I made some coos but nobody heard me. I started wiggling and rolled over to try and get to my dad. I rolled over again, and fell.

From the upper bunk on the long trip to the floor, with a hard *whack* I hit my eyebrow on the edge of a dresser. Then I fell the rest of the way and hit the ground on the right side of my head and on my right shoulder. My body was folded over my head until I flipped the rest of the way.

Blood streamed from my head as I lay on the hard ground alone, not understanding why there was so much pain and not knowing why this had happened. The pain was so unbearable that I wanted to die. I didn't want to be in this body when this body was a source of such intense suffering and agony. Just moments before, I had felt totally aligned with universal bliss, so connected to the Source of all things, and now I was experiencing the worst pain imaginable. It was confusing and disorienting.

All I wanted was to be held, but on the long way to the ground it was clear that there was no one there for me, that my need for comfort and connection didn't matter. And at just 5 months old, there was no way to make sense of this experience.

My spirit left for a few moments, trying to get back to universal bliss. I held my breath, trying to stay out of my body, wishing I could leave this earthly plane of unconscious beings and return to the pure love of the spirit realm. But breath came back into me, and I let out an agonizing wail.

As I lay there crying and bleeding, several people rushed to me, screaming in fear. The rush of fear coming at me from the crowd of disoriented and high people confused me even more.

"Oh my God! She's going to die!" my mom sobbed as she saw her new baby on the ground, bleeding, in pain.

"Let me see her," my dad said as he tried to stay calm and assess the degree of my head trauma.

I was in agony, my skull was fractured, I had a concussion, and blood was everywhere. This intense pain caused me to feel small and powerless, which had me feeling totally split from my connection to Source, fragmented from my alignment with God. My impulse to leave my body was an attempt to reconnect with Source. And in this impulse, I got caught between two dimensions, resisting the experience of being fully embodied.

In my pain, I needed a calm, soothing touch and to be held in love. But the adults around me were gripped with fear and under the influence of substances. Totally out of alignment with God consciousness, my parents' presence caused me to feel even less safe. Although I was close to death and wanted to die, I wasn't afraid of death—I was at peace with that realm. The presence of their panic caused me to dysregulate, fearing that this world wasn't safe for me and ultimately bringing me further away from my alignment with Source.

They projected all of the fear they had about me dying onto me, and that fear landed in my energetic system. I hadn't yet developed a sense of self; children are inherently boundaryless. Their fear became mine and I carried it around in my emotional and energetic body, as well as in my deep unconscious psyche, until I became aware of it many years later.

Being a newly embodied Spirit, before this experience I was without imprint and beliefs about how I needed to be in the world to earn love, approval, and safety. I was so connected to my vitality and my inherent trust in the world that I didn't yet know of fear and pain and abandonment. Because this trauma occurred when I was preverbal, my entire experience of life was influenced by it and I didn't even know it. With fear as my base emotion, and with a strong death urge that I couldn't recognize, my unconscious impulses in relationship with others and with myself had always been colored by this experience.

Disconnected from the wholeness of my being at 5 months old, I began to identify with pain rather than my essence. Clinging to my pain like a dog to a bone, I believed that I was my pain, that love was painful, and that I was unworthy of care and connection. Feeling broken and wounded, a part of me always wanted to die in order to get back to the bliss of being in alignment with Source.

To keep myself safe, I became "other-referenced," where I kept my attention out to assess my safety and acceptability. Leaking energy out of my head where the wound lived, I would leave myself to try to get connection. I couldn't see that the true sense of safety I longed for comes from my alignment with Source, so I leaned on other people to find that sense of safety.

While I was thinking that I was small and powerless in the world, the misbelief that I needed to stay in a tight box with limited range of self-expression to be safe was created here. I was accommodating, agreeable, and quiet in order to earn a sense of safety. If I asked for nothing, my unconscious mind reasoned, I would never be dropped again. This box felt like death since it kept me away from embodying my vast, expansive, powerful self that is my true nature. Fully embodying our alignment with Source is the most vulnerable and courageous thing we can ever do. It takes a tremendous life urge to be in touch with our will and embody our essence.

Collapsing around my will over and over again, the pattern of self-betrayal was second nature to me. Blind to my own unconscious wish to disappear, I tried to distract myself from the discomfort of not feeling like I belonged on the planet with various vices throughout my life. Drugs, sex, electronics, anorexia, shopping, overeating, and so on kept me disconnected from the light of my awareness. My breath became out of sync with my natural rhythm during the fall, and because that trauma lived within me unresolved I would frequently hold my breath. Not pulling life in was a symptom of my death urge, and I was keeping life out.

Eventually, over the course of several breathwork sessions, I had to give myself permission to go fully into my death urge so that I could find my will to live. I held my breath so tightly that I gasped for air, then held it in again. In an instant, I realized that I wanted to choose life—that I wanted to breathe in the sweet breath of life. I realized that my life has a purpose that is far greater than the pain of old trauma.

I had heard this story many times throughout my life, but it wasn't until I became a mom myself and was gripped with fear about my own newborn's safety that I began to see how deeply this wound had affected me. Because my postpartum anxiety grew to a dangerous level, I had to look within to see what was driving my intense fear. Projecting my fear of being unsafe in the world onto my own infant was very painful, and it was coming from a place in me that my conscious awareness couldn't comprehend. Our projections are the mind's attempt at making sense of the past, and once I had my own baby my mind diligently tried to make sense of all of the ways I felt unsafe in my history.

When I look at baby pictures of myself, I can see that I was concussed. Dazed. Disassociated. My needs and safety didn't matter even at a time that I was totally dependent on the adults in my life to keep me safe. From the moment we are born, we all want to know that we're safe to be in relationship. This fall conditioned me to believe not only that I am not safe in relationship but also that I'm not safe in my body. The ripple effect that this fall had on me was so deep and so extensive that I couldn't even see it because it was a normal part of my experience of being alive.

My baseline was fear. Fear of touch, fear of vulnerability, fear of pain, fear of being dropped, fear of being not enough, fear of not being wanted or loved. Since I was swimming in an ocean of fear, I couldn't see the water I was swimming in. It was just the way I was, the way life was.

Feeling deformed and unwanted, I never felt safe with either of my parents. Without an opportunity for a secure attachment, I became totally self-reliant, not trusting others to be there for me and closing off to vulnerability. But underneath this self-reliance there was a soft underbelly craving safe connection. Never feeling safe to allow myself to feel the craving of connection, I never again wanted someone after this fall—that was way too painful.

Physically, the impact of this fall was obvious. The scar over my right eyebrow, the way my right shoulder turned in and was lower than the left, the irregular curvature in my spine, and the constant pain in my head, neck, bicep, and back were daily reminders of how my parents had failed me. There was never a day in my life after that fall that my body wasn't in some degree of pain.

The dense scar tissue in my inner ear has brought me down with intense vertigo on several occasions. This happened a few times after feeling painfully emotionally dropped by an intimate partner, and it caused me to lie in bed for three days, spinning. When this happened, I reverted back to the newborn place of feeling scared and alone on the floor. Totally helpless.

My body felt like a fragile place to live, and relationships seemed like an unsafe thing to desire.

Very early on in my life I began to present a distorted face to the world. Off-center from the core of my being, disconnected from my alignment with Source, I started using strategies of my small self to try to find safety on this dimension. Never speaking to my emotional pain, dissonant perspective, or desire, I showed the world my light, my agreeable nature, and my flexibility. I was easy for everyone, making others more important than myself. And in the hiding of my pain and darkness, I started creating a life based on an inauthentic mask that subversively hid my truth.

Feeling fragmented, unlovable, and afraid of connection, I quieted my voice. These were all symptoms of feeling separate from Source, of forgetting my true nature. Believing that I was small and powerless, I tried to prevent myself from being dropped again by hiding. Not trusting others to be there for me, I started managing my inner world and pretending that I was okay when I really wasn't.

In one session, I imagined wrapping my infant self in a swaddle, held in the light of the Divine Mother. Deborah asked me if I wanted to be swaddled, and she took a blanket from her sofa and wrapped me tight. I needed that. I needed to feel held in love. I didn't know I deserved to feel cared for, and receiving this care opened me up in a new way.

Doing this deep work with my infant self while also being a new mom was powerful for me. I felt shame that I hadn't done this work before motherhood. I was dismayed that my children had been exposed to my anxiety and unhealed grief. Ultimately, though, through the sacred journey of my own healing, I came to see the power of healing into life with my children. Evolving and growing together, I didn't need to be perfect, I just needed to heal into my fullest expression. Rather than keeping me (and them, by extension) cycling through the same pain over and over again, my healing was a gift to my children. Embodying my wholeness, they are seen in their wholeness. Meeting my darkness and pain with curiosity, I'm able to be curious about their darkness and pain. Accessing the source of love and healing, I meet them from that deep place and they feel safe and secure in our connection. This is, perhaps, the greatest victory of all.

9
HONORING THE TRUTH OF MY HEART

"As you start to walk out on the way, the way appears."—Rumi

UNMASKING MY ESSENCE

For all practical outward purposes, Jason and I were a wonderful married couple. We created a beautiful home together, had wonderful children, and had compatible values around health, fitness, and lifestyle. Our routine was very comfortable. We had an unspoken agreement about our roles and our dynamic, and we both held up our part of the agreement with integrity and consistency. Our life was very wholesome and safe, just what I had always needed when I was a child.

Jason was a product manager at an outdoor clothing manufacturer and was passionate about the environment and adventure. Our kids attended private preschools with a focus on nature, kindness, health, and community. I had maintained my faculty position teaching online, but I had grown tired of my job at Boulder County Public Health. After all of the healing I had done with Deborah, I decided that it was time to start my private practice, which had been my dream since I was a young child.

From the outside, everything looked great. But the entanglement of our painful marriage dynamic persisted, and I habitually collapsed around my power and hid the full range of my being. Unconsciously I thought I needed to meet Jason in his conservative values to keep connection, so I tried to hide my magical, liberal self, a pattern I still carried around from childhood from trying to fit into societal norms.

When Jason glimpsed my magic and my ability to manifest what I wanted, he would call it "voodoo." Playing cards I would say aloud the card I wanted to pull next, and sure enough when I turned the card over the one I had voiced was there. He witnessed my ability to manifest parking places against all odds, get unusual job offers in the exact position I wanted, and be successful in the world even though I wasn't playing by the rules he thought the world lived by. Each time he called out my voodoo, I felt shame for being magical and tried to hide it from him.

Where before I felt like the wholesome child from "The Waltons" stuck in "The Addams Family," I now felt like Samantha from "Bewitched" stuck trying to appease Darren. I hid my powerful self and put on a guise of normalcy to try to let Jason think he had control as the man of the house. This antiquated relationship dynamic didn't fit what I wanted, but I unconsciously perpetuated it daily. Jason was afraid that I would surpass him and leave him if I claimed my power. Even though he was also working on himself, he expressed this fear more and more as he witnessed my evolution and growth.

When I dove into my study of homeopathy, Jason became more afraid of my witchy ways and was very resistant to this form of healing. He saw Deborah for sessions because I was so emphatic about it, but he seemed to be afraid to let go of his conditioned self because that's where his sense of control and safety was seated.

The more I was able to experience the magic of healing and aligning with Source, the more excited I became to work with clients. I could see people more clearly now and with greater understanding of the source of their pain. However, I had tremendous fear around launching my private practice. I felt like an imposter, as if no one would want to come and see me, and as if I was completely incompetent for the job. Becoming a healer had been my dream since I was 6 years old, and because this dream was so dear to my heart, I was terrified that I would fail.

Jason and I bought a new house when Tobin was 8 months old, one with a home office with its own entrance from the outside. Jason helped me paint my office in a Zen green, and I bought beautiful furniture to welcome my new clients.

I had the office—but I had no clients. I also wasn't well networked because I didn't go to graduate school in the area. I decided to create a niche in postpartum mood disorders and began networking with the amazing birth community thriving in Boulder.

When my first client called, I was scared and trembling, unsure of how to talk about my work or let her know how I could help her. I gave my best pitch about my training as a Gestalt psychotherapist and my history with teaching mindfulness meditation. I desperately wanted a client and would have seen her for free if that's what it took. When she asked how much I charged, I was afraid that I was going to lose her if my price was too high. I quoted her $60, and she quickly booked her first session.

When she arrived, she explained her history of sexual abuse, physical trauma, and early maternal death. As a new mom, the pain of her past was affecting her child negatively. She wanted to heal so she didn't pass on her wounds, and I was eager to serve her in her healing. Even though I had the wisdom, there was a part of me that was afraid to say something that would make her not like me. I couldn't see that my conditioned self was present in the session, just as it was with my intimate relationship.

While I knew I could do more for her than I was doing, she seemed to love her sessions. She cried, saying this was the first time she had ever had good therapy. My perfectionism wanted me to be better, though. I wanted to support her in full and total transformation. I knew her whole healing was possible, and I wanted to do more for her. But I couldn't figure out why the sessions didn't feel deep enough to me.

Around this time, Deborah referred me to a couples counselor because Jason and I kept circling around the same painful conflict, unable to see our way out. I was growing tired of trying to be perfect for him and believing his blame and criticism of me. I had been so conditioned to believe I was responsible for everybody else's well-being that I didn't know how to stop. Every time Jason expressed dislike for something I did, my inner perfectionist was triggered and I would get smaller and smaller to try to make him happy.

Because I was stuck in my story that Jason was rigid and controlling, I couldn't see how he was reflecting my own beliefs about me not mattering. He was an image of my own mind, here to teach me the very thing I needed to grow. I thought if he changed then we would be okay, but once we started working with our new couples counselor, Karen, I began to see my dysfunction in our dynamic.

At our first session with Karen, her presence allowed me to immediately trust her ability to see us beyond our words, much like Deborah. After we gave her a bit of history and let her know the dire state of our relationship, she had us find our Enneagram Type. I had studied the Enneagram in graduate school, and I knew that I was a Type 2 "Helper," but I had never used it in any practical way. After taking a short test, Jason typed himself as a Type 5 "Investigator."

Karen explained why this is important to know by starting from the beginning: when we are born, we are a newly embodied spirit, open to giving and receiving love freely. We don't yet have any ideas about what we need to do to earn love and acceptance. Around the age of 18 months we begin to develop an identity or sense of self. In psychology we call this our ego, which literally translates to the word "I." This is different from the way people use the word "ego" to describe someone who is full of themselves. The psychological ego is about who we think we are, our sense of self separate from others. This is the part of our psyche that experiences the outside world and reacts to it.

Early in childhood, we have formative experiences with our primary caregivers that shape our beliefs about our identity and begin to form our ego. We use these beliefs to guide the way we interact with the world, and they become our patterned way of engaging with others, also known as our personality.

The root word for personality is *persona*, and in Latin this literally translates to the word "mask." Our personality is masking our essence, that part of us that has been with us since the moment of our conception, and even beyond that—for lifetimes. Becoming intimately familiar with our mask, knowing patterns of thought and behavior driven by the unconscious beliefs we have about ourselves, is the very thing we need to differentiate from our ego.

When we can see our mask with clarity, we are in our witness mind, no longer identified with this small part of ourselves. From here, we can cultivate a relationship with our True Self as who we really are.

The Enneagram is a psychological and spiritual framework for understanding our mask so that we no longer identify with it. Having an ego is important. We need to have ways to navigate the world. Having a sense of self is vital in navigating this dimension. However, when we believe that reality lives in the thoughts, impulses and drives of our ego, we passively allow ourselves to be pulled away from our essence.

After Karen explained all of this, I looked at her with astonishment. This. All of this. This was exactly what I needed to be reminded of. I knew this in the depths of my soul but part of me had forgotten. The part of me that feels small, powerless, and insignificant had become so loud that I had forgotten about my infinite self. When I was 6 and again when I was 22, I had remembered my essence. However, I identified with my conditioning as who I was and that caused me to fall asleep to my True Self.

My mask (sometimes called a false self, fragmented self, or conditioned self) is not who I am. Even though my mind really believes that this is who I am, it is not. The world colludes with me in believing that I am my conditioned self, lauding me for my "helper" tendencies. But I am so much more than this. Learning how to engage with the world from my expansive, powerful True Self, learning how to embody my wholeness, was the next step in my personal development.

I was eager to learn more, but when I looked over at Jason he seemed perplexed. Slumped over in defeat, he seemed overwhelmed by the prospect of transcending his egoic self. The main motivation of the Type 5 comes from fear that they don't have enough and that they don't have the inner strength to face life. They're the most introverted Type, and they experience the world through their mind. Afraid of being intruded upon, they are very sensitive to other people's energy and they retreat into themselves. They want to specialize in something in order to feel secure in the world. Jason was identified with this way of being, and although he didn't like it, it was familiar.

The Type 2's main motivation is to earn love. Because they feel inherently unlovable, they want to help others, care for them, and seduce them in order to get the love they desire. To compensate for their fear of being not enough, a 2 becomes very prideful, believing that they are special. Type 2 individuals put other people's needs first, often not even knowing what they need, and then become the martyr.

This is an image-focused type that is very sociable and extroverted, and they experience the world through their heart. I could see for the first time how my personality appeared functional on the outside but came from deeply entrenched and hidden shame.

Karen told us that in her work, the Type 2 and the Type 5 are the most challenging to be in relationship together. But she assured us that if we did this work we could meet from a deeper place.

Jason and I both felt a deep resonance with our types, and we began studying our own Type and each other's Type in service of transcending our conditioning. We both committed to at least thirty minutes of daily meditation, and I bought the book "The Wisdom of the Enneagram" by Riso and Hudson (1999), which I read cover to cover.

I had been meditating throughout my life, always with profound results. With the newfound ingredient of knowing my Enneagram Type, I could see my conditioned self in meditation with more clarity. This clarity gave me distance, so I could cultivate my watcher mind with more mastery. No longer identified with the thoughts of the helper, I had space to cultivate a relationship with the truest version of myself, that part of me that's expansive and powerful and holds wisdom and truth.

"I wonder if she likes me," my conditioned self would think.

"Thought," I would say to myself, labeling my mind's ego chatter.

Then I would take a deep breath and turn my inner eye inward to the core of my being.

On and on and on, my conditioned mind worried about what others thought of me, whether I had earned their love enough, or what I could do better next time. Being identified with my conditioned self was exhausting and depleting. Understanding the unconscious motives of these thoughts allowed me to see my mask with clarity. From this vantage point I was empowered to stop indulging it. I would turn toward the vast and expansive space within all of that nattering, and I was able to witness my ego without being identified with it as truth or reality. From here, I was empowered to begin to cultivate an identity with my True Self as who I really am.

During that first session, Karen said, "Your True Self is that part of you that is never depleted. When you can see a solution to any problem, always go for connection, love, and trust, you know you are aligned with your True Self." As a Type 2, this was tricky for me. My ego thinks I'm being loving when I betray myself. My ego thinks that self-abandonment is the way to go for connection. I had to spend many hours in meditation, differentiating the manipulative tactics of my ego from the true and powerful presence of the True Self. Having glimpsed my True Self at various times throughout my life, I had a reference point to come back to. Understanding the difference between real love and ego love, I began to embody the source of love.

As I dedicated myself to this process, I spent more time in the quiet stillness that takes place beyond the thoughts. At first this practice happened quickly, where I would stop the stream, come to the silence, then be pulled back to the thoughts in an instant. But over time, with persistent practice, I began to spend more and more time in the stillness.

Sitting in the spaces between my thoughts was beautiful and breathtaking to me. In the silence, I could see how big and expansive I really was. When I stopped listening to my thoughts, everything arose with ease, grace, and power. In these moments, I would use my inner eye to look around the stillness for several moments before my mind started up again. The stillness was awe inspiring.

"*Be the body for God,*" I heard one day from deep within while sitting in meditation. It occurred to me in that moment that if I was to honor myself as a Sacred Being, I would be treating my body with tenderness and kindness. I'd be thinking loving thoughts toward my body, nourishing my body with the most vital, healthy foods, and moving in ways that felt joyful. I apologized to my body for blaming it for responding to my thoughts and actions. I apologized for comparing it to some idealized version and not appreciating it unconditionally. I dropped into deep love and gratitude for all my body holds for me, and I felt the delicious bliss of being in a body.

During some meditation sessions, my head would begin to turn, stretching my neck in very strange and often uncomfortable ways. I had no conscious control over the movements; my neck wanted to move and I surrendered. It felt as if my head was unwinding from my old head trauma and the strange movements felt good. I felt more aligned with Source when this happened, and less twisted or distorted. This is an experience I have had several times since, and it has contributed to miraculous healing physically and emotionally.

While I cultivated this practice, I was the mother of two young children, which can be the most depleting and challenging time of a woman's life. But every time my mind got caught up in a story about how much I do for my kids or how their needs are unending or how I wanted to run away, I would sit on my meditation cushion and reconnect to the place within me that is never depleted. I would drop into my heart and remember my love for them. From there, I was able to build and maintain secure attachments with my children, attachments I feared I had fractured with my postpartum mood disorders.

We have the power to focus our attention wherever we want. When our eyes are closed it can seem like we don't have agency of choice over where to focus. Passively using the power of attention to focus on our conditioned self, we live from our small, limited, shaped self. We feel disempowered, resentful, and stuck from this place. Learning to stop the stream of thought in its tracks, we empower ourselves to choose to focus our attention on our True Self. It can seem arbitrary or ineffective at first, especially if we think that meditation is about sitting in silence without any thoughts. But the mind thinks, so resisting that is fruitless. The work is really about being aware enough to stop the stream every time we notice it. Focusing on the silence between thoughts, even if the silence is just a fraction of a second, we cultivate expansive conscious awareness.

The more space we can put around our thoughts and actions, the more conscious we become in relationship to those thoughts and actions. So even a little bit of space is better than no space at all. In doing this rigorous practice, it becomes possible to connect to the part of us that is boundless, wise, and in flow with the universe. This practice reminds the ego who's in control and where we want to live from. No longer a captive to our thoughts, we're able to move forward in life from the truest part of ourselves.

This practice is not about vanquishing the ego or disenfranchising from it—we need our ego and our ego needs to feel welcomed and loved. This practice is about differentiating from the ego, recognizing that this is not our identity. We are not our ego. We are not our attachment wounds. We are not our personality or roles or pain. We are divine, sacred beings who are here to embody the Source that beats our heart, raising the vibration to the planet.

EMPOWERED WITH CHOICE

Aside from meditation, I wanted to bring the practice of taking my power back from my conditioned self into all areas of my life. With my expressive, affectionate personality that likes to please others, I started trying different behavior with friends. One night, I was going to a party with my 5-year-old daughter where there would be many new and old friends. Since my conditioned self was a chameleon, changing depending on who I was talking to, I decided to become a wallflower instead of working the room to earn approval.

Throughout the party, I felt incredibly uncomfortable. I wasn't extending myself in my typical social and curious way, and my mind was aflutter with anxiety. Since I wasn't following the impulse of my mind, I assumed that no one would like me. I wasn't trying to earn their approval, so I reasoned that I wouldn't have it. I went to the bathroom several times throughout the evening just to breathe and regulate my system. I kept looking around for alcohol to turn down the noise of my conditioned mind, which was loud and trying to get my attention. Since there was no alcohol at this kids' party, I just kept breathing deeply and feeling the extreme discomfort of not presenting my Type 2 mask to the world.

This seemingly simple exercise felt empowering to me: I could choose to not indulge my compulsory and habitual behavior and urges. No longer a recipient to my conditioning, I was consciously incompetent. I could see the fallacy of where I had been meeting the world, but I wasn't quite a master at embodying something truer.

I practiced similar exercises in not being appeasing and accommodating with close friends. I'd say "No" to requests for help when I was too busy or overwhelmed, and I expressed desires and preferences for times to meet and things to do. Of course, no one batted an eye, but this caused tremendous discomfort for me.

Soon after I started to shift my identification away from my conditioned self, Jason lost his job. I was gripped with fear, as was he. I wondered how we would feed our children, keep our home, or afford healthcare or our much-needed couples counseling. I had only four clients in my private practice, and I wasn't sure how to speed up the referrals I was slowly receiving. I frantically started looking for jobs, buying less expensive food, and I removed Tobin from preschool. I was afraid that we would be impoverished and without basic needs.

Even in this fear, I continued to sit in meditation.

Deborah once said to me, "When shit hits the fan, sit like your hair is on fire." And so I did. As everything around me seemed to burn, I sat and aligned with my essence.

My fearful thoughts were excruciatingly loud in my mind. I continued the practice of stopping them and coming into the space between, but I would quickly become gripped with fear. Over and over again I would do this, sitting for an hour at a time. For the first time in my life, I was choosing to meet my fear from my expansive True Self, which ultimately made my whole life expand. Instead of staying small and identifying with the fear, I used the fear to access a deeper connection with my alignment with Source.

This experience taught me that I am capable of meeting the stress of life as long as I am able to sit with it. Sitting with myself in the contraction and using the painful experience to come back to expansion, I was capable of staying in my life urge and not going small with my death urge. Like a training ground for my awakening, life brought me exactly what I needed in order to transcend my conditioned self.

All of us naturally expand and contract throughout the moments of our lives. In one moment, we feel good and trust the process of life. In another moment, we feel afraid and small in who we are. But when something big happens, like the breadwinner of the family losing his job, there can be intense contraction. When met with awareness, the expansion can be just as intense.

Although I wanted to wiggle away from my fear, sitting like my life depended on it when I was most afraid empowered me in ways that continue to impact my relationship with the world. Where I once wanted to control every aspect of life, I more easily flow with life while also choosing how to meet experiences with conscious choice and awareness. Even when something doesn't look how I think it ought to,

I have inherent trust in life when I connected to my innate wisdom and essence.

As I began to transform with this work of Enneagram and meditation, Jason tried. He really did. He sat in meditation daily, as suggested by Karen, and he took remedies from Deborah. Karen and Deborah were incredibly supportive and gave us extreme discounts during this time so that we could use this experience in service of our growth and evolution. But these struggles really exemplified just how different we were. As I grew more expansive and trusting of life, Jason continued to contract. He became fearful that I would outgrow him, and he desperately wanted me to stay small for him.

He became more adamant about projecting his fears and criticism onto me, and in the newness of my expansion I clumsily tried to set boundaries in order to remind myself that his fear was not mine. I wasn't willing to carry his fear and projections for him any longer. He would talk over me, tell me that my decisions were wrong, and try to tell me what to do. And I was unwilling to engage in that type of relationship any longer. I knew he was stressed. I wanted him to feel empowered. But I also could recognize that this was his journey and that I couldn't do it for him.

A few weeks into his unemployment, Jason and I were watching a movie after we put the kids to sleep. As we sat on the couch eating popcorn, we watched an old skater movie called "Grind." In one scene, the main male character's love interest is being slut-shamed by her ex-boyfriend, even though he was the one cheating on her.

In that moment, Jason vocalized his agreement of her being a slut.

"No way!" I said. "You can't put her down because some other guy is ogling her."

"She's a slut." He replied.

I was in total disbelief. I couldn't believe he had just said that. In my world, this girl, who had been loyal to her now ex-boyfriend even though he was cheating on her, was being pursued by a different guy who had a crush on her, and she was saying "No" to him. I couldn't see how he could blame her for this dynamic.

"But she ..." I tried to state my opinion.

"No!" Jason cut me off. "She wants him."

"He's the one ..." I tried again.

"No. Uh uh." He wouldn't let me get a word in edgewise.

Every time I tried to voice my opinion on the matter, Jason hushed me and spoke over me.

This went on for several minutes during which he shut me down every time I tried to speak. I grew more and more indignant with each hush. Voiceless. That's how I had felt in our entire marriage. He wanted me to stay quiet, complicit, and small so he could feel powerful and in control and big. I had colluded with that for too long, and in this moment I was no longer living from my small self. I was unwilling to collude any longer.

Since my conditioned self wanted to earn love and be okay with everything, I had never stood my ground with him. Before, I was desperate for love and approval, so I would never do anything that could potentially break connection. But this night was different. For the first time, I knew with everything inside of me that my True Self said "No" to this dynamic.

"I am your wife." I said sternly. "You don't have to agree with me but you do need to let me speak."

As I said this, he spoke over me again, not listening, not caring about my opinion, and squelching my voice.

"You don't have to agree with me but you do need to let me speak!" I said loudly as he continued to speak over me.

I became so flustered at trying to have a voice that every time he spoke I cut him off in the same way he did to me, trying to show him how it felt. My response was childlike, but I had never before had the gumption to even claim my voice in our relationship, so a younger part of me came online to attempt to hold my boundary.

My voice was raised and I had an intensity about me he'd never seen before. I became more childlike. "You are such a jerk!" I declared. "Why don't you go back to New Jersey where they like jerks?"

I was irate and mean as I clumsily tried to set a boundary, letting him know that I was not okay with this pattern anymore. He had become so accustomed to me staying quiet that he was shocked to see this other side of me after eleven years together. I was shocked, too. I had no idea where this ferocity was coming from, but everything about it felt right to me. I felt alive in our connection for the first time in a long time. I hadn't even realized how I was hiding my truth from him in order to keep our connection until I read about the Type 2.

In this moment with Jason, I blamed him for quieting my voice. I couldn't yet see that I had spent a lifetime of silencing my truth. I couldn't see that my conditioned self thought that people would only like me if I tried to be what I thought they needed me to be for them. I couldn't fully see my part in this pattern, but I knew that I wasn't going to participate in it any longer.

The argument about the movie quickly turned into an argument about our dynamic, and there was no coming to agreement on this.

All of the ways I kept myself small to fit into the box of our relationship exploded out of me. Jason was blindsided because he had no idea that I had been repressing these emotions all along. I had hidden my true feelings about the problems in our relationship for over eleven years, only speaking up occasionally. All in all, it had seemed as if we had a solid marriage. This is common for people in relationship with a Type 2; we are so good at hiding our pain that others have no idea it's there. They think everything is fine because that is the lie we embody.

I couldn't have revealed my dissonance earlier because I wasn't aware enough to even know I had been hiding it. I had been asleep to my authentic self and was meeting our relationship and the world from my small, conditioned self. I couldn't see my own manipulation. I couldn't see the way I hid and contorted. So out of alignment with my True Self, I couldn't even see how my interactions with the world were distorted.

Once the valve on the truth opened and I could see my mask of conditioning, I was completely unwilling to be complicit any more. And in the newness of this awareness, I was relentless in my anger. I told him all of the things I didn't like about him or about us. I told him all of the ways I tried to make everything okay when I was never okay with any of it. I told him how hard it was for me to be married to him. I told him that I didn't like the way he was in the world. And I told him that I never liked having sex with him. I told him that I had been living a lie, and I blamed him for not being different.

That night I moved into the guest room. Jason sat in the master bedroom in complete and utter shock. I was no longer available to work on our dynamic because the entanglement seemed too convoluted to actually build a real, authentic connection.

I couldn't see it at the time, but Jason was projecting his unhealed wounds from his mother onto me, as well as projections from his father, sister, and brother. Jason had always said he didn't like his mother and that he looked forward to her death. She was cold and controlling, and his dad was authoritarian, punishing him physically throughout his childhood. He was competitive with his brother, and his sister was the intelligent achiever he was compared to. The imprint of all of these early experiences was being placed onto me. Jason saw me through the lens of his unmet needs to feel empowered, so he tried to control me. He had an unmet need for affection, so he shamed my sensual way of being. He felt unseen and unloved as he was, so he criticized the way I was.

He didn't mean to do this; none of us do. But the mind is designed to help us navigate the world by using templates from past experiences to make sense of our current situation. When we lack self-awareness and understanding of others, we stay entrenched in old dynamics that aren't relevant to our current life.

He couldn't see me clearly just as I couldn't see him. The disowned parts in him were triggered by me, and he felt incompetent and not enough in our dynamic. He triggered my old wounds that were left unhealed from my relationship with my sister, where I always tried to be enough for her. I tried to be a good object for my dad, and so I put that onto Jason and engaged in that same pattern. My needs never mattered to my mom, and so I engaged with Jason as if my needs didn't matter. I was hard on myself, and in reality I didn't like myself. That self-loathing was reflected in him. He didn't like his mom, and that mother-wound was projected onto me (which is the birthplace of misogyny). But I was the one colluding with that story in my self-hate.

We were painful reflectors of one another's inner worlds, disowned parts, and unhealed old wounds. We forgot that we loved each other and instead tried to get the other to be our corrective experience, resenting the other for not being the healing that we longed for. Rather than using our experience and our words for connection, we used them as an attempt at controling one another, with mine being more subversive than his. I couldn't see how in my attempt at trying to make him happy I was trying to control him. I wanted him to be different, and I felt totally frustrated that he was perpetually dissatisfied regardless how hard I tried to please him.

The next day we went to see Karen and I told her and Jason that I was done. Karen commented during the session that it's not about whether I stay or go, but about who I become. I loved this so much, as it felt like freedom in my system. Who I was becoming couldn't stay in this marriage.

I had never thought I would get a divorce. Having come from a divorced family, I wanted to do marriage differently. But when it came down to it, I needed to leave the relationship in order to discover my own sense of sovereignty and wholeness.

When I told Deborah that I was leaving Jason, she said, "People are going to be surprised when you tell them. You're so skilled at making everything look really, really good."

I was surprised by this observation, and I could see the truth in it. My public face was all about loving being a mom, doing things as a family, and having all of the external things that represent a good life. With a nice house, good cars, vacations, and stylish clothes, I had been more concerned with the way things looked than the way our marriage actually was.

My private face was very different. Bitter, depressed, and lonely, I had been drinking copious amounts of wine nightly on and off since becoming a mom. I overate and carried a lot of extra weight on my body. I tuned out on social media, television, and shopping all in an unconscious attempt to ignore the despair I felt about my life.

Once I stopped participating in destructive behaviors in my private life and instead dedicated myself to my meditation practice, the light of my awareness was turned back on and illuminated the truth of my life. It no longer mattered to me if my public face was colored with divorce. I finally knew my worth did not come from my relationship status. I was more invested in living in alignment with my truth than I was concerned about what others thought of me.

Though I felt oppressed by Jason, I was complicit in this. I wasn't his victim even though my mind told me I was. He didn't own me even though a part of me believed he did. More solid in myself and more aware of my truth, I was changing into someone who clumsily engaged consciously with life.

In the months following my announcement, Jason became extremely depressed, fearful, and suicidal. He told me that I would never be able to afford to keep the house and support myself and the kids. He told me that I didn't appreciate all he did around the house. He told me that I was making the biggest mistake of my life.

It was true that I didn't have a plan. It was true that I didn't have a thriving private practice that could sustain my lifestyle. It was true that I had never supported myself on my own, and now I had two children to feed in addition to myself. It was also true that I had deep trust in the process of life, and everything inside me said "Leave this marriage." My whole system felt lit up, alive, and full of inspiration when I looked at the possibilities of my life without Jason.

I didn't want to date. I didn't want to be with anybody else. I wanted to do good work in the world. I wanted to enjoy every minute of my life. I wanted my kids to witness their mother empowered and in her strength. I wanted to be in my full expression in the world, and I didn't know how to do this with him as my husband.

This was not an act of selfishness. This was an act of truth. It was perhaps the first true thing I had ever done in my life. This was the first time I did something without fear of what other people would think and without trying to make things okay for everybody else. This was the first time in my life that I did something that stretched me beyond the conditioning of my persona in service of being in my authentic expression in the world. Yes, I was scared. Yes, I felt shame for breaking apart our family. But even more than that, I was saying "Yes" to a life that was bigger and more expansive than merely fear and shame.

Although I still didn't know what the next true thing would be for me, I was willing to take the first step and see how my path unfolded. Out of the darkness, I was choosing to move forward into the light. Becoming familiar with uncertainty was the only way I could stay the course.

10
STANDING MY SACRED GROUND

"Every woman that finally figured out her worth, has picked up her
suitcase of pride and boarded a flight to freedom, which landed in the
valley of change."
—Shannon L. Alder

FATE ENCOURAGING GROWTH

Telling my kids about the divorce was a very emotional decision. When
I was told that my parents were getting a divorce, I had felt abandoned,
responsible, and unloved. I wanted my kids to feel seen, held, and loved
in this transition, and Jason and I decided to do it together.

"Mommy and Daddy love you both very much. We also love each other
very much. But we have decided that we want to live in separate
houses," I said.

The moment the words came from my mouth, I could see the shock
run through their bodies. Their energy seemed to exude fear and grief.
Six-year-old Mylah started screaming, "NO!!!!" Tobin, who was 3 at the
time, sat silent and frozen.

While Jason comforted Mylah in her room, I stayed with Tobin. It was
a warm summer day and he wanted to play outside with the water table.

"I love watching you play," I said to him.

He seemed to be retreating into his own world, and I wanted him to
know that I was right there with him, watching him, attuning to him. I

asked him if I could play with him, and I reassured him that he was loved.

"I know this is confusing, sweetie, but Mommy and Daddy love you very much. We will always love you and care about what you need," I assured him.

As we played, I encouraged him to breathe deeply and I gave him aconite, a homeopathic remedy for shock and grief. Then Jason and I switched places, and I went upstairs to be with Mylah, who was in tears.

As she lay in her bed crying, I lay down next to her and began to stroke her hair.

"Why? Why do you have to do this?" she asked through her grieving tears.

"We love you with our whole hearts," I explained. "We also love each other. But we don't like living together anymore. I am so, so sorry, sweetheart."

"But where will we live? Who will take care of us?"

"You'll have two houses, and Mommy and Daddy will still both take care of you. We will always love you and care about what you need."

In this transition, my sole intention was to be attuned and available to my kids. Jason was in such grief that I needed to be solid to hold the emotional stability of our family.

"It's okay to be sad about this. Divorce can be so sad and confusing. Ask me all the questions you want whenever you want."

She liked this. She asked me several questions about why I didn't want to be married to her daddy, and I answered them the best I could.

I gave her homeopathic aconite and ignatia for grief and shock, and then we went outside to find Tobin and Jason. Mylah wanted to perform on her trapeze swing, and Tobin wanted to join in. Jason and I sat in chairs taking the role of audience, and it was the last time we played in this yard as a family. There was laughter and joy and love.

A few days after we told the children about our divorce, Jason became full of anger and rage. As he walked about the house, he glared at me.

"You are doing this to our family," he said. The blame was palpable. "I feel used, like you never loved me."

"That makes sense to me that you would feel that way. I'm so sorry for hurting you. I love you deeply, but I don't want to be married to you," I tried to explain.

Daily, Jason would explode in anger at me in front of the kids. As if I were water, I allowed his rage to move through me. I was present only to my compassionate heart with a sense of deep forgiveness. No defensiveness, no trying to explain our dynamic, no more apologies. This was my truth, and I claimed it with every cell of my body. Even though I didn't want to be with him, I had tremendous love for him. For the next few weeks I gave him all the space he needed to grieve and be angry. I took care of the kids while he locked himself in the master bedroom for days on end. All of the dreams, all of the energy, all of the hope that he had put into our family were disintegrating and he had every right to be mad at me.

The custody decision was hard for me. I had witnessed Jason treating Mylah the way he treated me: criticizing, oppressing, and demanding. I wanted to protect my kids from his anger, and all of the wise women in my life were encouraging me to go for the majority of custody. Every impulse I had wanted to keep my children close to me, and Jason was adamant about a 50/50 split. I was uncertain about how to proceed.

Jason was still unemployed, we were still under one roof, and the stress was beginning to build. He was so afraid about our financial stability that he resisted moving out for several weeks until it became apparent that I was fully committed to getting the divorce. At that point, Jason filed the papers, and began looking for a rental to move into.

Two days after he filed, I met somebody.

I wasn't looking for romance. I hadn't even thought about being with another man for over eleven years. The stress of our divorce was affecting me greatly, and a flaky, white rash covered my eyelids. I had been taking low-potency homeopathic graphites for the rash, and this was the first day that I looked normal or felt halfway attractive in weeks.

I was getting ready to take my car in to get serviced, and I put on makeup and a cute Boden dress and did my hair. As I got ready, I thought to myself, *"It's not like I'm going to meet someone at the mechanic's."*

Mocking myself for putting effort into my appearance, I grabbed my computer and said goodbye to the kids.

After I dropped my car off, I walked over to a hipster coffee shop in North Boulder called Amante. I ordered a soy latte, sat down, and open my computer to start working on my book proposal.

As I wrote, a man came and sat by me. He was tall and handsome, and he wore stylish clothes, nice shoes and hip glasses. His designer jeans fit just right, and his button-up shirt was the most flattering shade of purple. His camel-brown shoes had the perfect squared toe, and his glasses complimented his handsome face.

Although he looked a bit scattered and hurried, he wore a huge smile as he squeezed into his booth seat next to mine. I nodded at him and then we both proceeded to work on our computers.

His name was called when his order was ready, and when he came back with his coffee and croissant he thanked me for moving my computer case out of his way so he could scooch by.

"Are you a graduate student?" he asked when he saw I had a Word document on my screen.

"No. I'm a psychotherapist and a psychology professor. I'm working on a book proposal."

His look of interest invited the conversation to go deeper. It turned out that he worked for himself in marketing and had some good advice to give me for that section of my proposal, which I was struggling with that day. We exchanged names—his was Robert—and we talked some more about the marketing projects he was working on and about my private practice.

"I should let you get back to work," he said after a few minutes of talking.

I was disappointed. This was the first adult conversation I'd had in weeks that wasn't wrought with stress and pain. For a brief moment, I was more than a mom, more than a wife who was leaving her husband, and more than a psychotherapist trying to fill her practice. His interest in me made me feel interesting, and I was intrigued by who he was. I felt my heart sink when he shifted back to his computer.

We mutually turned back to our computer screens, but I could not focus on my proposal. I stared at the screen and tried to think of how to keep this handsome man next to me engaged in conversation.

His phone rang, and when he took the call he looked at me and nodded, as if to excuse himself as he walked outside. Soon thereafter, my phone rang. It was my mechanic telling me my car was finished. I hesitated to leave. I contemplated leaving him a business card but I didn't have them with me. I thought about writing my number down on a piece of paper, but that seemed desperate. So I packed up my computer and walked over to pick up my car.

As I walked, I thought about going back to give him my number, but I decided not to. Never to see Robert again.

I ran a few errands and when I went home I was happier than I had been in a long time. This brief encounter had put a huge smile on my face, and my heart was aflutter with excitement. I gave my kids a big hug and played with them for a while.

Jason was fuming. Seeing me happy angered him, so I tried to hide it.

Later that same night, I sat down at my computer to grade some papers for the Introductory Psychology course that I was teaching. Before logging into my online classroom, I checked my email. I was in total and complete disbelief that there in my inbox was a message from Robert. He had found me online and sent me a message. I was elated!

"Hi Harmony! It was nice to meet you earlier today at Amante," it read. "Sorry I missed you on your way out. Just thought I'd say 'Hi' this way."

I hadn't smiled this big for many years. This email ignited an excitement in me that I didn't even know I had been missing. I completely ignored the fact that he had Internet-stalked me. I desperately wanted to find a way to see him again.

"Hi Robert! I was going to leave you a card but I didn't have any on me. It was lovely to talk with you this morning and a welcome break from my proposal. I'd love to talk more with you about possibly working together. If you have some time later this week, my kids will be away and I'll have more flexibility," I replied.

Although I had no intention of hiring Robert for my marketing, it was the only way I could think of at the time to see him again. We arranged to meet at Amante the very next day, and when I arrived I saw Robert's eyes widen with excitement. I was wearing a maxi dress that was low cut and the perfect shade of blue to highlight my blue eyes. He was as stylish as he had been the previous day, and everything inside of me wanted to feel his body close to mine.

FLOODED WITH PROJECTIONS

It was a warm summer day and the coffee shop was bustling with patrons. I sat next to Robert on a stool at the counter, and we talked a bit about work. I felt nervous and a bit shaky, trying to figure out how I could be what he wanted me to be. Of course, I had no idea what he wanted me to be, but I was certain that who I was could not be enough for this sophisticated man. My conditioned self was running the show, and so much of my attention was on Robert that I didn't even notice that I was identifying with its impulse.

Robert asked me what I was up to for the day, and I told him that my schedule was unusually open because my kids were away for a few days with their dad and his family.

"You didn't want to see your in-laws?" he asked.

"No. I'm in the middle of a divorce, so I'm pretty sure they don't want to see me," I explained, as if I hadn't been waiting to tell him this.

"I'm so sorry to hear," he said. "How recent is it?"

"Very recent," I replied, being intentionally vague.

We drank our coffee and talked about kids. His son was at a summer camp and we looked at some pictures of him kayaking.

Although I had nowhere to be, I told him that I needed to go so I could work on my podcast. I didn't want him to think I was needy or clingy. I preferred men pursuing me, and I wanted to come across as independent and available for what could arise without seeming desperate. This self-protection technique was a holdover from my experiences with men, and I didn't yet have access to my authenticity to speak my truth about my desires. It was also driven by my projections from my dad not being emotionally available for me as a child. This prevented me from seeing Robert with clarity, just as it prevented me from meeting him from my mature, wise self. I was playing a game with him, and he seemed to be playing along with me. Although this action was out of integrity with the core of my being, this game was much more comfortable for me than being vulnerable and exposed.

Robert walked me to my car, and as I drove home I replayed our conversation, wondering if I'd ever hear from him again. Just moments later, he texted me.

"I would love to get a drink with you soon and continue our conversation," it read.

My stomach dropped and started fluttering with elation.

I couldn't believe he wanted to spend time with me. My self-esteem was so low from a long and challenging marriage that lacked passion and connection, just as my self-worth was so low from a lifetime of trauma and believing that I wasn't worthy of love. My mind immediately went to considering what I would wear on our date, as I believed my appearance was the most important factor in its success.

When I got home, I wanted to wait the right amount of time to text him back so I didn't seem desperate. But I didn't know what the right amount of time was. I sat in meditation and tried to sit with my excitement, wanting to stay embodied and connected to myself rather than manic and all over the place.

An hour later, I replied to his text and we made a date for the next evening.

The next twenty-four hours felt like an eternity to me. I had the house to myself and here I was, just a few days into the "cool-off period" of my divorce proceedings, already going on a date with an amazing, handsome man. I felt conflicted with excitement and guilt.

When I hadn't heard from Robert by 1 PM the next day with a place to meet, I became antsy. I started to text him that I would be with clients until four and I was wondering where to meet him. Before pressing send, I paused and witnessed my lie and manipulation. I had no clients scheduled for that day. This distorted and backwards way to get what I thought I wanted was completely unnecessary. I deleted the text, took a deep breath, and typed "Looking forward to seeing you tonight. Where should we meet?"

This simple, honest text took a lot of effort on my part. It felt vulnerable to let him know that I was looking forward to spending time with him, and asking him to commit to a place felt incredibly edgy.

We made plans to meet for happy hour at The Med, which is a happening restaurant in Downtown Boulder that is always bustling with college students and young couples. As I got ready, I contemplated wearing a sexy black and white summer cocktail dress and black wedges with a cork sole.

"It's too eager," I thought to myself. *"Wear something more understated."*

With a few more hours to decide on my outfit, I threw on a comfy dress and I drove to Deborah's to tell her about what was unfolding. As I told her about Robert, I shared with her the manipulative text impulse I had but how I had chosen something different. She seemed to be in awe of how my life was changing.

"Things are going to start happening quickly for you," she said, acknowledging how I was making better choices as I interacted with the world. "Your energy is freed up. You've been coming at your marriage with Jason sideways for so long. Now the universe can offer you what you want," she said.

Learning and practicing revealing our truth to the world is an essential component in living in alignment with the True Self. I was new to this practice, and I was clumsy with it. But with each and every effort on my part, my courage to try the different, truer thing was shifting my interactions with the world to a place of integrity rather than the manipulation of my conditioning.

"I am meeting him in two hours," I told her. "I didn't want to wear my dress over here. I think it's too sexy for tonight. I'm so nervous. I don't want to look too desperate, but I want to look sexy."

"Don't go small for some guy, Harmony," she said with conviction.

I liked that. It felt empowering. If claiming my sexiness was part of this experience, then I wanted to own it fully.

When I walked up to meet Robert, I was wearing a short, sexy summer dress with sexy wedge heels. I felt great about myself. Any fear I had about being too sexy dissipated the moment I saw his eyes widen with excitement.

We hugged and then walked inside the busy restaurant. As we sat outside on the terrace, we dropped the professional front and actually started to get to know one another. It turned out that Robert, who had grown up in Europe, had come to Colorado for college. He had planned on moving back to Europe, but he had gotten a woman pregnant during a one-night stand fourteen years earlier. The mother wanted full custody of their son, but Robert was committed to being a part of his child's life. After spending over $30,000 on a custody battle, Robert won 50% custody.

I told Robert that I wanted majority custody over my children, and he encouraged me to save my money. His story illuminated for me that unless the circumstances are extreme and dangerous for the child, it is a child's birthright to know both parents equally. I was surprised by how his story helped me soften to the idea of my children spending equal time with Jason, even though I considered myself the more competent and caring parent.

After some appetizers and wine, Robert and I decided to walk around Pearl St. The moment we stepped out of the restaurant, the rain started to pour. Robert smiled as he tilted his head up to receive the sensation of the water on his face, but I, in my little cocktail dress and wedges, recoiled from the rain.

Robert started walking toward his Audi convertible and asked me if I'd like to take a ride instead. We drove around the surrounding neighborhoods, taking in the beauty of central Boulder as it was washed clean with this shower.

He drove by his old house, telling me the story of how he had to move because of the black mold. In that moment, I looked over at him and our eyes met. We paused and the attraction was palpable. I reached over and put my hand on his, then I moved his hand to my leg. He smiled from ear to ear and let out a deep, masculine chuckle of excitement. Then he parked the car and we started making out with an intensity I hadn't experienced in many, many years. Right away, just seconds after we started kissing, Robert moved his hand to my underwear.

It was too fast for me. Fear surged through my body. I wanted him to stop, so I put my hand on his. After a short pause, I decided that I wanted to experience him. I couldn't recognize at the time that I unconsciously thought that if I stopped him I would lose connection. I also couldn't see at the time that a part of me believed that my pussy belonged to him, that his touch without consent was totally fine because as a woman I belonged to him.

With my hand on his, I felt more in control, and I started moving his hand over my vulva, helping him pleasure me. I was overwhelmed with sensation. It had been a long time since I had thought of myself as a sexual being. The windows were fogged up and it was hot inside. I was about to have an orgasm when, instead, I invited Robert back to my house. Jason still lived in this house with me, but while he was away with the kids I had the house to myself. My passion quickly overrode any guilt that I felt.

I led Robert to the guest room in the basement, which seemed like the most neutral place in the house to have sex. Slowly, Robert took my clothes off and laid me down on the bed.

As he crawled onto the bed, he looked over my entire body. "I like the look of this," he said as he gently caressed me.

This was the first time a man other than my husband had seen me naked since I had given birth. I felt nervous as he took me in, studying me as if I were a finely crafted piece of architecture.

"You are so beautiful," he whispered as he kept scanning my body with his eyes.

As he caressed my curves, I had never felt sexier in my entire life. In fact, I don't think I had never felt truly sexy before this moment. No man had ever looked at me like he did that night, just like no man had ever moved that slowly, taking me in with his eyes, before intercourse.

The way Robert touched me turned me on so intensely that I could have climaxed without any genital contact. In his appreciation for my body exactly as it was, I felt beautiful and worthy. As he massaged and caressed my vulva, he seemed to be getting so much pleasure out of being a part of my pleasure. And right there, in that moment, I was in so much ecstasy that I was completely unaware of the way my mind was being hijacked by hormones and projections.

I could no longer see clearly. All I could see was who I wanted Robert to be for me. I wanted this to be fate, for us to work together and live together and be happy forever together. I wanted to earn his love by being who I thought he wanted me to be, and I did that mostly by not having an opinion or a voice. The very same pattern that I had been doing for almost the entirety of my life, and the same pattern that had contributed to the dysfunction in my marriage, I immediately started repeating with Robert.

The fantasy of having another person come into our lives to complete us and make us happy and satisfied is fed to us through media and ancestry, and it can be challenging to see it as dysfunctional. It can seem like a normal part of falling in love, but it is actually quite destructive to real love. When we identify with the fantasy of our ego, we set ourselves up for disappointment and we set our potential partners up for failure.

Inherent in this fantasy is that a person will come into our lives and save us and complete us. There's a deep unconscious belief that we're not whole unless we're partnered, and this comes from a younger part that needed to feel loved in their split from Source. No relationship is here to complete us or make us happy. The experience of wholeness comes from our unbreakable connection with Source. Differentiating from the fantasy and our wounds, we can get clear on objective reality. Objective reality is our ability to see the things that are sure to exist independently of ourselves. Without projecting our fantasy onto the relationship, we can begin to see the objective things that have happened. From here, we can sober up and meet our relationships in a way that cultivates healthy connection based in truth and vulnerability.

PRACTICING STAYING IN MYSELF

After our encounter, Robert texted me often, asking to get together again. I was going through so much with my divorce—Jason raging at me, no childcare, no support—that I couldn't find a time to meet him. My mind was still steeped in a fantasy that we were meant for each other, and I was nervous with anticipation to make my fantasy a reality.

One month after my date with Robert, Jason finally moved into his new place. When the kids spent their first night there with him, I invited Robert over. I had been craving him since our last encounter, and I was nervous to finally see him again. My palms were sweaty and my heart was racing as I waited for him to arrive.

When he walked into my home, he immediately started kissing me and lifting up my dress. He was moving too fast for me and I wanted to slow him down, just like the first time we had kissed. I hadn't seen him in so long that I needed to get to know him again but asking for this felt impossible. Even though I was in touch with my needs, I bypassed my truth and let him take the lead.

He took my hand as he walked us to the sofa, and then he pulled me onto his lap. The moment we started kissing again, he promptly inserted his finger in my vagina. Shock and fear jolted through my whole system. This had happened to me so many times in my life, where men inserted themselves into me without consent, and I wasn't sure how to respond. I had gotten so many messages throughout my life that my body didn't belong to me that unconsciously I believed this to be true.

Sensing my fear, Robert paused with his finger still inside of me and we looked at one another. Afraid to lose connection, I didn't say a thing and instead resumed our make-out session. Desperate to please him and keep connection, I again bypassed my fear and stayed quiet, allowing him to touch me in any way he desired.

Even with all of the work I had done with Deborah and Karen, I was totally unaware that I was projecting Shane and Joe onto Robert. I was playing small and letting my young one take the lead. I was giving my power to my conditioned self by hiding my truth. At 38, I was still giving to get. I was being demure and seductive to earn love, and I was still under the delusion that my truth and my voice didn't matter. It would be easy to blame Robert for not asking for consent or for not being attuned to me, but since this is a pattern that I had been playing out for a lifetime, it was my work to overcome the way in which I silence myself.

But not on this day. On this day I tried to be what I thought Robert wanted.

I invited him to my room and we laid down in the brand-new king-size bed I had bought for this very occasion. Jason had taken our old bed, and when I got a new one I chose the large bed so Robert, who was 6'3", could sleep with me.

We had the most erotic foreplay I had ever experienced. Robert knew how to touch me in a way that ignited incredibly intense feelings of pleasure in my body. As he touched me, I reciprocated and was surprised by his soft erection. I tried not to personalize it, and we tried to have sex anyways. But his erection never got hard enough.

After our clumsily navigated almost-intercourse, Robert rested on the bed next to me and I snuggled up to him. I was trying to be okay with how this encounter had unfolded, but the disappointment I felt was devastating. After longing for this moment and fantasizing about how our relationship would unfold, my mind was buzzing with angst around how to make this work.

Robert fell asleep, and I lay next to him wondering why I wasn't enough for him, while simultaneously resenting him for moving too fast and then not delivering.

The buildup to this moment had been very intense for me. He was all I had thought about for weeks. Putting my children to bed, buying new furniture, and marketing my business were all done while the fantasy of him was in the forefront of my awareness.

All of that waiting and projection of love and need for connection disintegrated, and I felt used and sad and confused. My whole body wanted nothing to do with him.

Later that day, after he left, I texted him. "I noticed myself recoiling after you left" was all I said.

This was my clumsy attempt at being authentic. Since I was unable to do it in the moment, I was trying to let him know that what unfolded wasn't okay with me. I gave voice to my inner experience, but I didn't articulate why I was feeling this way.

"I'm so sad to hear that," he replied. "Do you want to meet and talk? I hope you want to see me again."

This was huge for me. I felt something unpleasant, and I told him. I spoke my truth, and he received it and stayed open to connection. I had never experienced this before in my life. A man that I was attracted to was open to hearing my dissatisfaction and pain.

My whole body softened.

We made plans to meet the following week and talk.

Robert lived an hour away from me. When I arrived at his small, quaint house, my picture of him began to fill out. Because of his stylish clothes and convertible car, I thought he was wealthy. He wasn't. He just had good taste and nurtured a polished image.

We sat in his small living room on his tiny, uncomfortable sofa while I held my Enneagram book.

"I abandoned myself in my living room the other day," I professed.

Confused, he asked me to explain. "What do you mean?"

"When you came in and started kissing me, I felt afraid because I had a need to get to know you again and talk. But I didn't tell you about it because your need felt more important to me at that moment. When I feel vulnerable, I have a hard time using my voice."

"I don't want you to do that with me," he said sweetly.

My heart melted. I felt happy that we were having an authentic conversation and he was able to be open to hearing about my inner world. This was a first for me. Literally, this was the first time in my entire life that I had honored myself with a man whom I wanted to want me who then stayed curious and open to me.

I went on to explain to him that I was a Type 2 on the Enneagram, and, after looking at the book, he typed himself as an 8. I explained to him how I was conditioned to abandon myself to earn love and to hide my truth so that other people felt important. We saw that he was conditioned to go for what he wants and to make his own way in the world. He protects his vulnerable heart and is invested in having things be the way he wants them, or he's out. My "other-referenced" conditioned self was contrasted by his "self-referenced" conditioned self.

Although we could see this pattern clearly, that awareness was short-lived.

When we spent time together, though I felt on one level that things were going well and everything was right, the truth is that I was working hard to be okay with everything. I continued to quiet my voice with him at every single turn. Weather it was about birth control, monogamy, or where to eat dinner, I let him take the lead and I stayed meek.

He was scattered, distant, and stressed about work most of the time. But in the moments of our connection, his brilliant world view and sophisticated taste in food and wine were alluring to me. The sex became increasingly blissful, and we would spend hours making love.

I was enamored with the way things seemed between us, but I was blind to the way things actually were.

Mistaking my fantasy of Robert for love, after dating for five months I told him that I loved him. Even though we only saw each other sporadically and I was hiding my truth from him most of the time, I was convinced he was the man for me.

"I love you. I know you're busy and we live an hour away from each other. I've really tried to not love you, but I can't help it, I do."

After hearing this, Robert said, "I adore you, too. I'm just not in a place in my life where I want a relationship."

I was taken back. I thought fate had brought us together and that I was doing a good job of being submissive for him. I thought that we were going to get married and be a blended family. We seemed perfect for each other in so many ways. Why else would we have met at Amante that day?

"I know you want to move back to Europe eventually, but we can make that work," I stated.

Our attraction for one another was intense, and I seduced Robert to try to get what I wanted from him. Even though he didn't really want a relationship with me, he came home with me that day and we made love.

For the next few weeks, Robert tried to be the man that I wanted to make him into. He made more of an effort to spend time with me and he was exquisitely loving when we were intimate.

Every day I thought about how I could get him to like me enough to be with me, how I could get him to change into the man I wanted: a man who wanted to be in a committed, long-term relationship with me.

It never occurred to me to find out if he was a guy *I* wanted to be with. Did I even like him? I never contemplated these questions, and honestly I didn't even know that this was an option. I was too caught up in my projections from a childhood being raised by an emotionally and physically absent father. I wanted to be enough for him, and I did that by trying to be the object of his desire as best I could.

It became clear to me that he only wanted me physically. Though he went through the motions of being a loving boyfriend, every touch or moment of physical closeness between us became an invitation to have sex. I felt like he was constantly pawing at me, but when I wanted to share thoughts and experiences in a deeper way, he wasn't as interested. I began to feel more like a tool for his sexual gratification than like an equal partner in the relationship. I felt hurt and abandoned all over again.

Pretending like this was okay with me, that a sexual relationship was enough for me, was my manipulation. I was giving him what he wanted so I could get what I thought I wanted. I couldn't see that through my lens he was an image of my dad. Trying to earn my worth through my seduction was an old pattern of mine, but this time I had children to consider. I had more awareness of my shaping, and I had just gotten out of a painfully dysfunctional marriage. I felt small and insignificant when I was with Robert, and I could no longer pretend that this was true.

I was grateful for the distraction that Robert was for me during a strenuous transition in my life, but after six months I was no longer willing to play this limiting and dissatisfying game with him.

"I don't want to do this with you anymore. I want a relationship with a man who wants to be with me," I said over the phone a few days before Christmas. I was in Sacramento visiting family but my mind was obsessing over Robert. I knew that I was off-center, and I wanted to come back to myself.

"I don't want to stop seeing you," he said.

"Right, as long as we play by your rules. I'm not okay with seeing one another sporadically for dinner and sex. I want a committed partnership."

He tried to talk me out of ending things between us, but I was in touch with a modicum of dignity and I wasn't going to abandon myself for him. When we hung up the phone, I grieved deeply. I cried more over my six-month affair with Robert than I had over my eleven-year relationship with Jason. Feeling sexy, desired, and separate from my roles of now ex-wife, mother, and therapist had given me hope and excitement about life. I had lost weight, my glow was back, and the world seemed larger to me than it had in a long time.

Self-betrayal is the subversive way we victimize ourselves. Empowered with conscious choice, we are a victim to no one. Becoming aware of the patterns of bypassing our truth, we can become clearer on how we project old experiences onto our current reality. Removing the veil of illusion that's been covering our eyes, we can take our power back from our conditioned self. We can stop the old pattern of collapse, deference, and self-betrayal, and we can begin to re-pattern ourselves with self-respect, self-trust, and self-honor. Holding ourselves in our dignity and sovereignty, we can stand our sacred ground.

AUTHENTICITY

I was feeling more alive and sexier than ever, but the part of my mind that perpetuates my body dysmorphia came back the moment I started creating a dating profile. After ending my affair with Robert, I realized that I wanted connection with a man, so for the first time in my life I created a profile on an online dating app called Bumble.

Feeling 300 pounds and undesirable, I was desperately afraid of putting myself out there only to be rejected. I didn't want my deepest fear of being unworthy of love to be affirmed on the internet. Choosing pictures was painful for me because I critiqued myself so harshly, and when I imagined men looking at my photos I imagined them critiquing me just as severely.

On top of wanting to present an appearance that men would be attracted to, I also found myself choosing words for my profile that were generally soft and likeable, wanting men to think that I was demure and accommodating in 300 characters or less:

"Affectionate, kind, and loving. I love to cook healthy, organic food. I practice yoga and meditation, and I'm passionate about making the world a better place. Enneagram 2. ENFJ. 2 kids part time. No smoking, No drugs."

Dating in the Boulder Bubble was surprisingly fun. With a population of highly educated, healthy, and successful people, I found that there were plenty of single men I wanted to spend time with. Many of the men on this app were attractive, intelligent professionals with a lot of good things going on in their lives (at least based on what I could tell from their profiles). And to my complete surprise, many of them were attracted to my profile and wanted to date me.

Within a couple of weeks of creating my account, I was going on two or three dates a week, which surprised my friends considering that I was recently divorced and had been saying that I didn't want to jump into another relationship. They had been supportive of my exploration with Robert, but they were concerned about how much I wanted a relationship.

"Give it time, Harmony. You don't want to start living for someone else, taking his opinions into account," my friend Carley had said to me about Robert.

"Have fun but take this time to get clear on what you want," my friend Madelyn said to me.

I agreed with this sentiment, but really I desperately wanted to be partnered. I tried to keep my dating life light, but a part of me was looking for my perfect mate. I wanted a man who could complete the picture of what I thought I needed.

When I wasn't dating or working, I was dedicating all of my time and energy to parenting my children in a way that created a secure base for them. The stress of the divorce had a huge impact on their emotional state, and my presence with them in their pain was welcoming, caring, and loving. I wanted their darkness to be seen and welcomed, and I wanted them to feel unconditionally loved by me. Being attuned to them and caring for their needs was incredibly important to me given how neglected I had been. Having fun with dating was an outlet that made this highly stressful situation easier. Because I was enjoying life, I was a better mother on the days I had my children.

I had been hungry for approval throughout my life, and my need for validation took over my dating endeavors. I was checking Bumble several times a day to see who wanted to date me. Having so many men interested in me gave me boosts to my ego that had me losing touch with the truth of who I am. My attention was continuously pulled to being attractive enough to get male attention and being chameleon-like enough to be able to fit any man's desire. My own sense of self-love was non-existent as my worth came from what they thought of me.

After marathon-dating for just three weeks post-Robert, I met a man named Eric who I thought was a dream come true. Eric's profile was thoughtful and intriguing. He was a social worker at a mental health institution, and he was passionate about personal growth. He was trained in Jungian shadow work and had an emotional sophistication unlike any other man I had ever met. He seemed to be a hippie, which I liked, and he posted pictures with many friends at festivals.

The moment Eric walked in to Pekoe Teahouse for our first date, I knew instantly that I wanted to be with him. With big brown eyes and standing at six-foot-three, he was the embodiment of a masculine man who was in touch with his deep interior.

He sat down across from me. "I am really nervous."

I was excited that he was already sharing his inner world with me. "Good!"

"Good?"

"Yes. I think that means you really care. Whenever I lead a workshop I get really nervous. Before it starts I go to the bathroom, look myself in the eyes in the mirror and say, 'Harmony, you are nervous because you care, not because you don't know what you're doing.'"

"I like that!" He smiled. "Tell me more about the workshops you lead."

I told Eric about my couples workshops and how I use the Enneagram to teach people how to become clear on how they were shaped in childhood so they can choose to meet their relationships from a deeper place. He told me about his work at the hospital and how he liked to dance and connect deeply.

As we sat at the table, we looked into each other's eyes and took many quiet pauses.

I didn't need to know anything about him because I already liked him. My body wanted to move closer to his, and I had to resist the urge to lean over and kiss him.

It was a short first meeting, about forty-five minutes, and when we hugged goodbye he asked if I'd like to get together again.

"I'd like that," I said without hesitation.

That night, Eric texted me and asked me if I'd like to see Michael Moore's new documentary, "Where to Invade Next?"

I thought it was strange that he was inviting me to see a movie for our first real date, especially since he had told me that he loves connecting deeply. But I agreed because I wanted to see him again, and we made plans to meet at the theater in two days.

On the morning of our date, Eric texted me and asked me if I would be open to going to an "Authentic Game Night" at the Integral Center instead of seeing the movie.

"My voice coach is in town leading this tonight, and I'd really like to go," he texted along with a link to the Facebook invitation.

The invitation read: "Authentic Game Nights are a guided process, in a safe and fun environment, where participants learn skills to connect with themselves and with others. We will explore embodiment practices, movement, easy dialogue, and relating authentically. You will learn a framework for connection that you can bring to your relationships and your daily life."

After reading this, I still had no idea what an Authentic Game Night was. I felt both nervous and excited about trying something that seemed so out of the box for me, and I found it humorous that we had been planning on going to go to a movie but instead he wanted us to do something that sounded edgy and vulnerable. Shifting my expectation of sitting in darkness together to playing authentic relating games activated a lot of fear in me, but I felt totally up for the challenge.

"I feel nervous but I'm willing to try," I replied.

"We'll be nervous together," Eric encouraged.

I found it charming that we barely knew each other and we were using emotional language already. I knew that this was a good start to something amazing.

That night, I met Eric at his place. He lived in a repurposed 1918 school house called The Village Co-Housing. It's an intentional community in Boulder where there is a focus on connection and relationship even though the residents live in separate apartments and houses.

Eric had helped to make this project into a reality, so he felt particularly proud as he showed me around.

We had planned to go to dinner before the games night began, but we were running out of time to go to a restaurant. Eric suggested we make something at his place instead, so I followed him to the kitchen to see what he had.

As he looked through his fridge, he spotted a large mason jar with green liquid in it.

"How about a kale smoothie? It doesn't taste very good but it has a lot of nutrient value," he said.

"No," was all I could say to that. "Let me look."

I was accustomed to men taking me to nice dinners and courting me with some level of sophistication. I was completely dumbfounded that Eric would even suggest we drink a green smoothie for dinner. I sort of laughed as I felt equally charmed and turned off by his bachelor ways infused with an unconventional style.

My private practice had filled up over the past few months since my divorce was final, and I had been seeing clients all day. I was really hungry, so I looked in his fridge and saw tofu, avocado, spinach, and carrots, which sounded like a good dinner to me. As I cooked us dinner, my mind was swirling in disbelief that I was cooking for us on our first real date. Again, this was me trying to be okay with everything but totally unaware of how this habit was playing out in the moment.

We ate dinner and drank wine from a box, and when we were done we walked up Broadway Street to the venue. The Integral Center was a community center for people who study Ken Wilber's Integral Theory, which brings diverse theories and philosophies into one framework. It was founded by a group of friends who created a relational practice to embody Integral philosophy. Housed in an old church in North Boulder, the Integral Center was a hub for relational transformation.

When we got there, there were about forty-five people waiting for the event to start. I could feel my heart rate elevate and my palms begin to sweat. I wasn't quite sure what I had gotten myself into.

The facilitator was a man named Jonathan. As we began, he invited everyone to stand in a large circle and close their eyes to connect to their deep inner self. My mind chattered with fear and Eric leaned into me and put his foot on mine to help me feel calmer and more grounded.

After several minutes, we opened our eyes to make eye contact with the other people standing in the circle. Jonathan asked us to walk around the room in silence, first looking at the ground, then looking up and making eye contact at the people we passed, then looking at the entire room as if we were in a museum.

"Find a person to stand in front of, and gaze into their eyes," Jonathan instructed.

As I stood in front of a woman with a small frame, sallow face, and thin brown hair, I felt extremely uncomfortable and could feel my face twitch. I quickly forgot my own anxiety when I looked into her eyes and noticed her sorrow and her fear. Or at least, it seemed to me that she was full of sorrow and fear. I never had the chance to check that out with her because a few moments later Jonathan instructed us to thank our partner and find someone else to stand with.

Once I was situated in front of another partner, a tall man who was only about 20 years old, Jonathan instructed us to tell this person what we saw when we looked at them.

My partner went first: "I see blue eyes, and a radiant smile. I see someone who looks together and happy. I see your teeth and your ..." It was time to switch.

I told the young man in front of me that I saw eagerness in his eyes and an intensity in his energy. I saw his short brown hair and crooked teeth. Then it was time to thank our partner and continue milling about the room.

We spent the whole evening doing variations of this type of connecting where we would offer our observations, assumptions, and projections of others and hear other peoples' about us.

For the final game, Jonathan instructed: "Now find someone to sit across from. Gaze into this person's eyes, check in with yourself to see what your intuition wants to tell them. What is something that this person needs to hear from your intuition?"

My partner, with her long red hair and radiant smile, went first. "You really are a goddess," she said to me.

I noticed myself wanting to deflect the deep compliment and immediately told her what had come up in me when I looked at her.

"Trust your intuition," I said.

She started laughing, "That is too perfect."

When I realized the beauty of this interaction, I started laughing hysterically. We both giggled for several minutes while the rest of the room quietly exchanged in this process.

At the end of the night I told Eric what happened between me and my red-headed partner, and he said with enthusiasm, "You really are a goddess!"

This felt so good to hear from him. I wished I believed it too, but at least the people around me could see something in me that I had longed to be in touch with.

The beauty of being witnessed by others who are invested in being authentic and revealed is that we can see ourselves more clearly. When seen in this way, our conditioned patterns of contortion and distortion where we hide parts of ourselves and present a mask to the world are magnified. Having our distortion magnified is the very thing we need to stop believing it and allowing it to guide our actions. Although uncomfortable and vulnerable, authenticity is the very medicine we need to live in alignment with the True Self.

We said goodbye to some people Eric knew, and in the entryway to the Center on our way out, Eric pulled me aside passionately. With his back against the wall, we looked intensely into one another's eyes. As I stood in front of him, holding his gaze, he leaned in and kissed me.

We made out for several moments as people walked past us on their way out. Then we walked back to his place, happily hand in hand.

"Do you have time to come inside?"

"Sure." I was relieved he had asked.

Once we were in his kitchen, he offered me a glass of water. After handing it to me, he walked to the other side of the kitchen and leaned against the counter while he watched me sip from the glass. I held his gaze in silence as I set the glass on the counter and started walking toward him.

"You. Are. Intense," Eric said emphatically as I moved toward him.

Hearing this, I paused, wondering if he was projecting or seeing me clearly. I didn't experience myself as intense, but I supposed it was possible. Once I could see how I would seem intense to him, I nodded in agreement and continued walking over to him.

I stood in front of him, looking up into his big brown eyes. He leaned down and we kissed passionately for a few moments.

"I want to pick you up and bring you to the futon," he said as he motioned to the mattress laying on his living room floor where a couch should be.

I paused and looked over at the short distance to the futon. "I'll walk," I said as I seductively looked up at him with a fierce look in my eyes.

No man had ever picked me up before, and even though my body was now lean, weighing the same as I had when I was anorexic in college, I was afraid I was too heavy and I was afraid of being dropped.

We made out on his futon for hours late into the night. Half naked, with our chests against one another, I had to slow myself down so as not to have sex with him so soon after meeting. He didn't seem to want to have sex, but the part of me that was accustomed to men moving fast was trying to figure out how to proceed with maturity.

Eric was 45, single, and attractive, and his longest relationship had only lasted two years. His experience around sex was very different from mine, considering that in the past fifteen years I had only been with two men (Jason and Robert). That evening on the futon, I tried to figure out what he wanted so I could give it to him.

Finally, at midnight, we agreed that it was time for me to go home. I left the house feeling dizzy with hormones. I felt like I was in love, unconsciously projecting my fantasy of relationship rescue onto him.

Eric texted me the next day, inviting me to dinner with his friends. I was excited that he wanted me to meet his friends so soon, and the group of us had a wonderful time walking Pearl Street together and getting to know one another over vegetarian food at Leaf.

The following week, Eric came to my house for dinner. And on just our fourth date, I told him that I didn't want to date anyone else. I explained that I had been dating a few other people, but I felt a deep connection with him.

"How did I get so lucky?" he exclaimed as he moved in for a kiss.

"I see relationships in terms of energy," I told him. "When we come together with someone, the energy between us is clean. And everything we do together either keeps that energy clean or mistunes it. I want to keep the energy clean between us."

I was hopeful that with our shared dedication for personal growth and communication we would be able to create a foundation for a healthy romantic relationship. Once we agreed to be monogamous, we went upstairs and made love.

My heart felt wide open as I experienced Eric for the first time. With his physical strength, he could move me around into sexual positions I didn't know were possible. Tantric and deeply connecting, our physical intimacy was active and heart-opening. But Eric's approach was focused on intercourse without giving any attention to the rest of my vulva. Never knowing how to talk to men about my sexual desire, I decided to focus only on the parts of our lovemaking that I did like.

For our sixth date, Eric invited me to take a dance class together called contact improv. In this dance, you find a rolling point of contact on your partner's body and you move together without breaking contact. You may start standing and then end up rolling on the ground. You may have one dance partner or six or more. It's a powerful dance that creates an experience of safe, sensual but not sexual touch with others, a gift so many of us don't experience in our everyday lives.

I was afraid to go when Eric first invited me to this eccentric form of dance, but because he loved it so much I reluctantly agreed to join him.

"I'll only dance with you, though," I bargained.

He agreed.

With my old head trauma, touch was scary to me. My body felt fragile, and I could easily get my ribs and cervical spine knocked out of alignment if someone jolted me in the wrong way. With my kids, with men, and in exercise, I often feared being hurt. Since most of the time

I ended up in pain from touch, I was guarded in my body. Even though my spine was no longer deeply affected by scoliosis, the residual muscular imbalance was something that I continued to work out with physical therapy. I was getting more stable and strong, but I still frequently went to the chiropractor and continued to seek out alternative body care, like fascia release, body stress release, and biodynamic cranial sacral therapy.

The lifelong pain I had carried in my body prevented me from totally trusting other people for safe touch, and the fear of being hurt or dropped was primal for me.

As the dance began, Eric and I sat on the ground with our backs together. We started moving back and forth, side to side, keeping a point of contact on our backs. It felt like a wonderful massage. Then with my body weight given over to him, Eric lay down and I rolled on top of him. I log-rolled over his body from head to toe, and it felt good to both of us.

After this warm-up, we followed the teacher's instructions and stood up to practice lifts. Standing side by side with our arms around each other's waist, I leaned into Eric and he lifted me up with one arm. After a few tries, and with my permission, he spun me off of his hip and I went flying through the air, landing on my feet.

I felt alive and invigorated. And I loved that I trusted him enough to allow him to lift me like that. We spent over an hour rolling all over each other's bodies, and it was intimate and profound in that it built physical trust between us. During the last ten minutes of class, Eric and I snuggled on the floor talking while everyone else continued to dance.

"I just want to know what you need so I can give it to you. I get so much from being with you and I want to give you what you need," he said.

Immediately, I started crying. No one in my entire life had ever cared about what I needed. People always seemed to be more concerned with what they needed me to be for them, and I rarely even knew what I needed.

"You're crying," Eric said as he held me close and wiped my tears. "That's what I needed," I said. "I just needed you to ask."

We all long for deep intimacy and deep connection; however, when we're identified with our conditioning we instinctively bypass the vulnerability necessary to create the connection we want. Afraid of being hurt, humiliated, rejected, or abandoned, we contort and manage ourselves to try to achieve the connection we think we want. Cultivating skills of authentic connection by giving voice to our truest truth, we can go for real connection without dropping ourselves.

11
CLAIMING THE SHADOW

"If you try to run away from your shadow, you will simply collapse due to exhaustion. Face the difficulties of life through love and faith."
— Amma

LIVING THE FANTASY

Three weeks after we met, Eric and I went to Tulum, Mexico together. He had planned this as a solo trip before we met, but instead it became a lover's getaway.

As a divorced mom with 50/50 custody, I was surprised by my spontaneity and ability to hop on a plane for a last-minute trip. Jason had agreed to keep the kids an extra day, and I met Eric down in Mexico part way through his trip.

He greeted me at the airport and we took a taxi to the ocean front room that he had reserved for us. With a deep connection and our open hearts, I was sure this was going to be the trip of a lifetime.

I had never felt as safe with a man as I did when I was with Eric. He was tender, caring, strong and emotionally intelligent. It was clear by the way he looked at me and introduced me to his friends that he was deeply in love with me.

"I must be at a new level of my development to be worthy of an amazing woman like you. You are beautiful, intelligent, and you have your life together. I feel so lucky that I get to be with you," he said on the long taxi ride to our hotel.

I grabbed the back of his head and pulled him close to me. In the back of the cab, we passionately made out on the hour drive to Tulum. Eric was the most affectionate man I had ever been with. His hands were always on me, at a restaurant, in the car, or walking down the street. His touch felt safe and connecting. He was also incredibly strong, and he would often pick me up and kiss me. I could surrender in his arms like I have never surrendered before.

When we arrived at our room, I was full of hope and excitement. But almost immediately when we got into the room, Eric started crying.

"I'm so tormented," he sobbed. "I just need you to know how much I suffer."

A bit shocked by this dark emotional release on our lover's getaway, I hugged him tight.

"What are you tormented by?"

"I don't know. Life has just been so hard for me. Everything is so hard and I have so much pain inside."

"What is it? What has been so hard about your life?"

Since we were both therapists, we both knew our own stories well. But Eric couldn't put any other words to his suffering. All he could say was that life had been so hard for him.

As he sobbed, I held him asking him what he needed from me.

"Just to know that I hurt inside," he said.

His pain seemed overwhelming, so I inquired more about specific childhood events, certain failures or heartbreak, and there was no one incident that Eric had that he considered hard or traumatic in his life. But he insisted that his life was hard. In my mind, I saw him as a tall, handsome, white man who had a graduate degree and lived in one of the happiest and healthiest parts of the country. His entitlement seemed obvious to me, so his torment was confusing.

We hadn't even explored the town yet and our vacation was less like the postcard image my mind had construed and more like a prelude to a psychiatric visit.

When we returned to our room later that night after exploring and having dinner out, things got worse.

We had just gotten into bed, when Eric said: "I don't think we should have sex."

"Okay. Why?"

"I just think if I go there fully with you now, I might get my heart broken."

Since we had made love before this trip, I was very confused. However, I was on my period and had just traveled all day so I wasn't in the mood anyway.

The next morning Eric told me that he wanted to do contact improv together. Naked, with oil.

Since this darkness that loomed in his presence made him seem fragile to me, I felt obligated to give him whatever he wanted in an effort to make this trip fun. Even though I wanted to go to the beach and enjoy the ocean, I took my clothes off, oiled up, and we rolled around on each other.

Eric got an erection, so we started making out.

"No. I can't," he said.

"Okay, that's fine. Whatever you need." I tried to appease.

My mind was full of confusion, and my heart was feeling played with. His needs and emotions were so big and prevalent that I focused solely on what would make him okay, staying flexible to what that might be as he was in constant flux. I didn't even know how to give voice to my needs, which were simply to have fun. I couldn't see that I was playing out my Type 2 patterning with him, as if he were an image of my mom, and I couldn't see that he was, in fact, conditioned as a Type 4. Type 4 individuals on the Enneagram are melancholy and self-absorbed. They are temperamental, dramatic, and self-referenced, trying to make significance out of their inner pain.

As a Type 2, I just wanted to give him what he needed without consideration of myself. I would notice my desire to go have fun and stop giving all of my attention to his inner suffering, but I would bypass my desire and push it aside thinking that what he wanted was more important because he was in pain. I couldn't see that my joy and exuberance was also valid and that I needed to make room for that to express itself.

Throughout this trip, we managed to swim in cenotes, bike to the Mayan ruins, and eat at some amazing restaurants. But every moment was colored by Eric's darkness and insecurity.

"I'm afraid we're going to go home broken up," I sobbed on our last day.

"Why?" he asked.

Because I don't like being with you, I thought to myself. *Because you're dramatic and there is no end to your melancholy.*

Because you actually don't care about what I need, you only focus on your suffering. Because you have never given me an orgasm.

"I don't know," I said. "This has been a hard trip."

"Really?" Eric responded. "We've had some hard moments but this has been the best vacation ever. I don't know what I would have done if you didn't come."

I was shocked. I couldn't believe that this trip was enjoyable to him. He seemed on the brink of a suicidal breakdown and I had never had a lover seem so conflicted about sex. We didn't have intercourse the entire trip, and we spent more time in our hotel room giving our attention to his melancholy than on the beach.

I felt drained and distraught, but I wanted to believe that my love could heal him.

"I want to meet your kids," he said on our way back to the airport on the last day of our trip.

"Really? We've only been dating for three and a half weeks. I want to wait six months before you meet them."

"I don't feel like I can really know you if I don't know them. I want to know all of you," he said.

That made sense to me, but after this challenging vacation and his deep melancholy, everything inside of me was screaming *"Don't do it, Harmony!"* My mom introduced me to every boyfriend and every lover she had when I was young. I had wanted more boundaries set for me, so I wanted to provide more boundaries for my kids. Against my better judgment, I agreed to make his desire more important than mine.

It was so automatic that I hardly even realized I was bypassing myself when I said, "Sure. We'll make a time when we get back."

The same night that I got back to Colorado, I facilitated my workshop, A Conscious Marriage, to a packed house. This workshop focused on how to use the context of one's relationship as a training ground to go deeper into alignment with the True Self and how to meet one's partner from this deep place. Teaching people tools of awareness and mindfulness, this workshop was intended to help them gain more self-mastery and awareness in order to see one's self and partner with more clarity, beyond the illusions of projections.

Aware that I was still learning how to do the very thing that I was teaching, I used Eric and myself as an example. I explained how as a Type 2, I want my love to heal other people. Driven by shame, I try to earn love by giving of myself, and this lives in me as not being in touch with what I need. I explained that being in a relationship with a Type 4 is challenging for me because the conditioning of his self-referenced ego is emotionally demanding. He thinks that he is good and okay if he gets what he needs, and I think that it's my job to give it to him.

The work of using our relationship as a reflection of our disowned parts highlights that our partner embodies the very thing we've disenfranchised. When I disenfranchise my needs, I am attracted to and attract men who embody the narcissistic tendency to believe that their needs are more important than mine. When my misbelief that I'm unworthy of love lives in the shadow of my unconscious, I am attracted to and attract a partner who holds the narcissistic belief that I need to be a certain way in order for him to be okay. When I disown my dissonance, I am attracted to and attract a mate who criticizes me and puts me down.

But my partner is not the "bad guy" in this. It's not his job to be in my wholeness so that I am happy. It's my job to claim and integrate my disowned parts and shadow. When I do, I become so solid in my alignment with the True Self that I get to consciously choose if I want to stay in the relationship or if I want to stay open to receiving a partner who genuinely cares about what I need because I know that my needs are important.

At the time, I was so enamored with Eric that I kept looking at him through rose-colored glasses. Ignoring his endless melancholy and deep depression, I was seeing him as the man I wanted him to be rather than seeing him clearly for the man that he was. I wasn't empowered with conscious choice because I was identified with my projections of him while also disowning my own darkness. Even now, when I don't claim my own shadow, I am blind to the shadow in the people around me. This was a huge blind spot in my relationship with Eric, perpetuated by lack of awareness that I was even doing this.

The next day, I became incredibly ill with flu-like stomach symptoms and Eric wanted to bring me some soup. Once he arrived, he became agitated that I needed care and that my focus was not on him.

"I shouldn't have come. I'm not good at this," he said as he paced around my living room just moments after he arrived.

I wasn't sure what he meant, but it seemed like he wasn't good at offering care to me even though he wanted to. My stomach was in terrible physical discomfort, unconsciously trying to digest the emotional turmoil of traveling to Tulum with Eric. In hearing that he wanted to leave, I felt dropped. I was mad that he wasn't more available to take care of me. If he was sick, I would have been doting over him and making sure all of his needs were met.

Once he left, my stomach started to relax and I was relieved he was gone. His presence made it harder to tend to myself, and I didn't have any attention to give to him. So soon after getting into this relationship,

I experienced great ambivalence about being with Eric. A big part of me wanted to break up with him, yet there was this other part of me that wanted to nurture the goodness between us.

In relationships, our distortion can be amplified when we don't give voice to our ambivalence. When there's a part of us that wants connection with our partner but another part that is uncertain, we often hide this truth because we're afraid that our ambivalence will hurt them. However, when we hide our authentic truth, our partner is unaware of all of the ways we are affected by their behavior. Only giving attention to the part that wants connection creates a false mask showing that everything is okay, and this is as big of a parasite to the connection as is the dark behavior that we're averse to in our partner. From this distorted place that is out of integrity with our truest truth, the relationship never feels satisfying because we're coming at it sideways.

SHADOW PLAY

Intimately familiar with his darkness, Eric was drawn to my light. Intimately familiar with my light, I was drawn to Eric's darkness.

Eric could see a fiery, fierce dragoness within me, and he wanted to support me in letting her out to play so that she didn't come out sideways in our relationship. Well versed in shadow play, which is a form of psychodrama where we would consciously play with our darkness, Eric encouraged me to embody the fire dragon that is my Chinese astrological sign.

Because of my pleasant, accommodating persona, I had disowned my fierceness throughout my life. Thinking that it wasn't okay to be a powerful, ferocious woman, I presented a distorted face to the world of happy and okay with everything. Eric was the first man who spoke about my powerful inner dragon and wanted to be in relationship with me around it rather than shaming me and wanting me to hide it.

Because of his encouragement, it was the first time in my life where I felt curious about the range of my darkness rather than denying it. Being with him, I felt like I had the permission I needed to embody a part of myself that I had been too scared to acknowledge. Roaring, fierce and intense, with Eric I playfully brought my shadow into the light of conscious awareness.

On our knees, facing each other with the palms of our hands touching and fingers interlocked, we looked fiercely into one another's eyes and roared loudly.

"ROAR!!!" I tried for a moment before I started to giggle. The young one in me who believed that it's not okay to be fierce and angry came to the surface immediately. I felt small and insecure, not knowing how to be intentionally fierce.

"GRRRRRRRR!" Eric growled as he held my gaze with strength.

"ROAR!!!!!" I replied, with more ferocity this time.

"GRRRRRRRRR…." He growled again, staying with the game.

"GRRRRRRRR….." I met him there with strength as I pushed firmly into his hands.

Once we were complete, Eric and I talked about what that was like for us, and I admitted that I needed more of this. I needed to gain mastery over my fierceness, and I was so appreciative to him for calling her out to play.

Claiming my disowned power, anger, and ferocity was an edge for me that I enjoyed exploring. However, claiming my disowned desire seemed nearly impossible with Eric. His desires were so constant and loud that I had to be extremely conscious of myself to give voice to what I wanted. Because this had been my pattern throughout my life, the ownership of transforming it was on me. I was dedicated to cultivating more mastery with voicing my desire, so I kept trying.

"What would you like me to pick up from Whole Foods? I'm headed out in a bit." Eric texted one day while we were making plans to cook dinner at his place.

I immediately started texting back "Whatever you want." Luckily, I caught myself and deleted it. For fifteen minutes, I took deep, regulating breaths trying to figure out how to ask for something.

I didn't know what I wanted for dinner. I would be fine with anything. But that wasn't the point. The point was that he asked and it was time for me to claim that I wanted something in order to build the muscle for asking for bigger things. Deferring my desire to others was my manipulative way of trying to earn love and keep connection, and the pattern was outdated. I was ready for something new, something truer.

"Chicken and broccoli," I texted back.

We ended up making a delicious dinner together that involved both chicken and broccoli. When I told him how hard it was for me to ask for that, he was perplexed. He was so self-referenced that he couldn't even fathom not being able to ask for what he wanted.

For all of the heartfelt love between us, there was also a lot of turmoil. Though he was committed to giving voice to his emotional world, it became clear that he really only wanted room to voice his own emotions and was not at all curious about mine.

If he did something that impacted me negatively, I would try to voice it: "I'm feeling hurt."

"No." He would snap. "You can't."

Confused by his dismissal of my emotions, I would try to stand up for myself: "You can't tell me what I'm feeling. I feel hurt."

"No. No, you can't."

He was a mirror to me, reflecting the part of my shadow that was ready to be illuminated. If I were alone on a mountain top I would have no idea that I was so skilled at self-abandonment. Collapsing around my will was self-harming, and I wanted to love myself with tenderness and care, just as I wanted a partner to love me with tenderness and care. It was my work to learn how to stay in touch with myself and not abandon myself, even if that meant rupturing connection.

I think that Eric felt too fragile and wounded in his own pain to see my experience as valid. He wanted to deny any negative impact he had on me so that he could be resilient. He was on antidepressants and sleep aids, and it was becoming increasingly clear to me that he needed treatment for suicidal ideation.

I didn't want to follow my impulse to fix him, though, that was the impulse of my inner young one who wanted Mom to be happy so I felt safe. I wanted to love him and support his process without being the savior. This was my great challenge, because I wanted him to be different. If chronic melancholy and selfishness formed Eric's dysfunction, chronic helping and self-abandonment formed mine.

Feeding into my ambivalence was all of the ways Eric was amazing and tender. When I would ask him what he wanted to do for the day, he would look me in the eyes and answer by saying, "Connect with you." My heart would melt and he would pull me onto his lap and we'd gaze into each other's eyes.

We would talk deeply, snuggle, and make love. We would spend time with his friends, and we hosted parties together. When I talked with him about my dissatisfaction with our sexual relationship, he was mortified to learn I had never had an orgasm with him. He put effort into learning about my clitoris and we tried to stay in communication about this. This worked at first, but soon after Eric regressed back to ignoring my need for erotic touch and I stopped asking.

It was easy for me to deny the negative impact Eric had on me because it was contrasted by how wonderful he was in other areas. He ended up being a caring masculine presence for my children. We had fun together at the Boulder Creek and walking around Pearl Street. My kids and I would spend time with him and his mom, who was like a surrogate grandmother to them with her sweet and caring ways. Our lives were intertwined with friendships and family, so the painful aspects could easily be brushed aside and ignored.

Eventually, his unwillingness to be curious about his impact on me was so consistent in our communication that I started losing patience with him. I wanted to claim something for myself that I had never claimed before. I wanted to give voice to my truth and my needs, and I wanted a caring partner who was curious about me. About six months after we started dating, Eric starting moving his stuff into my house without an invitation. I was feeling infringed upon and starting to resent his unrelenting presence. When I told Eric that I wanted to end our relationship, he begged me to try one last time.

We planned a road trip to Santa Fe to try and reconcile, and Eric packed the car while I saw clients. When I came out of my office ready to go, Eric was spinning with angst. He told me he needed to go for a run to calm down, but when he returned he clearly was not settled.

"I should tell you I hate road trips," Eric said about two hours into our six-hour drive.

"Maybe you can try to relax while I drive?" I said as an attempt to make everything okay.

It turned out he couldn't calm down. He was so agitated and restless that he made requests to stop every time he saw a rest stop. When we would stop, he would run around to try to get his energy out. But when he returned he was still on edge and filled with angst.

We eventually made it to the beautiful spa hotel I had reserved for us that was walking distance to the hub of town.

Similar to our experience in Mexico, this trip was plagued by Eric's melancholy and moodiness. He didn't want to have sex, and he didn't want to have fun.

Unlike Mexico, though, this time I took off by myself and went to explore the city. Not wanting to indulge Eric's emotional drama and wanting to honor my desire to explore the city, I told Eric that he could text me if he wanted to join me. He seemed fine with my decision, but this act of independence surprised him.

I loved exploring the city on my own. With no one else to attend to, I could follow my desire into any store I wanted. I bought some lovely jewelry, ate some delicious food, and took in the rich cultural history of the town.

Eric would come out with me sporadically. We would snuggle in the park, have dinner together, and we made our way to 10,000 Waves Spa and the Upaya Zen center. But if I wanted to see the museums, shopping, and explore the town further, I had to do it without him.

During our visit, we learned that Amma, the Indian guru who travels the world giving hugs, was in Santa Fe. My mom had gotten a hug from Amma, and I was in dire need of a good momma hug since it had been about eight years since I'd had one from my own mom. A hug from Amma is free, and people wait all night long to receive one.

Eric really wanted to go, too, so we packed up for the long night of waiting in line for the infamous hug.

Once we arrived at the event center, Eric was extremely moody and grumpy. Unable to give voice to what was going on for him, he went outside to take a walk. I felt dropped again.

For hours I sat by myself, feeling lonely and angry that he disappeared. I didn't understand how Eric and I could be deeply and intimately connecting in one moment but in the next he could be inaccessible and vacant. I had no cell reception so I couldn't call him, and I didn't know if he was going to make it back for the hug.

In his absence, I started talking to the handsome young man sitting next to me who was a dedicated follower of Amma. He had volunteered at her ashram in India, and so I asked him about the protocol of receiving a hug and what to expect.

"What do you get out of an Amma hug?" I asked him.

"You get whatever it is you need," he said. "That's different for every person."

Though I was still bothered about how Eric was acting, I felt excited and hopeful to get a hug from this legendary guru. I had no idea what I needed and I was eager to see how this unfolded.

We had arrived at 4 PM and were given our tickets for our place in line. Eric returned around 11:45. At about midnight, our numbers were called and we moved forward to get in the front line. The event was a big production with many attendants guiding the crowd and keeping an organized rhythm to the night.

When we moved forward to our place in line, the attendant asked if we wanted to be hugged together.

"No," I quickly replied.

I was fuming from his departure, and I didn't feel like connecting with him. He been gone for over four hours, and I was stressed by not knowing where he was and what he was doing. This hug was for me.

I went first and was ushered up to Amma's platform and told to get on my knees.

When it was my turn, an attendant guided me up to Amma and placed my head on her bosom.

Amma held me close and chanted a mantra in my ear.

I'm not sure what happened or what she was chanting, but halfway through my hug my body collapsed onto her in full surrender. It took my breath away.

Before I knew it, the hug was complete and Amma handed me some holy water, a rose petal, and a Hershey's Kiss.

Then I was ushered away, backwards on my knees, and given a chair to sit in as I watched others receive their hug.

As we drove back to the hotel, Eric told me that he was mad that I didn't want to get my hug with him. I responded that I was mad that he disappeared for hours. We fought the whole drive back. And when we got to our room, Eric made up a bed on the floor.

I felt so relieved. I didn't want him near me.

I was still in a daze from the hug. The deep surrender I experienced in Amma's embrace was still pulsating throughout my body. As I lay in bed, I could feel the love from Amma's heart move through every cell of my body. Blissful.

I could hear Eric tossing and turning in his bed, and I was okay with that. There was no part of me that wanted to be his savior from his suffering. I wanted to be with my own experience and show up for what felt like a rich transformation taking place within me.

In the days that followed, I felt softer and more feminine. I could see where I needed to surrender more in my life, and I could equally see where my clients needed to surrender more in theirs. This hug awoke in me the feeling of being like water. Where I typically wanted to control and make things happen, I was able to flow with what was happening without attachment.

I could see Eric's darkness more fully, and I could see how my attempt at trying to make that darkness go away was not in service of our connection or of my well-being. I was new to the practice of asserting what I wanted, but it seemed like our relationship couldn't exist without me abandoning myself.

On the long drive home from Santa Fe, I told Eric that I didn't want to be with him. He had an emotional outburst that was reminiscent of a toddler's tantrum, as if anger and rage would make me change my mind. I wanted a partner who was stable and healthy, and the more he raged, the clearer I became that I didn't want to be with him.

I had tried so hard in my marriage with Jason to make everything okay and please him. In this moment, I could see that the responsibility of Eric's emotional and mental health rested on him. Eric was not my responsibility, and I was ready to stop treating him as such. I still didn't know how to meet a man from my sovereign self, but it was becoming ever more obvious to me how painful it was to meet them from my conditioned self.

If my attention was always pulled to getting others to like me, to keeping connection, and to giving others what I thought they needed, I was meeting the world from my distortion. The young one in me who felt neglected and unlovable was running the show whether I was with a Type 5, 8, or 4. This is why it is level of evolution, not Enneagram Type, that matters in matchmaking. And in elevating our consciousness, it is more important to differentiate from our conditioned self and create an identity with our True Self than it is to create healthier behaviors or thoughts.

There is great liberation in being more committed to our own growth and evolution than we are to keeping our relationship. Our conditioning says that monogamous, heterosexual relationships that last until the end of time are the successful and acceptable relationships. This misbelief that has been fed to most of us keeps us feeling small and disempowered. When we believe our conditioned self we stop being curious about our own unique values and beliefs. If keeping the relationship is the most important thing, then we can easily leave ourselves, abandon our truth, and try to fit into a tight box that fits the context of the relationship. From this viewpoint, we are successful when we do this and the relationship lasts.

When we believe that our own personal well-being, dignity, health, joy, and vitality are the most important things, we feel empowered to choose what we are available for in our relationships. The spaciousness this stance affords gives us room to continue to grow and evolve. However, the vital element here is that we use the context of our relationship to continue to grow and evolve. Simply leaving isn't necessarily the right path if we're avoiding our growing edges. By meeting the edges of our own growth through the reflection of our partner while standing in our sovereignty and staying in our compassionate hearts, we will know with clarity when walking away is the truest thing we can do for ourselves.

12
PLAYING THE FIELD OF SELF-DISCOVERY

"Why are you knocking at every door? Knock at the door of your own heart."—Rumi

SEARCHING FOR THE NEW PARADIGM

It had been one year since my divorce, and I had spent almost the entire time in relationships, first with Robert and then Eric. After I broke up with Eric, I bought a jade yoni egg, which is carved of semi-precious stone and made to be worn in the vagina. The yoni egg is part of a 5,000-year-old tantric practice, in which empresses and concubines of the royal palace of China would utilize jade eggs to access sexual power, awaken sensuality, and maintain good health. I knew very little about the yoni egg when I bought it, but in my experience the practice was about creating a new relationship with my vagina and my pleasure.

The first time I practiced with my yoni egg, I spent over fifteen minutes preparing myself to invite the egg inside of me. Using my breath and vaginal muscles, I slowly and intentionally received the egg. It was the first time I had ever invited something into me (rather than having something inserted into me). Staying fully engaged with the present moment sensations and experience, this was the most connected I had ever felt with my own vagina. I was moved to tears by this experience. My vagina felt like mine, like it belonged to me.

I felt empowered with my muscles and my intention to "receive" the egg rather than "insert" the egg. In this practice I realized that being penetrated is very different when I am honored as the receiver, fully ready to invite my partner into me. Having a lover ask me if I'm ready to receive him before inserting himself in me would have been the very medicine I needed to feel honored as the receiver.

Aside from feeling more connected to my vagina, I experienced many other benefits from this practice, such as increased strength in my pelvic floor muscles, more connection with sensation in my vagina, opening up the central channel of my body aligning my chakras, and releasing old lovers' energy stored in my yoni.

I would sleep with my yoni egg inside me, and I would have dreams of ex-lovers. Then I would awake and feel lighter, more open, and more in touch with my emotions. Tears of compassion would well into my eyes and I felt more porous—less hardened to other people's pain. This surprised me because I experience myself as a very caring and compassionate person, but this practice aligned my root chakra with my heart in a new way.

As I was exploring a new relationship with my sex-center, I still wanted the validation, fun, and experience of intimate partnership. However, I wanted to get clearer on myself and what I was wanting before jumping into a relationship with someone new.

For me, jumping into bed with someone had typically led to jumping into a relationship. I decided that I wanted to really get to know a man before having sex with him, so I made a rule for myself: no sex until we've been on ten dates.

Since I was challenged in accessing my desire and setting boundaries with men, I wanted to try to approach each date as an interview for the next date. I wanted to stay in touch with myself and discover if I really wanted to spend more time with this person. I wanted to check in with myself to see how I felt in their presence over time and discover if I wanted to receive them.

Many years ago, one of my mom's psychic friends said to me: "Never go to bed with someone you don't want to be like. Your energies get all mixed up and you can't see them clearly anymore."

Although I understood this conceptually, I had never taken the time to get to know someone well enough before having sex. I wanted to continue to become healthier and more evolved, and I wanted to meet someone who matched my level of health. When I'm in my low level of health, I am very accommodating and codependent. It doesn't appear like a low level of health because I'm so caring and sparkly. However, self-abandonment invited narcissists into my life, and I wanted to shift this pattern.

Given my history of trying to earn love, safety, and value with sex, as well as not feeling empowered to say "No" to men, this ten-date rule was the absolute best boundary to set for myself. It gave me a sort of brake pedal that I had never had access to before. I was beginning to realize that I moved fast in order to find a sense of safety and control. I did this in all areas of my life when I felt unsafe, not just with men. In my speeding up with men, I was bypassing my vulnerability and objectifying myself. Slowing down afforded me the time and space to sit with the true experience within me that might emerge when I stop avoiding discomfort.

I put up a new profile on Bumble soon after I broke up with Eric, and I started chatting with men to see who I found interesting. The inner critic who ran my interactions with men kept running a story that I was too fat and that nobody would ever want to be with me. This was a very common inner script that I was accustomed to, and even though it was an outdated story I still believed it.

On the app, when an attractive, athletic man was interested in me, I felt exuberant and surprised. My worth felt validated and I would look over my profile to imagine how I seemed through his eyes. Looking at my photos, I could see that I was, in fact, beautiful. I had maintained a healthy weight for over a year, and I was fit, exercising almost daily. I had a sophisticated style that was equally unique and practical, and I had a light about me that people seemed drawn to.

But right behind that ego boost there was a deep fear of how this attractive man would be repulsed by me if he saw me naked. I didn't want to be with someone who wanted me because of the way I looked because I was afraid of ultimately disappointing him.

I made a date with a man named Ed. My friend Hayley came over to hang out with me in my master bathroom as I got ready. Ed was a business owner who trained elite athletes in Boulder. His whole life was fitness, and he appeared to be in amazing shape. I was being extra critical of myself, assuming that I would be too curvy for him in my size 8 jeans even though this was a healthy size for my frame.

I tried on multiple outfits, criticizing my appearance with every change of clothes. Frustrated with me, Hayley said, "You are a total bombshell. Look at you! You're gorgeous!"

I tried to take it in, but I quite literally felt like a fat child who nobody wanted to dance with at the junior high dance. My body shame was too loud for me to see the reality of the mature, beautiful woman I had become. Being so image-focused and so insecure, I was convinced that my appearance would cause me to be unworthy of love. Even though I was beginning to embody my magical, bright spirit in most areas of my life, my conditioned self still believed that with men I was my body, that I was an object for them to judge.

Wearing a short black dress and wedges, I walked up to Biter Bar on Pearl Street to meet Ed for the first time.

When I walked up to the patio where Ed was sitting, he looked me up and down with a smile and I felt relieved that he obviously liked the way I looked. As I sat there trying to get to know him, I thought about how I could continue to camouflage my belly with my dress. Every time he looked at me, I was afraid that he would discover that I wasn't fit enough to be with him.

We had a lot of fun on our first date. We ended up driving up to a lookout point on Flagstaff Mountain where we made out while we took in the beauty of Boulder.

I was comforted that Ed was into me as it unconsciously gave me reassurance of being worthy of existing. I didn't stop to ask myself if I was into him. Earning his approval was the only thing that pulled the attention of my mind.

On our second date we went on a hike up the Chautauqua trailhead. I was wearing my sexy lululemon yoga pants, hoping the high waist would hold my belly in. I could see him checking out my physique, and I wanted to be enough for him. Clearly I wasn't as fit as the athletes he coached, but hopefully I was fit enough.

After our hike we went out to dinner at Aloy Thai, Ed invited me back to his place.

I felt ambivalent. I had my new ten-date rule, and I was afraid that I wouldn't uphold it if I was in his home. But I was also afraid of disappointing him if I said no.

"I'll come over for a bit, but I'm not going to have sex with you," I told him matter-of-factly.

"Okay," he said, seeming to be less certain whether he still wanted me to come over.

At his apartment, Ed and I started to make out passionately on his couch. We told each other what we wanted to do with one another, and we grinded on each other until it became extremely hard for me to hold my boundary.

"What's your favorite position?" I asked him.

"Reverse cowgirl," he answered.

"I want you to turn me around and ..." I stopped myself before the words came out of my mouth. I almost told him that I wanted to have sex with him.

His hands were moving down my pants.

"My pants stay on," I quickly said as I moved his hand away, trying to remind myself and him of my boundary.

"Of course," Ed said. "You don't have anything to worry about."

He asked me if I wanted to come to his bed with him, and we stood up and walked to his room.

As he started taking his clothes off, my mind was active with fear. I wanted to slow down. I really didn't want to have sex with him. I could see how my messages were mixed and I wasn't owning my "No." I could see that my behavior was saying "Yes, maybe." I was trying to keep him interested in me, and I didn't know how to claim my boundary while still keeping connection.

I lay in his bed with my clothes on as he climbed on top of me with his clothes off.

He rubbed my body all over, and then he slid his hand down my pants. His touch felt so good and I didn't want to stop him.

A moment later, he started to pull my pants down.

"Don't," I stated firmly.

"Don't worry," Ed assured me as he continued to pull off my pants.

With my pants and underwear off, Ed looked at my body. I felt so vulnerable and unattractive. Then he started to go down on me. I didn't want him to. This was, after all, a form of sex.

I stopped him almost immediately and then I gave him a hand job, rationalizing that if he had an orgasm I wouldn't be too much of a tease.

I couldn't believe that I willingly walked into the situation and participated in it every step of the way. Once again playing small for some guy, I was so desperate to be liked that I was willing to be his object. My adult self set a rule, but my wound started to run the show, disempowering myself by believing that Ed's interest in me gave me worth and value.

I knew even before going over there that Ed wasn't the guy for me. Even though he was fun on our dates, when our conversations went to social issues he seemed racist and entitled. I was offended by his lack of empathy for the impoverished, and I was certain that he lacked self-awareness or desire to go deeper into himself. I felt shame for having gone this far with Ed because each moment with him felt like self-abandonment.

After Ed had an orgasm, I went home, never to see him again.

Ideally, men would instinctively honor women's boundaries and hold the stance as protector rather than inserting themselves into us. However, they have been conditioned to be masculine in the world in a way that has historically upheld their position of power. Since that story is quickly becoming outdated, men need to work on embodying the healthy masculine. But that work is their job. It is the job of the feminine beings on the planet to not disown our power as a way to find safety and value. We need to use our voice, hold ourselves in our truth, and stay solid in ourselves in the presence of men. Setting clear boundaries, saying "No," and calling out the impact of painful behavior will have us all shift the paradigm into a new and healthy updated version based on integration of the healthy feminine and healthy masculine.

EMPOWERED AND FUN

I had to regroup after my final date with Ed. While I was glad that I didn't have intercourse with him, I was disgraced by my self-abandonment. I was unclear about why I didn't own my "No." I betrayed myself for him, and I was appalled with myself for it.

The very next evening I went out to dinner with another man, Aaron. I wanted to meet Aaron because he was a naturopathic doctor; I was hopeful that he would embody the deeper understanding that I wanted to experience in partnership.

Although slightly awkward, Aaron was kind and attentive. He was an avid meditation practitioner and had spent a lot of time with an Indian guru, dedicating his time to consciousness and evolution. Although Aaron seemed wise and kind, there was something about him I didn't trust. When he talked about himself he didn't own any of his shadow behavior. He spoke as if he believed he was enlightened, and he seemed slippery, in a spiritual bypass of sorts, where he used his spirituality as a way to hide from suffering.

After a few dates, I wasn't curious to learn more so I turned my focus elsewhere.

This is when it became clear to me that my intention for dating wasn't about finding love in another. The whole point of me having different experiences with many men was to practice staying true to myself in the presence of a man.

I continued dating, and I dated a lot. The men were sweet and successful, and I enjoyed the process of getting to know myself and my desires more clearly with each date. From the outside it may have appeared that I was being frivolous with my dating, but what was happening internally was profound. I started to realize that interacting with men didn't need to be a disempowering experience where I gave myself over to them. Instead of losing myself to them, with each date I aligned even deeper with my True Self.

Then I met Jake.

When Jake and I first met, I was incredibly attracted to him. He was tall, dark, and handsome, with a chiseled jaw and heavily athletic build.

It was a cool September day, and we had arranged our first meeting at a coffee shop in central Boulder. Jake was new to Boulder, so we texted back and forth as I tried to direct him to the hidden café on the side of a store.

"Is it near Safeway?" Jake texted.

"No, it's on the other side, facing Iris."

"I have no idea how to get to you."

"It's around the corner from Safeway. I'm standing out front wearing a blue dress."

"I can't find it."

"I'll come meet you over there."

As Jake and I walked up to each other in the middle of the large, busy parking lot, he seemed flustered about getting lost. I felt a familiar fear: doubting that I was enough for him.

"You like to give directions," Jake said as he chuckled, alluding to the way I took control of the situation.

I started giggling nervously about the way I overcompensate for feeling insecure by seeming confident. "I guess I do."

We walked inside Red Rocks coffee shop and ordered our tea. As we stood at the counter, Jake gazed into my eyes in a way that both scared me and turned me on. His eyes were piercing and intense. All of the places in me that I try to hide felt jolted. It seemed as if there was no hiding from Jake, that he could see the depths of my soul with one look. And I liked it.

Jake was a men's relationship coach, and we sat in the coffee house drinking tea, talking about personal growth, our shared passion for psychology, and past relationships. Jake had moved to Boulder to be closer to the Integral Center, the place where Eric took me on our first date. He told me that the authentic relating practices there had changed his life, and he wanted as much of it as he could get. When he found out that I had been to the Integral Center before, he asked why I don't go.

"I'm a single mom solopreneur living twenty minutes from town. I don't have time to go to their events," I explained.

"I think you'd like it," he responded. "The work you do with clients sounds in line with what's happening there."

I took in the suggestion with little intention to go back to the Integral Center, but I was excited to spend more time with Jake. I was also dating a few other men. New Eric (as I called him) was a single dad living in Fort Collins. He was kind, engaging, and he took me on fun dates filled with good food, good wine, and laughter. I had plans to have dinner with New Eric one day, when Jake texted me:

"Meet me for lunch."

"Now?" I responded.

"Yes, now."

"I have a client at four, so if you can meet me near my place I have some time."

Since it was 2 PM when he texted me, I had already eaten lunch. But I wanted to see him again so I got myself together to meet him at a nearby taqueria.

At lunch, Jake spoke about himself in a way that was seductive. I felt drawn into him, and he asked questions about me in a way that had me feeling penetrated and excited.

We touched and massaged each other's hands, and we spent a lot of time gazing into each other's eyes. I was so aroused by our time together that after we ate, I invited him back to my house to show him my home office. Normally, I wouldn't invite guys I had just met online back to my house on our second date (especially with my ten-date rule). But I found Jake so attractive that I wanted more contact with him.

After I showed him around my house, Jake and I stood in my kitchen. He leaned against my kitchen island as I leaned against the counter opposite of him. Standing close together, Jake's eyes communicated to me an intensity of desire that ignited deep arousal in me. He looked like a hungry lion who hadn't mated in years and I was his prey.

His seductive gaze was alluring, and we held eye contact for several moments in silence. Slowly, Jake moved closer to me and then paused when his face got close to mine. The buildup was erotic as he moved in for a passionate kiss.

Pressing his body against mine with fierce desire, Jake picked me up and put me on the kitchen counter. His force was sexy and masculine and intense. Every part of me said "Yes" to his appetite for seduction.

After five minutes of an intense make-out session, Jake left so I could get ready for my client.

"You are so hot," he texted me when from his car. "Meet me at Convergence at the Integral Center tomorrow night."

"What's that?" I asked.

"It's a big Halloween party. I hear it's going to be amazing. I'd love to see you there!"

I hadn't been to the Integral Center since my first date with Eric, and I hadn't dressed up for Halloween in over ten years. The lack of fun and deep loneliness that I had endured for the eleven years prior to this moment had me forgetting what it was like to really let go and become uninhibited.

I was nervous and totally unwilling to go by myself, so I texted Hayley and asked if she'd come with me. Hayley was a single mom, too, and she loved dressing up for Halloween. She enthusiastically agreed to come, and the next day she brought over bags of costumes for us to use.

Hayley dressed up as Wonder Woman and I used her fairy wings and tutu, combined with a black and pink bustier that I had bought when I first started dating Jason. This bustier had been too sexy for Jason, and he had actually rejected me when I surprised him wearing it for our first anniversary. I had resigned it to the back of my closet for over ten years, and now I was resurrecting it to attend a wild party where my hot date would be.

When I looked in the mirror, I could see that my appearance—the hairdo, glittery makeup, and sexy outfit—was both hot and flattering. But my mind had a hard time owning my beauty. I never felt safe to fully own my sexiness because unconsciously I thought men would become even more assertive with me—internalized victim blaming. A part of me couldn't believe that I was leaving the house in lingerie, but another part of me was excited to be shaking up my life and doing something outside of my comfort zone.

"You look so sexy," Hayley assured me.

"Are you sure? I feel so strange wearing something like this out."

"No. You look hot. Wear that," she asserted.

When we arrived, the Integral Center was already packed with hundreds of people dressed in fun and super sexy costumes that made mine almost look like normal street wear.

As I walked in I was met with hundreds of widening, excited eyes, and I desperately wanted to not be seen. I felt my energy collapse and get smaller because in my mind I was overweight and ugly. Even though I could tell other people didn't see me that way, I perceived myself to be completely unattractive. I had a hard time enjoying my body because I was riddled with too much shame. Still fragmented with disowned parts swirling around in my psyche, I felt wobbly and unstable in my alignment with my True Self.

A few moments into the party I ran into Jake, who was wearing a hamburger costume with a "Gluten Free" and "Grass Fed" sign on it. He was the sexiest hamburger I had ever seen.

We sat on the couch talking for a while, and then Jake got up to go to the costume contest. Right away his friend Andrew took his seat and started talking to me.

After a short conversation about the booming real estate market in the Front Range, Andrew asked me out. Although I wasn't attracted to him and I was completely into Jake, I told Andrew that he could call me. I wasn't sure how to speak my truth, so I deferred to what he wanted. It was easier to say "Yes, maybe" than to claim my "No."

I quickly got up to go dance, and a gorgeous 28-year-old man dressed up as a caveman started dancing with me. Holding his cave man club, he gently hit the top of my head with it.

"What's your name?" I asked with confidence.

"Matthew," the young hunk replied.

"How old are you, Matthew?"

"Twenty-eight."

"I'm 39. Go dance with her," I said pointing at a younger woman dancing nearby.

He looked at her. Then he looked at me. And then he started dancing with me again. When he started hitting me over the head with his club again, I grabbed it and we started dancing with it as if we were in a tug-of-war. It was all fun and flirty until he accidentally hit my lip really hard with the club.

"Matthew ... Kiss it," I said, pointing at my lip.

He did as I said and kissed my lip.

"This is child's play, Matthew. Did hitting girls work for you in elementary school?"

He paused and thought about my question, and then continued dancing with me while I spanked him with his own club.

I felt empowered and sexy. I felt fierce and feminine. The playful dynamic with Matthew reminded me of the confidence that lives inside of me. Neither meek nor acquiescing, I was beginning to reconnect with my inner dominatrix where I have the ability to be in my power with men.

Disowning my power has been much of my downfall in relationships. When I ignored my power, it came out sideways in controlling and domineering ways. Eric had tried to get me to own my ferocity in our shadow play together, but I still felt too much shame about my own strength and deep fear that men couldn't handle me there. To own one's power with dignity and humility takes a strong life urge. The will to live along with knowing that we belong here in this life are needed to claim the true expression of power. I was just starting to access this part of me, and I wanted more.

I didn't see Jake for the rest of that night, but when we got together the following week he suggested we play a game of power dynamics. In the few times we had hung out, we had a few interactions where I told him what to do. I would give him directions on where to park, when to drink his tea, and where to sit. Every time I did this, Jake would laugh in the sweetest way and bring the attention to my behavior with grace.

"You seem to like to tell me what to do," he would say with a smile.

It was as if he were an aikido master using my power to unify us rather than separate us. Any shame I had about my impulse to control was alleviated, and I felt like I could relax into his masculinity.

The game that Jake suggested included him having the right to tell me five things to do. If I agreed, I had to do them, but there was a safe word if he asked me to do something that was too triggering or too edgy for me. I felt nervous about giving up control because I didn't fully trust Jake, but I was excited at the idea of being the object of his desire—when brought to conscious awareness this type of play can be transformative. Being objectified by men's subversive shadow is what frightened me. I wanted to see what would come of consciously being with this dynamic, so I reluctantly agreed.

"Five things ..." he said aloud as he thought about what he would have me do. "Okay, take this sweater off," he commanded.

I was wearing a red cashmere cardigan over lululemon exercise clothes, and the sweater seemed like an easy thing to give up.

"Now go stand with your hands against the wall."

I did as I was told. So far, I liked this game but I was nervous about not knowing what would come next. He walked over to me and kneeled down to spread my legs so they were farther apart. I turned my head to look at him.

"Don't look at me," he said with an authoritative tone. Clearly, he liked being in control.

Jake stood up and slowly and seductively walked around to my other side, taking in my body with his eyes. Gently, he started kissing my back and rubbing my body. I took a deep breath and moaned in complete arousal. He seductively teased me with his lips and his touch, and then commanded that I go upstairs to my bedroom.

As I walked upstairs, I contemplated whether he had one or two commands left.

I stood in front of my bed and he pushed me down. We started making out, and he told me to take his pants off for him.

"Go down on me," he commanded.

"No," I said.

"No?" he sounded surprised by my refusal.

"Nope," I took a deep breath.

I was having fun with Jake. I was attracted to him and I loved hanging out with him, but I wanted to stop playing games with men. This was our third date, and for the first time in my life I was slowing down sexually. I was clear on what I wanted, and casual sex was not on the list of priorities. I wanted to stop leaving myself for men, and I wanted to build the foundation for a healthy partnership. I wasn't sure if I wanted that with him, but I was clear that sex would likely impede me from being able to decipher such a thing.

We paused in the silence as he lay on top of me. I felt so much hesitance and insecurity in these long quiet moments as I tried to muster up the courage to voice my desire. I squirmed as I tried to wiggle away from saying anything at all. It would have been so much easier for me to just go down on him.

"I feel so vulnerable right now. I don't want to say this but I have to."

I squirmed some more, taking a few deep breaths.

"Once you hear it you're going to wonder why this is so hard for me, but here it goes: I want to get intentional about what we're doing here."

It took everything I had to say this, and I felt so much relief that I actually got the words out of my mouth.

"What do you mean?" he asked.

"I mean, what do you want to get out of this?"

"I'm in a place in my dating life where I'm having fun and want to date many people," he replied.

"I'm dating many people, too. And that's fine for dating, but I do not want to have sex with many people."

"I'm sort of in the opposite place. I'm exploring polyamory," he said.

I was annoyed that he hadn't told me this upfront. We were in my bed, half naked. I was so glad that I had paused our trajectory and asked for what I needed.

"Well, I have a rule that I won't have sex with someone I don't want to be like. All of the energies get all mixed together during intercourse, and I only want to invite energy into my body that I feel resonance with. I won't know if I want to be like you until I get to know you better."

"I like that!" Jake said with enthusiasm.

He laid down and pulled me close to him to snuggle. I rested my head on his chest, and we had an intimate and loving conversation about sex, which surprised me given I had just stopped our sexual game. Having him stay in connection with me around my "No" was relieving. I liked Jake, and even though I wasn't interested in polyamory, I still wanted to get to know him.

"How long do you think it would take for you to get to know if you want to have sex with me?" he inquired.

"Ten dates," I said with confidence, knowing that if I came to that conclusion it would be in part because he changed his mind about being poly.

"Ten dates?" He pondered this new information. "Okay."

I'm not sure if Jake took that as a challenge or if he wanted to see if I would like him enough to sleep with him, but after he left it became clear to me that what I wanted in a relationship was not in alignment with where Jake was in his life.

He was sweet and wise and handsome, but he was on an extended sabbatical from work and was dating several other women. I wanted a monogamous partnership with a man I could work with in the world, where I feel safe and loved and empowered. Even with the amazing connection and attraction, it seemed to me like our paths were headed in different directions.

Because I thought highly of Jake, I hoped we could be friends. The next night I invited him to meet me at the lookout on the night of the full moon to talk in person. We found a private spot where we sat on the cold ground and snuggled. Feeling nervous and awkward, I wanted to come right out and say what was on my mind before we started making out.

"I don't want to date you. I'm wanting a monogamous relationship, and you're in a different place."

"Are you sure you want to close that door?" he asked.

"Yes, I'm sure."

"I feel sad. I wasn't expecting this. I really like you."

"I was hoping we could be friends," I offered.

"No. I don't have feelings of friendship for you," he stated. "I like you more than that."

"I'm never going to have sex with you as long as you're dating other women," I said bluntly.

"Well I guess that's it, then," he replied.

We hugged and parted ways. No grief came up for me. No regret. No pain. It felt clean and right.

"Thank you for meeting me mindfully," Jake texted later that night. "It's a refreshing experience to be met this way by a woman."

It was refreshing for me, too. A younger, less mature version of myself would have had sex with Jake and hoped he'd fall in love with me, like I had done with Robert.

The practice of not distorting and contorting for men was new for me. Speaking my truth may seem simple and easy, but there's part of me that believes that I will die if I don't become what a man wants me to be for him. But here's the thing: I don't actually know what a man wants me to be for him. I only think I know based on experiences and the delusions of my own mind. In this interaction with Jake, I truly believe that what he wanted me to be was in my truth. If I had abandoned my truth, I would have been lying to both of us. When I manipulate the dynamic of a relationship to try to get what I think I want, none of my relationships feel satisfying or healthy. There is no real point for connection if I'm hiding parts of myself.

Being revealed and authentic is the practice of staying true to myself. It's an ongoing exercise of being self-aware enough to know what I'm feeling/wanting and courageous enough to speak on behalf of that awareness. I need to be willing to let go of relationships that are not meant for me in order to reveal my dissonant perspective. If I'm attached to getting what I think I want, then I do an inner contortion in an attempt to get that thing. But when I'm clear on my truth, I can offer it as a gift, vulnerably seeing what will happen. From this place, there is nothing to control. There is only the desire to be in an authentic and aligned relationship with the world.

This was my first glimpse at what life could be like when I am in my truth and sovereignty. I went home alone, but with me I brought my dignity.

13
AGENCY AND COMMUNION

"No matter how deep the issue is and no matter how long you have struggled with it, the possibility exists for you to be free, whole, and healed."—Brandon Bays

FOLLOWING DESIRE

"Do you want to go see 'Arrival' with me and some friends tonight?" Jake texted a week after I told him that I didn't want to date him.

I was surprised to hear from him given that he said he didn't want to be friends, but this seemed like a friendly invitation. I was on an awkward first date when I received the text, and I was happy to have an excuse to leave.

"Yes!" I replied. "I'm on a lame date right now. What time?"

"Haha! Meet me at the Boulder Cinema in an hour."

I made an excuse to my date about needing to leave early because of childcare and hurried up to go meet Jake and his friends.

Even though we were looking for different things in relationships, I could see something in Jake that was unique and mysterious. I wanted to spend more time with him, but I didn't want to be one of the many women swooning over him—my preference was to have many men swooning over me.

We sat next to each other during the movie, with his best friend and his friend's girlfriend in the next seats over. We held hands and I wrapped my arm around his bicep as we snuggled up throughout the film. While I thought this was going to be a friendly get together, it appeared more like a double date.

Once the movie was over, I offered to drive Jake to his car since he had parked far away.

"I signed up for both the Authentic Leadership and Facilitation Training and Alethia," I told him on the drive to his car.

These were two workshops being held at the Integral Center the following month. I had decided that I wanted to stretch myself and grow in community, so I signed up for both.

"Oh! I'm so happy to hear that! In my opinion, Alethia is the best orchestrated and held workshop I have ever taken."

He told me more about how being at Alethia was a profound experience for him, and moments later we were making out in my car.

"So this is friendship," I said.

He smiled and said, "Yes, friends. We can talk on the phone in bed in our underwear."

I told Jake again that I wasn't available for polyamory, and he told me again that he wanted more than friendship with me. We mutually decided not to hang out anymore, and I drove home with a sense of wonder about who this man was beyond what I could see with my eyes.

A few weeks later, I arrived at the Integral Center for the Authentic Leadership and Facilitation Training. I was hopeful to get more tools to be authentic in my leadership at the workshops I lead, but I was incredibly nervous and full of fear as I waited for the training to begin.

Chairs were arranged in a large circle in the chapel room. Housed in a large, maze-like church, the Integral Center has a pulse that is unique and unlike anything else I have ever experienced from a building. I realized that the building reminded me of my childhood home: a large, winding container for workshops that push edges and support transformation. I felt young as I sat in my chair, and I could feel my heart pound as every insecurity I had about being not enough raced through my mind.

Just then, Aaron walked in. Aaron was the naturopathic doctor I had gone on a couple of dates with, and seeing him made my heart race even faster. He came and sat next to me. With a warm, sweet smile, he asked me questions to try to catch up on my life. My brain was so hijacked with fear that I could barely think straight to answer him coherently.

Moments later, Jake walked in. My eyes widened and my heart continued to pound out of my chest. He came and sat on the other side of me.

"I didn't know you were going to be here," I said to Jake, remembering that just a few weeks ago I had told him that I was attending this workshop.

My attention kept going back and forth from Aaron to Jake and then to my own intense experience of fear and shame about being not enough. I was trying to regulate my system, but I was overwhelmed. The fear didn't make any sense to me, but it was so loud in my internal world that I was having an extremely hard time grounding and slowing down.

As the training progressed, we played a lot of authentic relating games, like the ones Jonathan had led on my first date with Eric. In this workshop, we were learning how to lead these games. One goal of these games was to practice staying in connection with ourselves while also connecting with others: Agency and Communion.

In a relationship, it's common to either place all of our attention on another person and listen with great interest ("other-referenced"), or place all of our attention on ourselves and talk about what's going on for us ("self-referenced"). In authentic relating, we try to have some attention on ourselves while also having some attention on others. This is where the real connection in relationships takes place. If I don't presence myself and reveal what's happening for me as an other-referenced person, I'm over in the other person's world and I leave myself. Similarly, if someone who is self-referenced doesn't stay curious about what's happening for the other person in the relationship, they stay in their own world and miss the point of connection.

It takes a lot of awareness to know our experience of ourselves and have the capacity to reveal what's happening for us, while also staying curious about another and having the ability to try to understand where they're coming from. This is why practicing in a container like the Integral Center can be so profound. Practicing with people who are not our family or intimate partners builds the muscle and expands our capacity.

Every part of me that felt fragmented, separate, unfixable, wounded, and unlovable was present at this workshop. I didn't yet have the skill to give voice to my experience of wanting to hide and retreat, which would have been totally welcomed by the attendees. My impulse to hide took over and I became very quiet. I participated in the games, but not in a way that was honest, revealed, and open.

"You seem apprehensive and quiet," Jake said to me on a lunch break. "Because you're so pretty, people are going to think you're a snob if you don't talk."

"That feels like a strange reflection to receive," I said, "I'm quiet because I feel ugly and unworthy."

"People can't see that if you don't express it," Jake encouraged. "Try something different."

On the second night of the training, I invited Jake back to my place to go hot tubbing. I now realize I was sending him mixed messages by asking him to be in intimate situations with me but still calling our relationship a "friendship." It's no surprise that Jake thought we were dating. I categorized us as friends to protect myself from feeling hurt that he was dating other women and to maintain a position of power with him wanting more than me.

After soaking in the hot tub, we laid in bed watching "Saturday Night Live." Before long, we were passionately making out.

"Let's have sex," I said impulsively.

"What? I thought you didn't want to have sex with me."

"I know, but it's been so long since I've had sex. I think I can do it now and then we can never see each other again." I was still trying to figure out a way to protect myself from getting hurt while also getting my intimacy needs met.

"I don't like the sound of that," Jake said. "I don't want to never see you again."

It was hard for me to understand that Jake could genuinely like me, care about me, be attracted to me, want intimacy with me, and also want to be with other women. It was also hard for me to understand why I was so attracted to him even though he was not available for the type of relationship I wanted.

Jake wasn't interested in having sex under those circumstances, so instead, we stayed in bed and gave each other orgasms without having intercourse. Again, I was surprised that he didn't drop connection with me after my convoluted attempt at intimacy.

The day after the training was over, one of the workshop leaders, Brian, emailed me and asked me if I'd like to get together for tea. I wasn't sure if this was a date or a friendly meeting, so I agreed to meet him because I thought he was a knowledgeable, interesting man.

When we went out the following weekend, we ran into Jake at the teahouse. I jolted with fear, not knowing how to proceed. We greeted each other with a friendly "Hello" and then Jake left to go volunteer at the homeless shelter. Brian and I got to know one another, but since I paid for my own tea I assumed that it wasn't a date.

The next day, Jake called me: "Brian called me to ask if we are dating. He said that he's interested in you. I told him that I thought you two would be great together. He's a really great person. I think you should go out with him."

"Really? That seems strange to me. I just took a workshop with him and he enrolled me in Alethia."

Because Jake spoke on Brian's behalf, I decided to accept his second invitation to get together the following week.

We met for a casual get-together at his place, and we shared stories of our past and talked about personal growth. A song came on that he liked, and he asked me to dance. As we danced, I could feel his erection, and the next thing I knew he was kissing me.

Soon after we kissed, it was time for me to leave. And a few hours later he called me.

"Harmony, since we kissed earlier I've been thinking that there are some things I want to tell you. I have a girlfriend. We're in a polyamorous relationship and she lives in California, but I just spent a week with her and you met her at the workshop."

He paused and I wondered who it could be; then I remembered the woman he was dancing with during the break at the training.

"Is it Annie?" I asked.

"Yes. And along with that, since I was just a facilitator in a workshop you took, and I enrolled you in Alethia, I think it's out of integrity for us to date. The Integral Center has a rule that we need to wait at least three months after being in a facilitation role with a participant before we can up level our relationship."

I was furious.

"I can't believe you didn't tell me any of this before," I said fiercely. "I'm going to be in Alethia next week with you there, and I feel used and betrayed."

"I know, that's why I'm telling you this now. I'm really sorry. I find you incredibly attractive. You're beautiful and successful, and I was overcome by my desire in the moment."

"I'm new to this, Brian. But if any random guy that I met on Bumble asked me out, kissed me, then told me he had a girlfriend, I would be livid. But on top of that, you are a leader in a community I just became a part of."

"I'm sorry. I don't know what to say. I was just following my desire and attraction."

"I don't think I can go to Alethia anymore. I'm so angry."

"Take your time making your decision. You can get your full refund back if you decide not to be there. And we can stay in communication about it if you do decide to come."

"If I come," I said, "I want you to stay away from me. I don't want you talking to me and you can't be in any of my circles."

"Of course. I'll give you all of the space you need to feel comfortable."

Later, I called Jake to tell him about what happened. I was incredibly upset about Brian's lack of boundaries and I was concerned about the safety of the participants. Jake apologized for encouraging me to date Brian, and then he told me that he would be at Alethia on support staff and he would be there for me if I needed. I felt comforted knowing he would be there, while also feeling afraid of being exposed in front of him.

Disowned power often colludes with misused power. White men, who have traditionally been in a position of power, have also traditionally misused that power. Women, who have historically been subservient to men, have been shaped to disown how powerful they actually are in order to find safety and connection. This antiquated, outdated story still lives within us and within the collective unconscious. Even though it's changing, we still need to do the work to not perpetuate it. White men need to stop following their desire and attraction as if they are entitled to have whomever they want, and women need to stop playing small and deferring to men's desire. What we want is important. We are important, and it's our job to treat ourselves as such in order to start shifting the old paradigm.

AUTHENTIC CONNECTION

Having a deeper sense that there was something for me to learn at Alethia, I decided to attend. It was the third week of January 2017, and I felt apprehensive and excited as I drove up that snowy Friday afternoon for the beginning of the workshop.

I wanted my time at Alethia to be about my inner process and growth, and not about men and dating. Since several men at the Integral Center seemed interested in me, I had decided that I wasn't going to date anyone from the workshop. Setting this boundary for myself before I walked into the Center was to help me own my "No" with more strength and keep my attention on myself. Turning men down in their attraction to me was still frightening. My inner 6-year-old was afraid that I would die or be assaulted if I said "No" to a man with conviction.

"Wear a spiritual condom," my friend Lyn had advised before I went to Alethia. She knew that men at these workshops always seem to be looking for a woman to date.

As the workshop began, we were sitting in a big circle starting to come together as a group. People were still trickling in as the woman to my right started talking to me.

"How are you feeling about being here?" she asked.

"Nervous. And you?" I replied.

"Nervous, too. I think it has to do with knowing that I'll be exposed in some way at this workshop and that kind of scares me," she revealed.

"Thank you for naming that. I think that's why I'm nervous, too."

We talked some more, and I learned that her name was Julie and she was visiting from California. Relieved to have made a connection with a kind and aware woman, I felt my whole body settle from the security and safety I felt with her.

Alethia began with James, the prime course leader, describing three levels of conversation. The first level he described was the informational level, where people exchange data. Topics such as what you do for work, what you ate for lunch, where you are from are exchanged in this level. The second level of conversation is the personal level. Here people exchange emotional information, how they're feeling, and what they're wanting. The third level is the relational level. This is the "I-Thou" of the relational field, where we talk about what our experience is being with one another.

One of the intentions of the work shop was to practice giving voice to the third level of conversation. Since we are conditioned to stay more surfaced in conversation, this practice would allow us to go deeper into connection with one another.

We paired up to practice authentic relating games aimed at building the skill of connecting by using the third level of conversation. After a few games, we came back together in a big circle and a man shared: "I'm noticing that I have a hard time being vulnerable. These games are really challenging for me."

Hearing a man share such a vulnerable insight in a large group of people ignited tremendous curiosity in me. The man who spoke was attractive and seemingly self-aware, and my whole body wanted to walk across the circle and hug him. I literally had to remind myself to stay in the circle. We hadn't even spoken to each other and yet I was interested in getting to know him more. And in this moment the boundary that I had tried to set for myself was not in my field of awareness—I was too in touch with my desire to recall this commitment I had made with myself.

Later that evening, the facilitators of the workshop talked about breathwork, which would be our next activity. Holotropic breathwork is the process of using controlled breathing in a quick, rhythmic pattern. People who practice this kind of breathwork sometimes feel trauma come up, which can be transmuted through the life-giving force of the breath. It's up to the practitioner to stay with the breath as old pain arises. Rather than going into the pain and trauma, the goal is to stay expansive and in your life urge with your breath. The more able a person is to keep breathing in this pattern no matter what, the more likely they will have a rebirthing experience.

Because I had experienced rebirthing a few times with my mom and Jane, breathwork at the Integral Center felt familiar, deep, and empowering.

I spent the next two hours in an amazing rebirthing experience where I touched on five major traumas from my past.

The first trauma that arose was about feeling hurt and unloved by my lovers. The second was not being held in love by Jason while giving birth to our children. Then I felt the old pain from head trauma, where I realized for the very first time that I had anger about my fall. The fourth trauma was not feeling securely attached with my mom. And the fifth was grieving the loss of my umbilical cord after my own birth.

As each trauma came up, I met it with an expansive holding of love, and I excavated it with vocalization that was loud and powerful. I screamed and I cried with so much power that I forgot there were other people in the room with me.

Cory, a staff member at the Center, supported me in an incredibly loving, respectful way. He was there to give me what I needed as I breathed, and I asked for it at every turn. Pressing firmly on my sternum, snuggling, rubbing my head ... whatever I needed, he was right there offering it to me in the most loving way.

And at the end of the rebirthing, I felt bigger and more grown up.

I was also disoriented, so when people got up to leave for the night I stayed to try to integrate this intense experience before driving home. Jake offered to support me in getting grounded, and we snuggled on the couch as the building cleared out for the night.

"When I realized it was you who was screaming so loud, I had deep respect for you," he said.

"I'm glad to hear that because I was so in my experience that I forgot other people were in the room."

I looked up at him and we started kissing. Feeling connected to Jake felt safe and grounding to me. I wanted to invite him home with me, but instead I decided it would be a good idea to sleep before the rest of the weekend unfolded. I was still conflicted about dating someone who was polyamorous and I was in total denial that I had my own version of polyamory, since I was dating several men.

The core authentic relating practice at the Integral Center and at Alethia is called circling. Circling is a relational meditation practice where three or more people gather in a circle and put their attention on one person with the intention of trying to understand that person's inner world. The person who is being circled gets to just be themselves and express or name whatever is true for them as it arises.

The facilitator and the participants of the circle are tasked with welcoming everything that arises both in the person getting circled and within themselves. The idea is that we are simply 'being with' this person without offering advice or trying to fix them or change them in any way. We use "ownership language"—language that is inarguable, without assumptions, and in service of lessening projections—and the people in the circle offer vulnerable insight into how it feels to be with the circled participant's experience. This offers the circled participant an authentic reflection of their impact on the world.

The whole second day of the workshop was centered on break-out circles for every participant. I had never experienced circling, and although I did have some valuable understanding about communication and language, I felt afraid of doing something wrong as a participant. Since this was a relational practice and not therapy, I was completely uncertain about how to show up authentically and be present in my truth.

I felt even more afraid when it was my turn to be circled. Since I was a master at hiding, being seen and exposed was not something I was excited about. I was much more comfortable in the facilitator role, and being a participant was a huge stretch for me.

When I walked into the room for my circle, Michael, the facilitator, seemed rigid and closed. He had arrived at the workshop a day late, so I hadn't had any interactions with him. When I walked in the room, he didn't greet me in a warm or inviting way, which made me uneasy.

As my circle began, I noticed myself feeling guarded and unsafe. Michael reminded me of Jason, and I instantly projected onto him all of the things I assumed about him based on my experience with Jason. Unconsciously, I used his apparent coldness to deduce that he didn't want to know my true experience, that he wasn't capable of understanding my world, and that he wasn't a safe person for me to open up to.

We started the circle with everyone standing, then Michael instructed everyone to sit except for me. I was triggered by what felt like a command to stay standing, when in truth I could have done whatever I wanted at this moment.

"You seem guarded," Michael observed.

"Yes. I'm not sure why. I think I'm afraid that I won't have sovereignty of choice," I said, referring to the fact that I was the only one standing.

We talked for a bit about how I didn't want him to tell me what to do, and the participants were encouraging me to just sit. I felt controlled and was trying to stay in my dignity.

"If you were going to wear a sign, I think it would read something like 'You're not the boss of me,'" he said.

"Right. It's more like, 'I'm the boss.'" I said proudly.

"What else would your sign say?" he asked.

"Thoughtful, kind, soft. I want to be kind toward myself, and I'm working with my fierceness. I'm born the year of the fire dragon, and sometimes I breathe fire. This is how I protect myself when I feel unsafe."

"Do you feel unsafe now?"

"Yes. Extremely. This is so uncomfortable and you seem so cold and rigid and controlling. I'm trying to appease you without losing my dignity. It's hard for me. I never used my voice in childhood, I never spoke my truth and I enabled everyone's dysfunction."

"It sounds lonely."

"Yes. I suffered a lot, alone, for not using my voice."

It was beautiful. This circle allowed me to be witnessed in my pattern that was typically destructive to my intimate relationships. Having people be curious about me there, without trying to offer me advice or fix the pattern, felt healing and regulating.

I was pretty fierce with Michael, and the participants in my circle were excited that I had this side to me. The men in the group encouraged me to access it and women at the workshop celebrated it. I had tremendous shame around my ferocity, and even my shame was being welcomed in the circle.

After this circle, my whole system was lit up with excitement.

I approached Michael privately on a break, and I told him that I felt hurt by his lack of interest of building rapport at the beginning of my circle, and that our first interaction led to me not trusting him. When I was finally able to find words for why I was guarded with him, I could see Michael's whole body soften. In this interaction, I learned a powerful lesson about myself: when I am hurt and don't clear it with the person I have the resentment toward, I shut down and allow my resentment to come between us.

Taking this even further, when I hide my truth from one person, not only is that not in service of my connection with that one person, it's not in service of my connection with anyone. Having clean relationships with the people in my life makes it so I can have a clean relationship with all people.

I felt more integrated and empowered for having had this experience. Although this wasn't the circle I would have chosen, it was the circle I needed. I needed to be face-to-face with a man with whom I felt unsafe and be witnessed in my power and welcomed in all of that.

The number of women who have been violated by men is so enormous that men are tasked with embodying gentle patience to cultivate safety in relationship. With the files of evidence from the past stored in our psyches, our whole system can tighten with self-protection in the presence of a new man even if there is no obvious reason for the fear. As women, we need to honor ourselves in our process and not bypass our body's fear response. When we hide our apprehension and don't give it a voice, it is still there in the relational field, influencing our interactions. The simple act of revealing our guardedness and our fear brings it to the awareness field so it no longer drives the impulses of the unconscious mind, allowing our story to update.

VULNERABILITY

Later that evening, we played an authentic relating game called "Anyone Else?" In this game, someone stands up and reveals something about themselves, and then asks "Anyone else?" Then anyone who also has that experience stands up. The person who spoke can then add onto it and step forward to see if anyone else had this other part of the experience, too.

During this game, Charles, a tall man in his fifties, stood up and said, "I am single, anyone else?"

I stood up and noticed an attractive man my age standing as well. Our eyes met. Nervous, I immediately looked away.

Charles took a step forward and stated, "And I don't want to be, anyone else?"

The attractive man and I both stepped forward, looking at each other.

"Thank you," Charles said and then we all sat down.

That man and I learned a lot about each other in this game. We learned that we were both Jewish, we had both had a life-changing spiritual experience, we both were certified yoga teachers, we didn't do drugs, and we both loved our work.

I learned that he had never been married and didn't have any kids but wanted a child of his own.

He learned that I was divorced with kids, and that I married someone I had a conflictual relationship with.

After this game, we took a short break and we found ourselves getting water at the same time. "Hi. My name is Tim," the man said, extending his hand to shake mine.

"I'm Harmony," I said as I reciprocated.

"You really learn a lot about a person in this game," he stated.

"Yeah, most people don't look at me and think 'Jew,'" I said, joking about my blonde hair, blue eyes, and round nose.

"Right, I would have never thought."

"I went to a private Jewish school for elementary, and I never felt like I fit in there because of the way I look," I shared.

"Where did you grow up?" Tim asked.

"Sacramento."

Then he turned away and started fumbling through his things. Sensing his withdrawal from me, I turned toward my bag and started fumbling through mine as well.

"You look familiar to me," Tim said suddenly.

"Me? I don't think so. Where do you work?" I replied.

"I think it's from the yoga studio I go to. You teach?"

"Oh, no. I used to teach when I was in college and graduate school. I'm a psychotherapist," I replied.

Tim looked away, taking in this new information about me. "Cool," he said with a smile.

Then I sensed him pull away again as he turned back to his bag of belongings.

The day went on with more circles and authentic relating games, and at the end of the night we did a group practice called "Hold/Hide Nothing." Before we did the practice, the facilitators talked about cost of holding a resentment or grievance toward another person and how that gets in the way of authentic connection. When we are actively hiding our truth because we're afraid that our truth will rupture a connection, we actually inhibit the connection from flowing.

One facilitator used an analogy of a clean windshield between two people. When I have an interaction with someone and I'm holding a painful impact from that experience, it's like a splat on the windshield. If I don't open up to the other person and let them know that I am holding this feeling about them, that splat stays there. Over time, if I continue to not bring my truth to the people around me, we can barely see one another anymore beyond the splats of the past. This can easily describe part of the reason why most of my relationships have ended.

There's a specific process they teach at the Integral Center for bringing what they call a "Hold Nothing" to someone, which means bringing up a resentment or other feeling that we are holding against someone. The first step is to state your intention to the other person. Since the reason we bring Hold Nothings to others is to enhance our connection, we say this explicitly.

Sometimes people bring Hold Nothings as a way to try to control or change the other person. In a relationship, we're either communicating for connection or we're communicating for control. Self-awareness and inner processing can be important before communicating our truth in service of connection. Our truest truth is a vulnerable thing to offer when we let go of expectation or any attempt at control. If we're not in a place of wanting connection, we're not ready to bring a Hold Nothing. Sometimes it can be helpful to process or vent with a friend or therapist first in order to see the situation more clearly and drop into our hearts.

Once we explicitly state our intention to the other person—that we have something we want to talk about and we're bringing it to them to strengthen our connection—we then ask the person for consent, checking in to see if they want to hear what we're holding.

So, I might say to someone: "I have something I want to talk with you about. I'm bringing it to you because I want to feel closer to you. Are you available to hear it?"

If the person says yes, we proceed using a process similar to nonviolent communication (NVC), a practice developed by Marshall Rosenberg and the NVC community.

First, I state the objective thing that happened: "When we were talking about the movie, you spoke over me when I was sharing my perspective. Do you remember that?"

It's important to start by getting shared reality on the interaction before moving forward. It's also important to not infuse judgment into the objective thing that happened—to just stay objective. When both people agree on this objective interaction and agree on what happened, we go to the next step.

Next I would say how I felt when that happened, emphasizing what story I was running about what happened: how the experience lives in me. How it feels.

For instance: "When we were talking about the movie and you spoke over me, I felt angry and stifled. My story is you didn't want to hear my point of view and that you think your ideas are more important than mine."

Then I would ask the person to reflect what they heard and share the impact that it has on them. "It sounds like you felt angry and stifled when I spoke over you. Hearing that, I notice I feel sad. I want you to feel heard by me and I wish I would have been more open to you in that moment."

On the night of Alethia, Tim and I were seated next to one another in the big circle when we were given instructions about how to do Hold Nothings. Once we learned the process, we were then invited to practice doing them with each other. Tim turned to me and said, "Harmony, I have a Hold Nothing for you. It's in service of our connection. Are you available to hear it?"

I was shocked as I searched my mind for a way I might have offended him.

"Oh ..." I said, disappointed.

"No, it's a golden one," he assured, meaning that he was holding something sweet that he wanted to share with me.

"Oh! Yes. I'd love to hear it!" I was relieved but still very nervous.

"Earlier when we were talking after 'Anyone Else?' I really wanted to move closer to you and talk more, but something inside me pulled me away. I'm afraid to stay open ... I have this armor," he revealed.

I took a deep breath.

"Let me make sure I'm getting this. When we were talking earlier you wanted to engage with me more, but instead your armor came up and you're wanting me to know about it. Did I get that?"

"Yes," he replied.

"Hearing that, I feel warmth in my heart and a lot of gratitude toward you for telling me this. I also feel some sadness about the armor and I notice myself wanting to hear more."

We gazed into each other's eyes with our knees touching. I wanted to move closer and touch him in some way.

"I am a very affectionate person," I said, "and I really want to give you a hug right now."

Tim's face lit up with a huge smile. "Can I hug you?"

"Yes," I said with an equally huge smile.

We sat in the chairs hugging for several minutes while the rest of the participants busily talked about their Hold Nothings with their exercise partners.

Tim's strong arms felt so comforting and I softened into his body.

"Oh! I have a Hold Nothing for you!" I said excitedly.

"Okay. What is it?"

"Earlier, you were late getting back from lunch, and we played a game before you returned. I missed your voice in the big circle and I wanted to know what you would have said."

"Okay, so earlier when I was late coming back from lunch, you guys played a game, and you wanted to hear what I would have said."

"Yes. Do you want to play the game now?"

"I don't know how to play the game," Tim said.

"Well, I was there. I can teach you."

"Okay."

"The game was called 'If you really knew me, you'd know...' You finish the sentence and reveal something about yourself. I'll go first and share what I said."

I took a deep breath. Realizing how intimate and vulnerable this was, I started to squirm.

"I'm feeling really shy now, but I'm going to do it anyway. If you really knew me, you'd know that I can't see my own physical beauty because I have too much body shame."

Tim looked at me and said, "I feel a lot of empathy. That seems like a common human experience and I can relate to it."

I was surprised by his words. Tim was a tall, handsome man with big, muscular arms and a defined chest. I felt comforted knowing that he understood how I could have a hard time seeing my own beauty.

"Okay. Your turn," I said.

"Okay. If you really knew me, you'd know that I am terrified of human interaction."

I felt shocked as I took this in.

"I'm imagining that's why you're here," I stated.

"Yes," he said.

"And I'm also imagining you feel safe with me since you just revealed this to me."

"Yes," he said again.

"I want to hug you again," I said.

"Okay."

We embraced again, this time moving to the floor to get closer.

After a long, sweet embrace, I again became aware of the room full of people.

"I have a few Hold Nothings with other people here. This was so great. Let's connect later," he said.

The next day was the third and final day of the workshop. I was hoping to spend more time with Tim, but when we returned from lunch, I found out he had left the workshop entirely. When I noticed he was missing, I asked one of the support staff what happened to him. It turned out that when we registered for the workshop he knew that he had to leave town on Sunday afternoon. I was extremely disappointed that I didn't get to say goodbye.

My world felt like it was expanding, and life felt like it was in Technicolor after Alethia. I experienced deep connection with many women who had participated in the workshop, and I was hopeful for new friendships with strong women. My clinical skills were heightened because I was more present and engaged with my clients. Rather than following clients on the train of their story, I was more attuned to their energy and body language, so I could bring them back to their present moment experience, which is vital for real healing to happen.

I was also more present with my children than my busy mind typically allowed. I could see them for the mystery of who they were, not assuming that I knew anything about their emotional world or needs. Where I once tried to fix their problems and project my solution onto them, I was able to be in relationship with them from a place of sovereignty and dignity. Revealing the impact of their words and actions while staying curious about what was happening for them, our connection was deeply honoring of our humanity. Without a hierarchy, I met them from my wholeness.

While I was more present with the people near me, I was also deep in a fantasy about Tim and me being together forever. I saw our connection as fate, as if we were brought together to meet all of each other's needs and desires. This fantasy kept pulling the attention of my mind, and I eventually started believing it.

Like an alcoholic who is deluded that she has control over reality, this part of my mind craved the fantasy of love that I had picked up from romantic comedies, from watching my mom move lovers into our house too quickly, and from believing the messages of my conditioned self. When Type 2 individuals feel safe, we move in the direction of the Type 4. This means that when I feel a connection with a man, I believe that the inner feelings and fantasies are truth.

This pattern was very destructive to my intimate relationships. When I did this, my relationships took place in my mind rather than in connection with the person I was fantasizing about. Relationships only happen in the present moment. My mind took the past interactions I had with Tim and started projecting them onto the future. I set myself up for disappointment by blocking the real intimate connection from emerging.

I had plans for Tim that he wasn't privy to or in agreement with. My mind wasn't able to be present with the actual events that had occurred. It wanted to make them more meaningful. Our current and future relationship was taking place in my mind, and not in actuality with Tim. I was making him into an object for my fantasy, which was the very thing I was repulsed by when men tried to do this with me. I didn't actually know Tim well enough to decide if we should be together forever, but the part of my conditioned self that wanted a man to save me, to fulfill my longing to be enough, to make my life complete, took over and in that I lost contact with myself.

In order to have full agency of choice, I needed to be fully aware of the messages and projections I was experiencing. I needed to be sober, not under the influence of these fantasies. I could not meet a man from my wholeness and sovereignty if there was a part of me that thought I was incomplete without him. And I could not allow a man to have agency of choice with me if I hid my inner world from him and tried to be what I thought he wanted me to be. If I thought I needed my fantasy to come true in order for me to be happy and okay, then I contorted and managed myself to try to get what I think I needed.

Because I had a challenging time unlearning this pattern, after Alethia I started working with a spiritual teacher named Barbara to support the dissolving of this pattern. This part of myself—the "fantasy girl," as she called it—does not originate with me and is not qualified to choose a capable mate. On the realm of my higher self, Barbara and I worked to dissolve this sabotage pattern from my energetic field. As we did this, I could feel the fantasy girl become darker and more insistent on running the show. Barbara put the fantasy girl on a spiritual restraining order, asking all of my angels and guides to disqualify her from coming with me with dates or choosing my mate. Eventually I could see with my conscious awareness that she was completely gone. To my relief, I haven't had the experience of "fantasy girl" since.

14
FINDING REAL LOVE

"Your task is not to seek for love, but merely to seek and find all the barriers within yourself that you have built against it."—Rumi

RELATIONSHIP SCHOOL

I was elated when Tim found me on Facebook and started messaging me there. After catching him up on the part of the workshop he missed, we made plans for when he returned from his business trip. The first time we got together was two weeks after Alethia and the day before I started T3. T3 stands for "Train the Trainer" and it was the Integral Center's nine-month certification program in circling. I had glimpsed the goodness of authentic relating and I wanted more. From the one weekend at Alethia, I was better equipped as a mother, as a friend, as a psychotherapist, and potentially as a romantic partner.

I had lunch with Jake the day before T3 started. When he told me that he had also enrolled, I told him that I wanted to renegotiate the terms of our friendship.

"I met someone I really like, and I want us to have more boundaries in our relationship." I started to cry. "I'm afraid you won't want to be my friend."

"I love you, Harmony," he said.

"I love you, too," I replied with tears streaming down my face, "and I'm afraid that you don't respect me enough to be my friend."

"Is that what's going on for you? I was saying the opposite, that I respect you so much that I want more with you. Of course I'll be your friend." Jake gave me a big hug. "Can we still snuggle?" he asked.

"We'll see how it goes," I answered with my typical "Yes, maybe," leaving it open because I was afraid that saying "No" would rupture the connection.

Jake seemed both sad and understanding. "I want you in my life, and if that's as a friend then I will show up that way. I'm happy for you."

Later that same night, I went over to Tim's house for dinner. He had made a vegetable stew for us in his gorgeous mountain home. Tucked up in the foothills, there wasn't another person, car, or house as far as the eye could see.

On our first date, I learned that Tim was a business coach trained in the Enneagram, somatics, and high-level communication techniques. He traveled the world for his work teaching businesses healthy communication and conflict resolution.

"Are you a 2?" Tim asked as we sat on his deck eating his delicious vegetable stew.

"I am such a 2," I replied. "With a strong 3 wing." My Type 3 wing caused me to be extremely image conscious and a master at deceit. The thing I deceived others about the most was the way I felt, hiding that I'd been hurt by them. At that time I couldn't see that I also have a strong 1 wing, where my perfectionist tendencies and striving to be good influence much of my behavior. "What are you?" I asked.

"Guess," he replied.

"Hm ... I don't know you well enough yet. Keep talking and I'll figure it out."

That night, Tim and I had a stimulating conversation about human behavior, conflict resolution, communication, and relationships. Between my nervousness and excitement, I could barely eat.

"I'm thinking you're an 8," I said an hour after arriving. "You're protected from vulnerability, and you want to make your own way in the world," I explained.

"Nope. Keep guessing," he said.

I thought it over. He wasn't a 4, because he's too closed off. Maybe he was a 5, because he was afraid of failure. I ran through all of the numbers and finally landed on one.

"You're a 1!" I exclaimed.

"Yep," he smiled. "I want to do things right, and even though you can't see it on the outside, on the inside I'm terrified of getting it wrong."

Everything about being with Tim felt wonderful, until we went to snuggle on the couch. As we lay together on the sofa, I felt like I was snuggling with armor. I kept trying to be okay with it, trying to find a way to soften into his embrace, but his energetic armor felt solid and impermeable.

As I tried to feel closer to him, all of my insecurities started bubbling to the surface. Suddenly my body dysmorphia was triggered and my body seemed enormous and I was wrought with insecurities. My mind was racing with thoughts about how if I were sexier, skinner, or somehow different, he would open up to me.

"I'm curious to know what's going on with you," I said.

"Why do you ask?" he replied.

Not aware enough in the moment to articulate my experience, I became even more nervous. Revealing what was happening within me seemed impossible in this moment. My attention was on him as a point of reference. If he relaxed, I could relax.

I tried to muster up the courage to speak on behalf of my inner world.

"I feel vulnerable," I replied.

"Why?"

"Because I like you, and I'm a 2 and my significance comes from what you think of me," I painfully joked about my Enneagram shaping.

I turned away from him to try to come back to myself. I closed my eyes for a few moments and tried to focus on my breath.

"I'm feeling nervous, too," he revealed.

He moved my body down on the sofa and he lay on top of me. We snuggled and pressed our bodies against one another, softening into each other. I wanted him to kiss me as we breathed heavily into one another's mouths. Every time I thought he was going to move in for a kiss, he would change directions. But before I knew it, it was time for me to go home. I had a sitter watching my kids, and it was a school night.

Tim walked me to my car. We looked up at the stars. From his mountain home, the sky was majestic and overwhelmingly beautiful. We hugged goodbye, and I drove home swirling in a mixture of excitement and fear. When men move slowly and don't kiss me right away, I assume they're not interested in me. I was hoping I was wrong about this, but I had a feeling that he wasn't interested in pursuing me. I tried to ignore this feeling and clung to my fantasy about what I wanted for us.

The next day I started T3.

I walked into the chapel room of the Integral Center, and all of the chairs were arranged in a large circle. I was excited that two people that I had met from Alethia were enrolled, and I felt comfort seeing Jake.

There were twenty-four participants in total, with about the same number in staff. Forty-eight people filled the room with authentic desire.

As our course began, Ryan, one of the prime course leaders, described the crucible that is T3. "There's an alchemy that happens when these three things come together: circling, personal growth, and community. We unlearn our cultural conditioning, practice being conscious humans together, uncover who we really are and learn that it's okay to be in our full expression. Remember, it's about getting real, not getting it right."

Excitement and anxiety surged through my body on hearing this introduction. I knew in my gut that this was the thing I had always needed but never knew existed. My propensity toward perfectionism had always made me try to get things right, which had kept me from getting real. My training and experience with psychotherapy and homeopathy was solid and valuable, but learning to be in authentic connection with community was an idea that both frightened me and enlivened me.

I wanted to be fully expressed.

I wanted to speak my truth.

I wanted to claim my power, desires, and boundaries.

I wanted to honor myself in the presence of men.

I wanted to meet the world beyond my conditioned self and practice being an integrated human.

I wanted to be witnessed.

I wanted to be receptive to the reflections of others.

I wanted to learn how to stay in connection even when my old wounds wanted to keep me on an isolated island that was familiar, safe, and lonely.

I wanted to let go of control and allow for the transformation to unfold.

I was so ready for this.

Trembling with fear, my mind kept trying to contain my anxiety. I felt so unsafe in relationships that my trauma response was triggered hugely in this container. Even in the presence of intense fear, the part of me that wanted to change and grow and evolve was louder than the part of me that was afraid. It was as if my death urge was at odds with my life urge. The part of me that played small was fighting with the part of me that wanted to be in my full expression. My box of conditioning was constricting, and I wanted to break free from it so that I could stand in my expansiveness rather than retreat in my contraction.

Trauma and conditioning happens in relationships with others. This means that deep healing also happens in relationships with others. The therapeutic relationship of counseling can be extremely healing: however, sometimes we need more. Sometimes we need to be witnessed and held in a transformative container of other human beings who also want to heal. Fear can try to keep us from exploring such communities. Trust can allow us to take the leap anyway and feel the aliveness of our own vitality as we grow and evolve beyond the old stories.

HUMILITY AND DIGNITY

On the second day of T3, we played a game of "Anyone Else?" During the game, a participant named Joel, who was tall, handsome, and fit stood up and said, "Earlier when Sheri was talking about desiring harmony among her housemates"—he turned and looked right at me—"I thought about desiring Harmony. Anyone else?"

I immediately started giggling, and as I looked around the room several people were standing up. I looked over at Jake and he remained seated. I internally pouted for a micro-minute.

All this attention was a surge to my ego. I felt special and seen and wanted. My mind was aflutter with how special I was to be called out in the big group on the first weekend in such a big way by such a gorgeous man. The young one in me who had been neglected was elated to have so much attention.

After he said this, the part of my conditioned self that craved validation like a drug addict was ignited and I became internally prideful. Pride is the passion of the Type 2, and it's what the mind of this type chews on. Cultivating humility is one of the virtues I practice nurturing, but here my prideful ego was out of control.

"I'm so special because men are attracted to me. I'm special because my name is Harmony. I'm special because people like me and come to me for help with their problems. I'm special because I'm good at what I do. I'm special because I'm blonde but I'm Jewish. I'm special because the most handsome man at this training just stood up and told the whole group that he thought of me when he heard 'I desire harmony.' I'm special."

It was painful to have all of this pride run through me. The thoughts of my specialness were so loud that my mind contracted around them. Identified with my conditioned self, I was looping through thoughts that were keeping me from true connection. I felt slightly manic with how special I felt, and this was a stark contrast to the deep experience of insecurity I had felt with Tim the night before. My prideful ego was polarized from the collapse of my trauma. Off-center from the core of my being, I couldn't regulate and come back to my home base.

Dignity is the opposite of collapse. Humility is the opposite of posturing. Unable to stand in my dignity, my mind was posturing with specialness so that I could try to find validation for my worth. Unconsciously believing that I didn't belong on this planet, in this body, or at the Integral Center, my mind was searching for a reason for my life to have value. Somewhere in the shadow of my mind, there was a belief that my value came from what other people thought of me—or more specifically, what men thought of me.

Later that same night as I was on my way out, I stopped to talk to two of the participants. We were talking about love and dating and sex.

"I haven't had sex for almost a year," I confessed. "I'm dating a lot, but I want to get to know someone before I have sex with them."

"What?" Chris said. "You're talking crazy to me. I can't even imagine. I've never waited to have sex with someone in my whole life. I meet someone, have sex, and we are in a relationship."

"That's what I used to do, and it didn't work out well for me. I met someone recently at Alethia. I'm super excited because I think that there's a lot of potential for us."

"Who is it?"

"I'm not going to tell you. You know everyone in Boulder." Chris was a local performer and was well known in the area. I felt really guarded about my feelings toward Tim because I felt so insecure in our connection.

"Come on, tell me," Chris pleaded.

I thought about it for a moment, said no a few more times, and then I pushed through my hesitation and I said his name quickly, "Tim."

"Oh. I know Tim. Tim … what's his last name? Is it Tim H … I can't remember his last name but I know who you're talking about."

"I knew you'd know him! His last name does start with a H. I feel so vulnerable and nervous." Every ounce of insecurity I felt about Tim jumped to the forefront of my mind. I felt exposed in this reveal, and I was afraid of being judged for being not enough for Tim.

"Why? I don't get it."

"I am so insecure. My mind says I'm too fat for him, that he's too attractive for me, and that I'll never be enough for him."

Chris looked at me and scanned my body up in down with a look of disbelief on his face. "Girl, you're crazy."

"Argh, you don't understand." I was so frustrated. "Please. Don't tell anyone. Keep this totally confidential."

"Of course. And Harmony, you are so beautiful. You are so enough for him and for anyone you want."

I got up, walked to my car, and cried as I drove home. Tired of this painful pattern, all of the shame and self-loathing that lived within me started bubbling to the surface. Thoughts of being not enough, unworthy of love, and disgustingly unattractive looped through my mind.

When I arrived at my house, I knew I'd be unable to sleep. Even though it was late, I sat on my meditation cushion for twenty minutes and tried to find my center. Once the timer went off, I texted Tim "T3 is so crazy. Hope you're enjoying California." And then went to sleep.

At 3 AM I woke up to go to the bathroom. I checked to see if Tim had texted back. He hadn't.

On my way back to bed, I caught a glimpse of myself in the mirror. I wasn't fat. I wasn't ugly. It was as if I was seeing myself with fresh eyes, and I couldn't understand why I would think such deprecating thoughts about myself.

"What are you doing to yourself?" I said aloud as I started to cry. "You're amazing. Why do you keep doing this to yourself?" Grief from the depths of my soul poured out as tears. I was crying for the lifetime I'd spent being unkind to myself.

"You think you're too fat or not good enough for love. But you are. Look at you. You're an amazing person. You're beautiful. You do wonderful work in the world. Your light shines so brightly. Stop doing this to yourself," I bawled with tears and snot running down my face.

For the next five hours I cried every tear I had in my body. When I couldn't cry any more, I got up and prepared for the third and final day of our first weekend of this nine-month training.

I arrived at the Integral Center early because I needed support. I felt hugely triggered and I didn't want to isolate myself in my pain. This instinct to seek connection rather than isolation was new for me. Since my conditioned self wants everyone to think I have it all together, showing up in tears and wanting connection was a growing edge that felt so right.

I walked around the maze-like building and saw no one. The facilitators were in a team meeting and no other participants had arrived yet.

I sat in the kitchen by myself, anxiously awaiting human connection. A few minutes later, a fellow participant named Zack walked in and our eyes met, mine red and puffy from a night of crying.

"I need a hug," I said through my watery emotional state.

"Okay," Zack said as he set his belongings down and opened his arms. I moved in for a hug. In this loving embrace, I surrendered to receiving his care and love. To want co-regulation with and soothing from another human being is a natural part of human suffering that I had never given myself permission to admit I needed.

After several moments of this nourishing and healing hug, Zack lowered his arms and gazed into my eyes. "Here's a flower," he said, handing me a lily. "I picked it this morning for someone, not knowing who, and I think it was for you."

I started bawling again, this time with so much love in my heart. "Thank you," I said as I wept and hugged him.

The day began in the chapel with the chairs arranged in a big circle. I had hoped other people would be bawling, too, but when the room got quiet, I was the only one. I could not stop crying. Zack sat next to me holding my hand, and I held the lily on my lap.

"My attention is on you, Harmony," Nichole, one of the prime course leaders said aloud.

The room got quiet and all of the attention was on me.

I shook as I cried, feeling shame for having such loud emotions while also being relieved to have attention on me. "Something happened last night that caused my heart to break open."

"So your heart is breaking open right now?" she asked.

"Yes," I cried.

"I like knowing that. It had looked to me like something else was happening."

I still didn't fully understand why this trigger was so deep and intense, so I couldn't articulate anymore to share. When Nichole moved on to another share, my mind was so hijacked with emotions that I got up and went into another room. Frank, one of the assistant course leads, followed me and offered me support.

"My heart. It hurts. It hurts so badly," I said as I cried.

"Do you want me to put pressure on it?" he asked.

"Yes." I took his hand and placed it on my sternum, pushing down to show him how hard I wanted pressure.

I didn't know how good this would feel, and I was surprised that Frank knew to offer this touch to me. My chest felt tremendous relief under the pressure of his hand. "I can't stop," I said as I cried, feeling shame for the deep well of emotions moving through me.

"I don't need you to stop," he replied.

I needed to hear this. I needed full permission to feel. I had never in my life felt like the people around me had room for my emotions, so I locked them away and pretended that everything was okay, that I was okay, even when I wasn't. Especially when I wasn't.

This crucible, full of strangers and new friends, ignited my old pain and trauma and conditioning in the most intense way so that I could be purified of the old story. As we heal, we get to our wounds at deeper levels over time. Even though I had transcended this pattern of self-loathing in college, I needed to get to it at a deeper level in adulthood.

In my mind, I needed to hide my pain to get connection. Here, at the Integral Center, revealing my pain was the path to connection. Revealing my authentic experience, this practice welcomed all of the parts of me in a way I didn't know was possible in a relationship. With each experience that I had in this magical building, I was learning how to be genuinely myself in the presence of others. And it was powerful.

Frank's capacity to welcome me in my trigger allowed me to feel safe enough to purge much of my old grief. This grief was beyond story; but I had walked around with it daily for my entire life. I let it move through me until I felt totally complete in my experience. With Frank's presence, I felt my body soften. My heart felt more open, and I felt lighter.

The rest of the day I was blown out. Feeling disembodied and spacy, I wasn't tracking others in the same way I typically do. There was no part of my attention going to earning love and approval. I wasn't trying to get validation. I wasn't concerned about what other people thought of me. My inner world and self-care were the loudest part of my experience, and I was able to show up for myself in a way I never had.

Later that night it was time for my circle, and I had requested that Ryan circle me because he had a soft masculine presence and was skilled and slow in his method. I thought his attention might be regulating for me.

Ryan and four other participants were present in my circle as I sat in a large, comfy chair. I asked for the lighting to be just so. I asked for a blanket. All of the people there were willing to give me what I wanted and were excited to see me taking care of myself.

Ryan began the circle by setting context. He explained that we would spend the next hour trying to understand what it's like to be Harmony. As they tried to get my world, they would share what it's like to be with me, owning their experience and not projecting their story onto me. We would begin by connecting with self in a short meditation, and then we would open our eyes and connect with the others in the group with brief eye-gazing.

After eye-gazing with one another, all of the attention was on me. "So here we are, in Harmony's circle, and it looks like you're already in an experience," Ryan said.

"Yes," I cried. "That's a good word for it: 'Experience.'" I started laughing hysterically. My laughter seemed maniacal as I cried. "I'm sorry. I can't stop," I explained.

"I don't need you to stop. Does anyone here need Harmony to stop laughing or crying?" he asked the group.

Everyone said "No."

I felt relieved. I didn't need to manage myself for them. They could handle me processing and discharging my emotions in the way I needed. My whole body relaxed. I softened into my comfy chair.

"It seems to me like you're really enjoying that chair," Ryan named. "It's like you really know what you need and you are midwifing yourself through this process."

"I like hearing that, that it looks like I'm taking care of myself in this process."

"Yeah, and it's like the more you take care of yourself and know what you need, the more engaged I feel to give you what you need, too, to support your process."

"What a great perspective. My taking care of my needs invites you in to support me in that. Wow." I was amazed at this revelation and really resonated with this message.

"I'm just sitting in this expansive state, this vastness. It's like, my whole life I have had this tension between my pedestal of specialness and this shadow aspect of a deep fear of being unworthy or not good enough. I've been working the tension between these two opposing energies my entire life, and yesterday the combination of Joel standing up in 'Anyone Else?' and then a vulnerability hangover with Chris was the perfect concoction to release this tension."

"Oh. So that's what's going on with you right now—a Joel/Chris concoction helped you to see these two opposing energies you've had your entire life, and now there's like this relief in not having to hold that tension anymore."

"Yes," I said, taking a deep exhale. "And I've been working on this for my entire life. Literally. When I was 5 years old, I rebirthed for the first time. When I was 6, my mom took me to a transcendental meditation center and I started a meditation practice. When I was 7, I did my first firewalk. Seriously, my whole life I have been working on myself, and now as I sit here it's like all of the tension is gone. I feel amazing!"

Ryan reflected what I said and then asked the group for impact. As it turned out, seeing me in this state offered hope to others that they might someday overcome their own polarities and feel more integrated. Seeing me in this newness and openness inspired them to access that place within themselves.

As this first T3 weekend ended, I felt totally and completely one with vast, expansive essence. I felt light, free, and soft. Although still disembodied, I wasn't as contracted around my Type 2 conditioning. Something had shifted. It wasn't as if my specialness and fear of being unworthy weren't there within me, but I felt more welcoming of these parts of me and less identified with them. I had compassion and love for myself at how this conditioning had affected my experience of life in such huge ways.

I could see for the first time how my old head trauma imprinted this idea that I am inherently ugly. My physical body was deformed from the fall and my energetic body had hardened around that wound. I was seeing the world through this lens and deciphered my worth based on this wound. Since my own parents didn't even protect my safety when I needed it most, my wound told me that I was unwanted, that nobody would ever love me. That I wasn't safe in the relational field. This imprint had guided all of my actions and motives in relationship with others.

"You think I'm ugly, and you don't want me, so I need to earn your love," was the unconscious projection.

In the presence of loving witness and community, I could see that this story was outdated. For the first time, I could see my inherent beauty and worth. I could see that my value didn't come from my appearance, that I wasn't an object to perform or be perfect for others. This was new and profound for me, and it let me begin an inquiry about how circling can heal attachment wounds.

Wanting to feel unconditionally loved is an experience all beings long for. Needing to know that our parents will be a secure base for us when we reach out for them or when we're struggling, we all long to feel safe in connection with others. When our parents fail us in welcoming us unconditionally and are unable to meet our unending needs, we begin to manipulate the environment to try to find love and power.

The wound of not having a secure attachment with our parents is the thing that drives us when we are in our distortion. Within the framework of a set amount of time with more than one person giving the circlee attention in a clean and dignified way, where there are no projections or attempts to fix or change, we begin to trust relationships. And from this place, we feel welcoming of our authentic expression and feel more sovereign and whole.

After that first T3 weekend, I was feeling so aligned with my lovability and worthiness that when Tim told me that he was only interested in a friendship with me, I felt grateful to hear his truth, rather than disappointed. Where I would have once felt shame about being not enough for him, I felt love for myself and excitement to be open to meeting someone who wanted to experience this with me.

My heart felt incredibly wide open, and from this place I felt fully aligned with the True Self. Without my conditioned self pulling my attention and causing me to feel separate and powerless and small, I accessed oneness, where there is no separation between any of us.

The way I treat others is quite literally the way I treat myself. The way I treat myself is quite literally the way I treat the world. When I am judgmental toward myself, I judge you. When I try to control myself and try to be perfect, I try to control you and have high expectations of you. When I think I'm special, I am intimidated by you because I think you're the special one. When I'm afraid that I am not enough, you will never be enough for me. When I don't trust myself to honor my truth, I will never trust you.

Similarly, when I embody my True Self and see myself as powerful and expansive, I see those same powerful qualities in you. When I treat myself as if I'm the body for God, I treat you as the Sacred Being you truly are.

In my longing for love from another, I come from my wound and want you to fix me. Being driven by thoughts of not being worthy of love, I don't love myself. And when I don't love myself, there is no way that any love you offer me will seep through the wall of self-protection I carry around my heart.

This is the beauty of understanding projections: the people in my life are reflecting to me every part of myself that I disowned and that lurks in the shadow. The people in my life could not trigger me if I was fully integrated and aligned with my wholeness.

Having a community of people witness me with openness and curiosity was messy and stretched me in ways I didn't know were possible. Seeing my shadow reflected back to me through them, I began to claim the parts of myself that I had historically disenfranchised. Claiming that I was manipulative, that I wanted others to think I was perfect, and that I was fierce brought me more in line with the core of my being. Stripping away the box of conditioning that kept me bound, I was able to own my shadow and fully embody my darkness. I had felt caged in by my conditioned self, but this experience let me see that the door to the cage was always open. I simply needed to walk through it.

When we claim our shadow, we have more mastery with our darkness. When we disown our shadow, our darkness drives our unconscious impulses, thoughts, and actions. We have less agency over our actions and thoughts, and even when we try to create change, everything feels difficult and challenging. In the calming of the parts of us that we would rather hide, we have more conscious awareness over where we are meeting the world from and what we are reflecting. In noticing our manipulative tactics to get what we want (e.g. giving to get, disowning our desire, etc.), we can give this a voice. "I notice there's a part of me that thinks I need to earn your love by not having any needs." This simple claiming brings the shadow to the light, and from here everything begins to change.

15
AUTHENTIC LIVING

"Authenticity is a collection of choices that we have to make every day. It's about the choice to show up and be real. The choice to be honest. The choice to let our true selves be seen."—Brené Brown

THE NEED FOR SAFETY

As T3 progressed, I was enjoying the exploration of owning my authentic truth in community. I was getting better at honoring myself with men and using my voice with clarity. However, the unconscious way that my history influenced my interactions in intimate relationships was still murky to me. In the rest of my life I was an empowered, strong woman. I happily parented my children with love and tenderness, I had many deep and supportive friendships with other fierce women, and I was a powerful healer with my clients. Because my pattern was only showing up in my sexual relationships, I wanted to gain deeper understanding about how my identification with my trauma was getting in the way of experiencing deep connection and intimacy with a man.

I had always said that I had never been molested or raped, and even though I acknowledge to Deborah how I had been violated, I still ignored the impact of my past traumas. Ignoring my wounds left them unhealed because I disowned my pain. Unconscious to their existence, my unhealed pain would come out in ways that surprised me. I would feel intense fear when walking down the street; I was totally closed off from real intimacy with my partners; and when I sensed a man was attracted to me I would either become seductive, flirtatious, or put up a strong energetic boundary. The instincts were so automatic, I hardly even realized I was indulging them.

Staying in my alignment around my children and other women was easy for me. I felt safe in these connections, so my wound wasn't triggered. Even though much of my pain was caused in relationship with my mom and sister, my attachment wound mostly got projected onto men because this is where I felt most vulnerable. When I did notice myself get triggered with friendships or my children, I could easily regulate and find my voice to speak my truest truth. With men, it seemed as if I impulsively played the game of love to try to keep a sense of power because I was deeply afraid of them trying to use their power over me or abandon me.

In my past I had believed that my body was an object that men were entitled to judge and touch and do with as they wanted. Men colluded in this misbelief with me, and they treated me like a possession. My humanity was ignored by my partners, perpetrators, and lovers. I was conditioned by my parents to be a good object, and in this I learned to ignore my own pain, denying my inner experience and quieting my voice.

I didn't know that I deserved a safe lover. I didn't have a template for a caring, loving man who was curious about my inner world. My history was colored by multiple encounters with men where I felt victimized and powerless, but still I didn't consciously know that I was afraid of men. A part of my mind was blind to other people's predatory behavior toward me because I was conditioned to believe that this was normal. I was also skilled at disowning my anger, my power, my pain, and my desire. Even though my mature self knew that I was powerful and important and not an object to be used, a younger part of me needed the system update.

During weekend six of T3, I started to see my patterns with men more clearly and I wanted to gain deeper understanding about why I was so distrusting of men. I viewed men as either pathetic and weak or dominant and callous. Some part of me was always testing men to see where their weakness was, where their hidden agenda was, whether they were viewing me as an object. I was testing to see if they were solid and secure so I could decide if they could meet me in my power and see me as a magical human being with a vast inner world who could not be possessed.

"These guys follow you around like dogs," Jake said to me about the many male friends I had in the community.

276

I was very flirty with the men of the Integral Center, seducing them but never actually wanting them or dating them. "I'm never going to have sex with you" was my stock reply when a man expressed interest in me. I wanted affection, I wanted to be wanted, and I wanted attention. However, I knew that I would never be with any of them. Choosing celibacy gave me space to mature, work on myself, and evolve in a much-needed way. However, the seductress in me was still unconsciously leaking sexual energy as a misguided way to garner power.

Experiencing the validation my ego wanted along with the sense of safety my deep unconscious wanted, I was learning how to maintain some semblance of a boundary with men while also staying in connection in the presence of sexual energy. Because this pattern was so unconscious, I couldn't see that my conditioned self (what I now call the "unhealthy feminine") was playing a game that kept me looping in my identification with my wounds. I also couldn't see that this identification caused me to be attracted to and attracting unhealthy masculine men who colluded with my seductive and accommodating conditioning.

As we heal and grow, we loop around the same general patterns and wounds; however, each time we get to them at deeper levels. We develop more mastery and profound awareness when we come back around to a pattern and work with it consciously. As we become less identified with the conditioned self and the wounds of trauma, we create more space from them, differentiating more fully and embodying our wholeness with greater capacity.

A part of me thought I should be more enlightened, that I should have been beyond these games and this desire for validation. But because it was happening, using it as the path to deepen my awakening was my task.

Throughout T3, Jake and I were developing a deep friendship under the new terms of our relationship. We still touched each other and snuggled, but that was the extent of our physical relationship. He held space for me when I was emotionally triggered. He would come over to my house to spend time with me when I was sad and messy, and he asked for my support when relationships with the people in his life became triggering. He seemed to be able to see me more clearly than I could see myself, and I came to trust his perception even when I felt shame about what he was pointing out.

We also had a lot of fun together dancing, laughing, and playing Cards Against Humanity and raunchy authentic relating games late into the night with other friends from our T3 cohort. In this connection, Jake became my best friend.

I trusted him more than any man I had ever known. I told Jake more than once that I trusted him more than anyone, but he didn't want to receive it. Afraid of being placed on a pedestal only to fall because of his human imperfections, he didn't want to hold that place in my life. I didn't understand this. To me, he was the epitome of a wise, healthy masculine man: caring, solid, and strong.

At the start of weekend six of T3, we began by playing a game called "Fly on the Wall." In this game, a participant is a fly on the wall while a group of other participants talk about them. The person who is the fly on the wall has control over what level of gossip they want to hear (level 1-3), and a staff person is sitting with them eye-gazing and holding compassionate space as they listen to what's being said about them.

This exercise is intended to trigger the person who is the fly on the wall in service of bringing to light the disowned parts within them. When we look at our triggers in connection with community and in circling, we become more integrated and whole. Shadow feelings and fears drive us less, and we're able to meet life with more clarity and presence when we meet our triggers in this way.

On this Friday evening, we broke out into small groups to play Fly on the Wall. When it was my turn to be the fly, I was disappointed that my gossip gang was saying stuff about me that didn't ping any of my triggers.

"She's a Queen Bee ... the leader of the popular crowd," one woman said.

"I think Harmony might be a witch," another participant stated. "But a good witch," she added.

"I find Harmony extremely attractive," one man said.

I gazed into the eyes of the staff person holding space for me, smiling at what seemed liked very superficial perceptions of me. I wanted something much deeper and more in service of bringing my shadow motives to the surface.

"I have a story that Harmony tests men and that no one will ever be good enough for her," one man said.

My eyes widened and I smiled with excitement as I felt the ping of this truth. I was happy that my shadow with men was being illuminated, as this was what I had been wanting to shift. Swirling with newfound awareness and clarity, my mind was abuzz with thoughts about men, my sexuality, my subversive motives, my manipulative behavior, and my tactics to find safety and control.

After everyone had a turn, we went back to the big group to share about our experience. Zack, who had brought me the lily on the first weekend of T3, was crawling out of his skin in a trigger and raised his hand to share.

"It was said in my fly on the wall that I essentially show up here like a big pussy, and I'm wanting to check that out with the group," he said as he was looking around anxiously.

Ryan reflected what he heard him say, "You were told that you show up like a pussy and you want to know if the rest of the cohort sees you that way, too. Is that right?"

"Yes. I want to know."

"Okay. Raise your hand if you think Zack shows up like a pussy," Ryan said.

As I listened to this, I held my hands in my lap thinking to myself "*I am not engaging with a poll that uses female genitalia as a synonym for weakness.*"

"Can we use a different word?" Linda, one of the course leads, hollered from across the room before anybody raised their hands.

"YES!" I yelped as I raised both of my hands triumphantly.

All of the attention went to me.

"I said that to piss Harmony off. That wasn't the actual word they used. I just wanted to trigger Harmony," Zack confessed.

A look of astonishment came over my face. I was in total disbelief that my dear friend Zack would want to passive aggressively hurt me by using language that was oppressive against women. My pussy had been grabbed, objectified, used, pounded, and hurt more times than I could even quantify. Men had inserted themselves into my pussy without consent, without care for my pleasure, and without regard to my humanity. My pussy had never felt honored, cherished, loved, or valued during sex. Ever. Not by me and not by my lovers. Never being seen as the strong source of life that it is, my pussy was ready for a new story that was not influenced by oppression and power dynamics. I was ready to claim the power of my pussy for myself, and I was not willing to stay quiet in this community setting and enable misogynistic oppressive language about my body to violently be used to hurt me.

I could understand that Zack had been conditioned in this way. Growing up on the East Coast, being called a pussy was a threat to his masculinity. I could get that he was in a trigger about this and wanted to find a sense of strength and power by hurting me, a woman who is powerful and strong. But I was not willing to passively allow him to power over me by using colloquial language about my genitalia.

The rest of the large group share was a blur to me because I was so intensely triggered. When we took a break, Zack came over and sat next to me.

"I'm not available for connection right now, Zack. I'm too triggered," I said.

"No. I want to talk."

"I'm not available for that," I insisted. "I'm really angry." As I said this, I smiled. This was a defense mechanism because I wasn't accustomed to owning my anger. Unconsciously, a part of me thought that if I delivered my anger with a smile, I'd be safe from harm.

"You're not mad. You're smiling. I'm not moving," Zack said as he claimed the seat next to me.

"I'm not available for this, Zack. Please give me space."

"No. I'm not moving." Zack crossed his arms and refused to move from the seat next to mine.

Angry at his attempt to exert his power over me, I put up the coldest, sharpest energetic wall I could and I refused to move. I was not going to let him win, and I shunned him for the rest of the night.

The next evening we were doing carpet work, which is a dedicated amount of time to follow up with people about Hold Nothings and other processes or conversations that have gone unfinished. When I sat down on the carpet, Joel crawled over to me and said seductively, "I have something I want to tell you."

"Okay." I smiled.

He looked at me as we sat in silence, then he looked around, checking to see who was sitting near us. I waited to hear his Hold Nothing, not knowing what it could possibly be. His eyes looked down at the short black dress I had on and he said, "You look so gorgeous in that. I mean, wow. Nicely done, Harmony."

I giggled with nervous excitement. "You seem turned on."

"Yeah ... I am."

I gasped with surprise. Joel and I had an extremely flirtatious relationship since the first weekend of T3. He gave me piggy back rides, he'd pick me up every time he hugged me, and we were clearly attracted to one another. But he was seven years younger than me and I knew I would never actually be with him intimately. There was something about his flirtation that I loved, but I also popped out of myself with him, trying to be the fun flirty girl he wanted rather than the authentic, solid woman that I really was.

Right after Joel said this to me, a group of people crawled over to talk with us. It's a rule during carpet work that you don't walk anywhere, so the room is filled with people crawling or sitting on the floor. We all started talking about our Fly on the Wall experiences, but my mind was still on what Joel had just said to me.

I went home that night feeling a mixture of emotions as thoughts of men fluttered through my mind. I was feeling validated knowing that

Joel was attracted to me, but I was disappointed that I was getting off on his desire for me because there was a part of me that still believed this is where my worth came from. I was still angry about what Zack said, highlighting for me why I test men: if a dear friend of mine could try to exert power over me as I tried to set a boundary, men are not to be trusted. And I was still very much intrigued by being outed for the way I test men and my misbelief that no one will ever be good enough for me. This seemed to be the unconscious drive that had me locked into a pattern with men that prevented intimacy.

I had always believed that if I found the right man, all of that would change. But I was starting to see my side in the dynamic. If my history says men aren't safe and I treat all men as if they are part of this old story, I collude with the story and keep myself and men playing out projections rather than meeting them from my essence and seeing them beyond their conditioned self. When I disown my truth, my own projections can actually induce in men the behavior that I most fear. Also, if I'm afraid that I'm not good enough or worthy of love, I put that onto men and see them as not enough for me, inducing that feeling in them.

The next morning was Sunday, and when we convened in the large group Ryan asked everybody to point to a person they're interested in hearing from. The people who had the most points were invited to share. Two other women and I had the most points, and when it was my turn Ryan said, "We'd like to know what's going on for you, Harmony."

I took a breath and paused. "I'm afraid of men."

Ryan looked surprised at this share. "You're afraid of men," he reflected. "How does that fear show up in your relationships?"

"I test men. I try to see where the point of power is. I'm testing to see if they'll try to use their power over me or if they'll collapse when I'm in my power. I seduce them. I play with them. And I think that none of them will ever be good enough for me."

"Wow. I'm surprised by this. I'm a man. Are you afraid of me?"

"I don't fully trust you. Like 80% I trust you. I think you'd collapse if I were to fully own my power with you."

"Okay," he said. "Is there a man in your life that you do trust?"

My mind started scanning for a man in my life I trusted. My dad I trusted a lot, but not to hold me in my emotional power. He tended to collapse and drop me when I was in that place. I had a lot of male friends, many of whom I trusted mostly, but not all of the way.

"Jake," I said with certainty as I looked across the circle at him.

Jake jolted with surprise.

"Jake. He's the only man in your life who you feel safe with and fully trust."

"Yes," I said, shaking with how vulnerable I felt at making this reveal in the presence of the large group.

"Jake, Harmony, are you two willing to stand in the center of the circle?" Ryan asked.

"I'm willing if you are," I said to Jake.

"Yeah, of course," Jake said.

We met in the center of the circle with over thirty people looking at us. We stood facing each other, gazing into one another's eyes.

"So here he is, the only man in your life you feel safe with," Ryan said.

I smiled as tears started streaming down my face. I nodded in agreement. This felt so true to me.

"And I'm sure you've tested him," Ryan pointed out.

"Yes." I giggled as I thought of all the ways I'd tested Jake throughout our relationship.

Jake smiled and laughed, too. "Yes, she has!" he agreed.

"I'm wondering, what does it feel like to be here with him now?"

I took a deep breath and scanned my body with my inner eye. "I feel my feet on the ground," I said. "I also feel my belly, solid and strong. And I feel my heart, so open and full of love."

"How's that for you, Jake?"

"Oh, I feel my heart so big right now," he said as he put his hand on his heart with tears in his eyes.

"I want to hug you," I said.

"Yes," Jake said as we came in for a long embrace.

After a few moments, Ryan asked the person sitting next to Jake to move so that I could sit next to him. We held hands and breathed in the beauty of what felt like a ceremony honoring our relationship.

Until this moment, I couldn't see the water that I was swimming in. I couldn't see that I had been drowning in an ocean of fear toward men, and that this unconscious fear kept me isolated while I longed for deep intimacy. My fear of being dropped by a man or overpowered by a man kept me totally guarded against vulnerably sharing myself.

I had reached out for my dad at 5 months old, when I fell, and he hadn't been there for me. Because of this, I projected onto all men that they wouldn't be there for me when I needed them. This story was reinforced over and over again throughout my intimate relationships. But I couldn't see that in this fear, I stayed guarded and dropped the men in my life first, inducing the very pattern that I didn't want.

I had also tried to be perfect for my sister, taking her criticism personally and believing her story that I was responsible for her pain and anger about our family. I projected this onto men, trying to be perfect for them and believing that I was responsible for their well-being and happiness.

And I had also picked up my mom's story about men, that men are not safe in their desire. This was confused with the other story I picked up from her that my worth comes from men's desire for me and that I need to submit to their affection. If I didn't, my unconscious mind believed I would die, which I learned from my history lesson at Jewish school at age 6.

Unconsciously, I had continued to collect evidence throughout my life to support these projections. Until Jake. Having one man in my life who I totally trusted - and honoring that experience as totally sacred in the presence of our community - began to transform me in a deep way.

As we sat in the big circle, Jake leaned over and said, "That was the most powerful experience for me, being named as a safe man in front of the whole group. Wow, I am so overwhelmed right now. I love you, Harmony."

"I've been trying to tell you how much I value our friendship for months and you never take it in. I love you and I am so grateful to have you in my life."

We held hands and took some deep breaths as the rest of the large group shares continued.

The only reason anyone ever wants to exert power over someone else is because they feel weak and powerless. When we truly claim and own our power, we empower and uplift all of the people around us. When a man is able to uplift and protect the women in his life, he is embodying his strength. Similarly, when a women encourages the men in her life to become even more powerful, she is standing solid in her power. Empowering our children, our parents, our lovers, friends, and community, our connection to our power strengthens. There is no other. How we treat the people in our lives is, quite literally, how we treat ourselves.

When men disown their inner feminine (which is the ability to "be with" and stay receptive) and when women disown their inner masculine (which is claiming their desire and taking initiative) we end up with a fragmented society. Integrating our inner feminine and masculine energies is the way to create balance and harmony on the planet. When men claim the part of them that is soft, receptive, and open—just sometimes—and when women claim their desire, initiative, and boundaries—again, even just once in a while—the yin and yang energies come together. Each side of the yin yang symbol has a little dot of the other, and this is the same quality we need to cultivate within ourselves: A little bit of feminine (yin) in the masculine men (yang), and a little bit of masculine (yang) in the feminine women (yin).

SETTING CONTEXT

Over the next three months, my friendship with Jake deepened, as did my personal growth journey. I was doing breathwork regularly in private sessions. When I first started private breathwork sessions, I would come to a place where I didn't want to breathe. My neck felt constricted as if a noose were around it, and I would turn blue from lack of oxygen as my breath didn't want to flow. I didn't have any control over this. Although I was not intentionally holding my breath, my unconscious death urge was being brought to the surface.

Ultimately, I had to go deeply into my death urge so that I could find my will to live. I would gasp and moan in agony as my throat stayed constricted. Trying to fight my death urge was useless. I needed to surrender to it so that I could eventually choose to pull life in with my breath. The moment I chose life and started breathing again I felt empowered in my resolve. A natural and easeful rhythm of breath began, and I didn't need to expend any effort at all. My breath breathed me. Choosing to be in this body for the first time since my fall, I knew I wanted to be here. My spirit felt like it belonged in this human vessel and on this earth.

The more time I spent breathing consciously in a rhythmic pattern, the softer and more whole my energetic system became. Areas of tension in my head, neck, face, and back relaxed. I started seeing myself and the men in my life with deep understanding and compassion as I released old trauma and hardened energetic wounds. From the vantage point of my inner eye, I became fascinated with the wound of my head trauma, and eventually the dense energy started moving and I could see my sparkly light in that area of my system. I could see my inner beauty, and that beauty started being reflected out into the physical world where I saw my divine exquisiteness represented in my physical form for the first time.

Between the relational work of circling and the energetic healing of breathing, my old head trauma and attachment wounds related to it were beginning to heal on a deeper level. I wanted to be embodied in my True Self and I was beginning to trust myself in my power to do so. I was accessing my inner fierceness, becoming more solid in myself, less distorted and less manipulative. I was learning to speak my truth and navigate relationships when they were challenging. I was beginning to own my beauty and feel sexy in my body, enjoying my curves and giving myself permission to care about how I looked rather than resisting my desire to focus on image. I felt like I was growing up into my mature self, integrated, whole, and powerful.

Not being in a romantic relationship during this time made it possible for me to stay in myself and keep my healing and evolution my priority. My friendships were deep and satisfying, and Jake was my dearest, closest friend. The depth of our friendship was so beautiful to the entire community that I was constantly asked why we weren't together. Every friend, acquaintance, and new person in the community would inquire about our connection.

"Do you want to be with him?" my friend Julie asked.

"No. I am perfectly happy with our friendship as it is."

Daily, someone would tell me that Jake was in love with me or that we seemed perfect together. I was physically attracted to him, I trusted him more than any other man I had ever known, and he was the most strong and loving presence I had ever experienced when I was in grief or fear. I loved Jake dearly, but I wasn't sure that he would be a capable partner for me. He didn't work, and he could hardly care for his own basic needs. He was aimless in his life, and he was still exploring polyamory. I had children and a thriving private practice and a dog and a home. My fear was that Jake would feel like another responsibility; someone who needed me rather than someone who could meet me in all aspects of life and contribute to the goodness I had cultivated since my divorce.

"What's going on with you two?" Alyssa, a member of our T3 cohort, asked us one night at a party.

Jake was lying on the couch and I was sitting on the floor in front of him. He was caressing my hair and outlining the bone structure of my face, gazing at me with love.

"We're friends," I replied. "We met via online dating over a year ago. He's the reason I know about circling and the Integral Center, and we have a deep friendship with a lot of love."

"Yeah, but you two could have an even more special friendship if you had sex. You could be special friends," said Alyssa.

"You can't put us in a box," said Jake. "Our friendship is too unique for that."

At this point, there were four other people gathered around us trying to figure out our relationship.

"I want you two to get together," said Sheri. "I think about it all of the time."

"Really? Why?" I asked.

"You two are so perfect together. You're both powerful and wise, and you're so beautiful."

"Is this a poly vs monogamy thing?" Alyssa asked, who was polyamorous.

"In part," I responded.

"You know you have all of the control," Alyssa stated to me. "What is this guy going to have to do for you to finally have sex with him?"

I paused to think about that question. I didn't have an answer to it. I just knew that as things were, I wasn't interested in being sexual with Jake.

"This is the most beautiful friendship I have ever had. Maybe there's no defining it," I said.

"Okay," said Alyssa, "It's like relational anarchy, like you're neither friends nor lovers. It's undefinable."

Jake and I looked at each other and paused.

"I love you," he said.

"I love us" I said, "as we are."

The group of friends interested in our love wasn't satisfied with the state of our friendship. They wanted more for us, and over the next month, I started to want more, too. And it seemed like Jake was starting to think about us more because he started to look at me as if he was totally in love with me.

A few months later we completed T3. It was October when Jake and I started to get serious about collaborating on a workshop together. One day he came over to my house so we could outline our offering.

"After we work on the content of this presentation, I want to talk about our love," he said.

"Okay." I wasn't sure what that meant but I wrote it down on the agenda. "I want us to talk about a marketing video for this presentation, and my marketing expert wants us to include two things in the video."

"I'm not comfortable with that," Jake said with his voiced raised and an intensity on his face. "Is the video going to influence the content of our workshop?"

"I don't think so. I want to tell you what the two things are and let you decide."

"No! Tell me. Is it going to influence the content of our presentation?"

"I don't think so. Please let me tell you so you can decide." I sort of giggled because I was scared and confused. This conversation was starting to seem convoluted to me, and I didn't understand why he was so angry.

Before I knew it, Jake had an intense tone and energy about him. "The content is more important than marketing! I don't want the marketing to influence the content!"

Every time I tried to tell him what the two elements were, he spoke over me. It was as if he were an angry dog barking at me and I couldn't get a word in edgewise. I was confused and afraid. I just wanted to tell him that my marketing person wanted us to include our "Why" for the workshop and what we thought people would get out of it. But I was never able to say that because Jake left my house so triggered that he was shaking.

A few hours later I got a text from him. "I don't think I can be friends with you after that."

This interaction didn't make any sense to me. This conversation could have been easy and quick. We didn't need to include the pieces if we didn't want to, but I had wanted to let him know what some options were, so that we could get on the same page.

Over the next two months, Jake and I had very little contact, and when we did meet our friend Jarrod mediated our conversations. Jarrod was a very skilled circler who had a Master's in social work. He offered to meet with us because he was passionate about self-actualization through the challenges of relationship. With Jarrod present, we processed this one event on three different occasions.

In these mediated discussions, I dedicated myself to not personalizing Jake's experience and to "get Jake's world." I wanted to know what was happening for him in that moment, and I wanted to be heard by him about what was happening for me. As it turned out, Jake was scared about the possibility of the integrity of our work being warped by marketing strategies. This made sense to me, but I still didn't understand why he reacted in the way he did.

"I was wanting to tell you that I wanted to be with you that day. I was feeling vulnerable and excited," he said.

I felt my heart melt. My whole being was elated knowing that he wanted me, but since we hadn't spent any time together over the past two months, I had begun dating someone else and hadn't told him yet.

It was December now and two months had passed since our argument. I invited Jake over to a holiday party at my house. I had been casually dating a man named Matt for two months, and I was leaning against the counter, flirting with him, when Jake walked in holding a bouquet of flowers.

"You came!" I said with a huge smile on my face as I gave him a big hug.

"You seem so happy," he said.

I was happy, and I was also scared of hurting him or Matt. I felt awkward and unsure of what to do next.

"Do you two know each other?" I asked as I took the flowers and looked for a vase.

They looked at one another in a way that was neither warm nor friendly. "We've met once before," Jake said.

I walked away to trim the flowers at the sink, and when I turned around Jake and Matt were talking with each other. I felt overwhelmed with a rush of adrenaline, not knowing how to navigate this burgeoning love triangle. I awkwardly avoided both Jake and Matt for the next few hours.

As the party progressed, I socialized and hung out by the fire pit and had a glass of wine. A few hours passed and I gathered everyone in the living room to play instruments and sing. There were some very talented musicians in the house, and I was excited to get everyone together in one space.

I was getting snacks from the kitchen to bring to the living room, and when I came to find a seat, Matt was sitting on the floor and Jake was on the couch.

"Come sit by me," Jake said as he made room for me.

We snuggled up next to each other on the couch for the first time in two months. Since Matt and I weren't seeing each other exclusively, I felt okay about snuggling with Jake, but I didn't want to drop Matt, either. When Matt and I had first started spending time together, he had asked me why Jake and I weren't a couple, a common question men I dated asked me since Jake and I were so close. I had told Matt what I would tell everyone who asked, that we were just friends and this was how we wanted it.

Since it had been so long since Jake and I had hung out, it felt good to come back into connection with him. However, a lot of my attention was on Matt, and I felt torn about sitting near Jake. The truth is, I wanted to make everyone happy, and I had no idea what I wanted. I didn't know who I wanted to sit by or who I wanted to connect with. I was totally out of touch with my desire.

Matt left early, saying he wasn't feeling well. And Jake was the last guest to leave. We talked outside by the fire pit until three in the morning, laughing and being us again. I felt excited to have my friend back, and I was happy to forget about the previous argument and move forward. But I was uncertain about what was next for us.

The thing that I easily forget is that my relationships are a reflection of me. Everything I think about another says something about me. Even though my mind thinks *"The man I love will never want me,"* this can be translated into *"I don't love myself or want myself as I am."* My self-love has historically been very conditional and dependent on the way I looked and how successful I was. I ended up projecting this onto men and believed that they viewed me in the same way I did. I also twisted this into believing they would never be good enough for me.

There was no part of me that thought Jake wanted me. Even with our history, the community rallying behind us, him telling me that he wanted to be with me on the day of our argument, there was no part of me that thought we would ever get together.

Two days later, Jake and I met for our final meeting with Jarrod. When we scheduled this meeting, Jake and I still weren't spending time together or talking. Since we were now back in connection, Jarrod suggested we get clear on the context we wanted for our relationship.

"You two have never come to an agreement on the context of your relationship," Jarrod said, "and it seems like now might be a good time to do that. What I want you to do is go into separate rooms, write down the context you want … this is about how you want to be with each other … what are the guidelines for your relationship together … then come back in here. You will hand the paper to the other person. One person will read the other's proposed context aloud, but you won't reply. You won't say a word about it. Then the other person will read the other's proposed context, without reply. You'll eye-gaze for ten minutes, then you won't process this for one week."

Jake and I agreed on this process, and we went to separate rooms to write out the context we wanted for our relationship. As I sat with my blank paper, I felt scared and vulnerable. I still didn't fully understand Jake's anger that day at my house about the marketing video, and we hadn't spent enough time together after that for me to get a sense of our connection after our time away.

Also, I was starting to date Matt and I was interested to see where that was going. We had plans to go salsa dancing the following week. I found him extremely attractive and wise.

After thirty minutes, Jake and I came back together and handed each other our proposed context. I was shaking with anticipation. Without a clue about the context he might want, I was scared about how he was going to react to what I wrote.

We decided that I would read his first:

"I want to be in a monogamous relationship with Harmony, where we cut off all other connections where there can be possible sexual leakage."

I was shocked. I had no idea he was going to write this, and the proposal went on. There were three pages of detailed guidelines for how we would navigate this relationship, including not having sex for three months.

Once I was done, tears started streaming down my face. "I never thought I was going to be enough for you," I cried. Since we agreed not to process, I got up and went to the bathroom and sobbed. After several minutes, I came back and got ready to hear Jake read my proposal aloud.

"I want to be in a relationship with Jake where we explore intimacy together while also exploring with other people."

Jake looked up at me in shock. This was the very thing I had told him I didn't want to do with him when we first met over a year ago. He continued to read my two-page document, outlining the exploration of vulnerability, trust, and communication I wanted. Then he set the paper down and we eye-gazed for ten minutes.

After the ten minutes, Jarrod walked in and asked how we were doing.

"We wrote down very different things, and I think it would be great if you'd be willing to process this with us," I said.

Jarrod agreed to spend some time with us processing our context, which was truly a gift because I'm not sure we would have been able to navigate this on our own.

"Jake wrote that he wanted a monogamous container with me for three months where we don't have sex with each other and where we cut out all potential sexual leakage with other people," I said, updating Jarrod. "And I wrote that I wanted to explore sexual intimacy together while also exploring with other people."

"Okay, it sounds like Jake wants more with you than you do with him," Jarrod said. "How's that for you, Jake?"

"It feels terrible," he said. "I put my heart on the line and my story is that I was more vulnerable than Harmony."

Jarrod spent some time trying to gain understanding about the way Jake was feeling; then he turned to me. "It sounds like you want to stay open to other people. Is there something that you want to tell Jake but maybe you're afraid to?"

I paused and fear rushed over me. I was thinking of Matt and how I couldn't tell Jake because he would be hurt and not want to be with me if he knew I was seeing someone else.

I stayed silent, frozen by fear.

"I get it, Harmony. Your relationships with other people would be impacted by this context. I get it," Jake said.

I felt relieved. Jake said the thing that I was too afraid to say, and I took that as confirmation that I didn't need to tell him about Matt.

"Yes. It will. It will affect a lot of my relationships," I said. "I don't know how I feel about your context. Let me make sure I've got this: you want me to stop giving any of my attention to other men, give all of my attention to you, but then you don't want to have sex with me?"

"Yes."

"No way! I'm not going to agree to that. If we're going to be together, I want to be with what wants to happen between us. We've been friends for over a year, and we've never had sex. We know each other so well. I'm not willing to stop the flow of my sexual energy all together for you and then not have someone to give it to."

"You want to be with other people!" he exclaimed.

"That was before I knew you wanted to be with me," I said.

Jarrod reflected what we said, then he encouraged us to spend time together over the next week without talking about context. "Just let this all settle in and see how you feel next Sunday."

The entire next week, Jake courted me. He took me to sushi, brought me several bouquets of flowers, and told me how deeply he loved me. It was mid-December, and we snuggled up in front of the fire and watched *Elf* together. We were more physical than we had been together since early on in our relationship, and it felt good to be more romantic and sensual with him.

Our week together was lovely, and when we met the following Sunday to talk, we decided to first go for a hike, then come back to my house for dinner. It was a sunny but chilly December day, and Jake wanted to show me his secret spot up by Mount Sanitas. He had just gotten off the phone with his mom, and he seemed triggered by their conversation.

"She never asks me about myself," he said. "She wants to tell me about all of the little things in her life, but she never asks about me. Then when she senses that she's losing me, she starts a fight. It's like the only way she knows how to feel connected with me—to fight."

"That sounds painful," I said.

It's hard to explain what happened next. I've never experienced anything like it before, but Jake seemed to disassociate then started treating me as if I were his mom. He was full of angst toward me and nothing I said was right. He kept telling me that I was selfish, that I was saying the wrong thing, and he seemed extremely dissatisfied with my attempts to keep connection with him.

He took a few deep breaths and centered himself. "You're not my mother," he said, as if he needed to remind himself of that.

Neither are you, I thought to myself but didn't dare say.

Jake was projecting his mother-wound onto me, and since I didn't feel entangled with him I didn't personalize what was happening. However, I also didn't recognize that this was part of the way Jake engaged in his intimate relationships. It was the first time it had ever happened, so I figured it was circumstantial to his recent conversation with her.

When the hike was over, I felt relieved. Aside from our conflict over the marketing video, this was the most stressful time I had ever spent with Jake. I was hoping that he would be able to move through his experience consciously, but at dinner he maintained a hardness with me that was difficult to be around.

Once we ate, I lay on the floor in front of the fireplace and Jake came over and started rubbing my body. Before I knew it, he was pressing really hard into my hips.

"Stop! That hurts," I said.

Jake persisted, pressing even harder when I said stop.

"What are you doing?! That hurts!" I took his hand and tried to push it away.

"Say the safe word," he said, alluding to a word we had agreed upon to use if one of us were in a big trigger or ever needed the other to stop what they're doing.

"Plant!" I yelled. "Plant!"

And he stopped.

"What the hell is wrong with you? I asked you to stop. That hurt so badly. Why on earth would you keep doing that when I asked you to stop?"

"It's not my job to care-take you. You need to say 'plant' when something is too much for you."

"No. It's your job to be a responsive partner who cares that you are hurting me!" I exclaimed.

"I'm not willing to do that," he said.

"Well we shouldn't be together, then," I said.

Jake was a boundary pusher. This was something I loved about him in our friendship because it helped me to see my edges and grow. But in the context of romance, I was feeling more unsafe with him than I could have anticipated, and I think my lack of boundaries had him feeling unsafe, too. This was undoubtedly ripe ground for learning and growth, but I was a clear "No" to being treated this way.

"Your context feels like control to me. It doesn't feel like love," I said. "I don't want a relationship that I need a safe word for, and I don't like the way you treat me. I think I liked you better when you had your attention on other women."

"I'm just trying to make it so we have the best possible shot at long-term partnership," he said.

"I don't want to be in a long-term partnership where I feel controlled. This is my thing with men. I'm extremely codependent and I give my power away and that is not in service of long-term partnership."

"I'm afraid that my jealousies will get triggered with you and come between us. Eventually I want to be able to trust you to have friendships with men, but right now I need this to feel secure," he revealed.

Knowing why he wanted this had me feeling compassion for him, but every time I looked at his conditions for being with me it seemed like he was trying to put me into a box, to take away my power and thwart my creative energy.

"The entire time we've known each other, I've been single. You don't know how I am in a monogamous relationship. I am so loyal and caring. All of the touch I give everyone else would be given to you," I explained.

"There are so many men in this community who want to be with you. I need you to stop giving them attention so I know that I'm the most important person in the room to you," he said.

"When I try this on, I feel like I'm in a narrow hallway and I need to fit into this small parameter for you to feel okay. That doesn't work for me. I'm a no to this context."

"Okay. Fine. I give up. My heart is on the floor here," Jake said with tears in his eyes. "If you don't want to do this with me, I'll leave. But you have to know, Harmony, our friendship is going to change. I'm not going to be as open to you anymore."

"I understand and I feel sad about that, but this context as you've presented it isn't something I want with you."

When Jake left that night, I felt sad about losing our friendship, but I also felt more solid in myself for owning my authentic truth with him. This represented so much growth and progress for me. In saying "no" to Jake, I said "yes" to myself and to what I wanted. I wanted a relationship that felt empowering and liberating. I wanted to feel more expansive and big for being partnered, not confined and managed. I wanted a partner who felt secure in himself and was so solid in himself that he could meet me in my strength and power.

From the outside, we seemed perfect together. But as Jake started to think of me as a potential mate, his attachment wounds were triggered. The young one in him who wanted to feel safe with his mom was trying to figure out how to contain my feminine power so he could access his masculine power. It was as if he saw me as his enemy rather than his teammate. After each attempt I made to get on his team, he shunned me and reprimanded me. Because I had spent so much time cultivating my sovereignty and differentiating from my wounds, I didn't collude in this pattern as I had done with previous partners. I stood my sacred ground and happily let him walk out the door.

As we start to heal and evolve, our growth is reflected in the outer part of our lives first, then makes its way to our inner circle. For example, as we begin to heal, our interactions with community and work get healthier. Then our connections with friendships, family, and children start to flourish. The last area of our life to be affected by our growth is our intimate partnerships. Our attachment wounds are triggered by those closest to us, and becoming consciously competent in our interactions with our intimate partner can be the most rigorous spiritual practice. Not colluding in the dynamic is the first step in that. Even when we don't know the healthiest response, not reacting from the wounded place is the beginning of being empowered with conscious choice and right action.

16

THE TEST

"Because it is happening, it is the path to enlightenment."
— Pema Chodron

DISENTANGLEMENT

"I just had an amazing circle and I want to tell you about it," Jake texted me two nights after I had said "No" to his context proposal.

"Do you want to talk on the phone? I just put my kids to sleep," I replied.

"Can I come over? I want to see you."

"Okay. We'll need to be quiet."

When Jake walked in, he asked if we could lie down and snuggle. "I want touch," he said.

He followed me up to my room, and we lay down in my bed. Jake seemed softer and more open than I had ever seen him. He typically had a hardness about him, an East Coast edge that came across as intimidating or demanding. Tonight, he was shaking and on the verge of tears.

"Ken circled me and I was being hard and defensive to everyone in the circle, then he asked me if I was wearing my mother," he explained.

"That makes sense to me," I said. "I had been thinking that same thing but didn't say it. After you talked to your mom the other day you seemed harder and more controlling with me."

Ken was Jake's mentor, so he could say something like that to him and Jake could receive it. As a therapist, I tried to be careful about how much analysis I offered the men I dated, so I chose to be discerning when I saw this pattern emerge in Jake.

"Ken said that I need to learn how to stay open to receive care. I realize I have been so hard with you, and I want to be softer."

My whole system softened hearing this, and I melted into his arms. We kissed and held each other close and caressed each other's bodies.

"I love you so much, Harmony," he said through his tears.

"I love you, too, Jake. I love you so much," I said as I squeezed him tightly.

The fluidity and softness between us was nourishing to my soul. I had been craving this. This felt welcoming and vulnerable and beautiful.

When he left, I felt deeply in love with Jake for the first time. We spent the next week negotiating our context, with both of us knowing that we wanted to find a way to come to a mutual agreement on our relationship. Feeling Jake's vulnerability removed my feeling of being controlled. He seemed more open to my perspective and curious about what I was wanting.

When Christmas Eve arrived, it was my forty-first birthday. After spending the morning with my kids, I dropped them off at their dad's and I called Matt to tell him that I no longer wanted to see him. Right after we got off the phone, Jake came over to celebrate my birthday. He walked in my front door carrying four dozen roses and a birthday cake. Seeing him took my breath away.

"This is just a small representation of how much I love you," he said. "I want you to breathe it in. Smell this rose and breathe in my love."

He put a rose up to my nose and I breathed in his love. "It's beautiful."

"I'd like to give you a massage in front of your fire place."

"Wow!" I said with a smile. "I feel so loved."

He set up the massage table, and as he touched me I continued to breathe in his love. Thirty minutes into the massage I started crying. I lifted my head and said, "I get it. You know me. You know all of me—my light and my dark—and you love me. You love all of me."

With a look of love and amazement, Jake said, "That's why I love you, Harmony. Because of who you are—all of you."

My heart burst open and I cried a deep cry. I had wanted to feel this for my whole life, to feel fully seen and loved, like I didn't need to hide my truth or try to be perfect for a man.

I turned over onto my back and Jake kissed me. "Can I finish your massage?"

"Of course," I said with a smile.

I kept my eyes open to observe the man who loved me and whom I loved dearly massage my body and shower me with love and affection.

When the massage was finished, we sat in front of the fireplace eating dinner.

"This feels like love to me. I'll say yes to the context from this place," I said.

"Wait, are you saying yes to the context I proposed?"

"Absolutely. If I feel loved by you, I don't want to snuggle with other men or leak sexual energy. I want to give all of my attention to you. I want you to do the same—no watching pornography or leaking of sexual energy either. Also, I want to make love to you."

"Wow. I love that you said that about pornography. I think that's important for me to not leak sexual energy either. And I'm open to changing the part about our sexual relationship. I just don't want our time together to become all about sex. But I guess we've known each other for so long that I don't think that will happen."

We agreed that we would be in communication about our sexual desire, and I was overjoyed with an open heart. Later that night when our friends came over for an impromptu birthday party, everyone was happy that we were finally together.

After everyone left, Jake and I made out in my bed, trying to resist the impulse to make love. He spent the night, and the next morning, on Christmas day, he talked on the phone with his mom and dad. He was triggered by the phone call, but we talked about what was happening for him. As he shared about his trigger, I touched him and snuggled him. There's a part of me that wants my love make everything better for the people in my life, which seems kind and caring but is also a pattern of enmeshment that comes from fear.

After lunch, we went to the movies to see the animated film "Ferdinand," and when we came home I prepared dinner for us while we continued our negotiation about sex.

"I think we should give each other tantric massages," I said, "where the goal isn't climax but we explore giving each other pleasure and learn each other's bodies."

One of the principles of tantra is that bliss is our original state. We need to use our breath and our awareness to access our innate bliss on our own and in connection with another. We need to be in our life urge to access true bliss and share it with a partner, without objectification or performance. Because we harden around our humanity and lose touch with this original state, people look to other people, food, drugs, porn, and so on to try to find this experience. Even though the mind tries to project out to find the bliss, it always lives within us—we just need to turn toward it with breath and conscious awareness.

"I like that," Jake said.

His gaze turned toward the ground as he was sitting in the recliner of my living room. I was in the kitchen making dinner, feeling good about the conscious way we were choosing to navigate our romantic partnership. Then, everything switched. Jake looked up at me with a glare in his eyes and raised his voice.

"You make me collapse around my masculinity! There's no room for this part of me here! You only want me when I'm collapsed!"

I was surprised by this shift and extremely confused.

"It sounds like there's a part of you that you want to have present in our relationship, and you have a story that I don't want that part of you. Did I get that?" I paraphrased what he said in an attempt to understand where he was coming from without personalizing his emotional trigger.

"Yes! You don't want my strong masculinity!" he said, still angry.

"Jake, I'm not sure what's happening here. I love your masculine strength. In fact, it's one of the sexiest things about you. If you feel collapsed around your masculinity, don't blame me for it. I just wanted us to find a way to explore our sexuality without intercourse, because that's what you wanted."

"You're right. I like that idea. I think I should go." He looked disassociated as he stood up and walked out of my house without a loving goodbye.

When the door shut, I collapsed in tears. The extreme between deep intimacy and ruptured connection confused my system and I started feeling insecure in our relationship. To be the recipient of his projection around his masculinity was painful, and in his sudden exit I felt dropped.

Alone on Christmas evening, my mind tried to make sense of the change in this relationship. Jake's trigger was intense and deeply distorted. I was confused about how he could switch so quickly from loving and kind to blaming and full of rage. I didn't feel responsible for his collapse or his anger, but I was devastated that our connection had been broken. Mentally I tried to imagine what was happening within him to cause his sudden trigger, and I noticed an impulse to try to be perfect for him so we could come back into our intimacy bubble.

This was already harder than I had anticipated, but I had agreed to a three-month container with Jake and I wanted to stay open to seeing what would emerge from our relationship. That night I decided that we would likely not be long-term partners, but since we had a rich history of intimacy and love I wanted to give us time to try.

When we come together with another person in an intimate relationship, it can be challenging to decipher the difference between the veils of our own projections and seeing one another clearly. Noticing the impulse of our conditioning is important information in staying solid in our alignment with the True Self. We often match the frequency of our partners, where we mirror the vibration of the most intense energy in the couple. Vibrating at our own frequency in our alignment with Source is the outcome of differentiating from our attachment wounds. This means that when our partner is struggling, triggered, or in a state of low mental health, we don't change our vibration to match that. In our attachment wounds, we match other people's vibration to keep connection. In the differentiation from our attachment wounds, we keep our alignment with Source as our primary connection and we vibrate at that frequency.

EMBODYING THE HEALTHY FEMININE

Early in this context with Jake, I was mostly vibrating at my own frequency and was individuated from him. However, there was a twinge of my attachment wound starting to surface when he was triggered. I noticed myself trying to please him, thinking his pain and his needs were more important than what was happening in me. Whether I was with my children, friends, or clients, my attention would wander to him and I started looking at him as my point of reference rather than staying aligned with Source.

The next week there was a pre-New Year's Eve party at the Integral Center. New Year's Eve landed on a Sunday, and over 300 people attended this party on the night before. Jake and I planned to meet at my house to strategize how to navigate the web of past romantic interests at the Integral Center, and I made an elaborate dinner for us to enjoy before leaving for the event.

As I waited for Jake, I got dressed in a sexy backless red lace dress with black boots. My long wavy hair was perfectly coiffed, and I had on more makeup than typical for me.

I watched the time tick by, trying to occupy my mind and resist the urge to be upset that Jake was over an hour late. I decided not to text him because I didn't want to come across as needy. My character structure believed that being understanding and accommodating for Jake was more important than what was happening with me.

I didn't want to start an argument and I wanted to keep my eye on our planning strategy. So when Jake arrived, I gave him a hug and a kiss as if everything was fine. On the surface, everything was fine. It was easy for me to ignore his tardiness because feeling connected was more important to me. In hindsight, I could see how sharing my truth would have been the thing that would have strengthened our connection; however, in the moment I was nervous about going to this party together and I wanted to move forward with our planning.

"Dinner is ready," I said as I walked over to the table where I had already served our meal.

"Why did you go to all of this trouble?!?" Jake raised his voice when he realized that I had put hours of effort into our dinner.

"I told you that I wanted to make us a nice dinner so we could talk about how we want to be together tonight."

"But we're going to a party!" he yelled. "I didn't know you were doing all of this."

"It's okay. I'm not mad," I tried to calm him down. "Let's just eat."

He became quiet, his face clouded by anger.

"I don't know why I make things so hard on myself. I was trying to figure out what to wear, and I'm so bad at getting out of the house."

"It's fine. Let's eat and get going to the party."

"It's not fine, Harmony!" he yelled. "You went to all of this trouble and I wasn't here!"

"I'm not mad, and I don't understand why you are. I made us dinner. Let's eat and talk about our plan."

With growing anger, Jake sat at my kitchen table quietly, refusing my touch or Pollyanna reassurances that everything was okay. After several minutes of loud silence, I got up and changed out of my dress and put on my sweat pants.

I came back downstairs decidedly staying home, hoping he would go to the party without me.

"Are you trying to start a fight? Do you want this?" he asked me in a tone that intimidated me.

"I just wanted to have dinner with you. If you feel bad that you were late, then own that. Don't blame me for this fight." I wasn't fighting. I was trying to be okay with everything. I wanted to be okay with his lateness and his anger, but I wasn't okay with his blame.

"I think I'm hungry. I haven't eaten all day," Jake said. "I'm a bear when I don't eat."

He started eating and I put my dinner away, not eating a bite. I sat at the table with him, watching myself close down.

Before in my life, I had a blind spot in my awareness preventing me from seeing other people's distortions. This was in large part because I couldn't see my own. However, because I had been working on myself and my relationships with men over the past few years, I had more awareness about my own distortion and more conscious choice about how I wanted to be with Jake. Although my conditioning still caused me to try to keep our relationship harmonious, I wasn't willing to passively receive his projections as truth about me.

Once he apologized for the way he behaved, I took a deep breath, put my dress back on, and we drove to the party. On our way to the Integral Center, we agreed that we would stay together, not dance with anybody else, and if at any moment one of us felt jealous or insecure we would give a hand signal and we would drop what we were doing and come back into connection.

As we circulated throughout the building, we talked with many of our friends and evaded many past romantic interests. It seemed like around every corner there was someone he or I had dated. And at each turn, I became more triggered and full of fear. I didn't want Jake to be jealous of the many men who wanted my attention, and I was afraid of hurting my male friends' feelings, too. I genuinely liked these men as friends, and I was afraid that they would be confused and hurt that I was ignoring them.

Jake and I found a small room with a DJ where we didn't know anybody. We both agreed that this was safe a place to hang out for a while. We danced together, enjoying our escape from the web of exes until Jake's ex-girlfriend walked in. The moment I saw her, I looked over at Jake.

Once he noticed her, he asked, "Do you want to leave?"

I wasn't sure that I wanted to leave, so I stood there silently.

Jake grabbed my hand and pulled me out of the room. "Let's get out of here. We can sit in my car and get centered."

When we got to the car, we were both laughing at how crazy that was for us.

"We're not going back in there," Jake said. "That was too much, too soon."

As we drove home, I noticed a growing trigger of disdain about his ex. I had never thought much about the women Jake dated because I didn't think we would ever be together. As we navigated this new territory of monogamy, I was repulsed by his choice in past lovers. My mind kept looping with thoughts about how immature his ex was and how she seemed like a Barbie doll. This trigger was coming from the place in me that was adamantly against being controlled like an object by Jake. I was projecting my trigger onto his ex, but the underlying unconscious thought was about overcoming my own self-betrayal and self-objectification.

All night long I went on and on about how I didn't like his last relationship, and all night long he defended it. He told me that he wouldn't have been ready for me had he not been with her. But for me, that was the problem: seeing her reminded me that he was not ready for the level of relationship that I wanted. He wanted me to play small for him, and I reluctantly obliged. Disgusted with myself that I was trying to be a perfect object for him, I was angered by seeing his ex and realizing that she was a reflection of my shadow that I didn't want to see or claim.

That night we barely slept, and the next day we were completely worn out emotionally and physically.

"I want to stay home tonight," I said. We had plans to go to another New Year's Eve party at a friend's house, but I ached deeply in my soul. This was all too much for me.

"I want you to go. Get loved on by our friends. I'll come a little later."

"Okay," I said without resistance.

He seemed happy that I agreed to do what he said without question, and my sense was he would have liked this to be the status quo.

I went to the party alone, and as I talked with my friends I anxiously awaited his arrival.

"I don't think this is going to last," I said to my friend Julie. Since meeting at Alethia, Julie had moved to Colorado and we developed a deep and beautiful friendship. "This is the hardest relationship. I feel like I'm being strangled all of the time, like I can't breathe."

"I think you two just need to get through this," she said. "You just need to see it through. It's been building for so long. It just needs to run its course."

"I think you're right. I just don't know how much more of this I can take."

A moment later, Jake walked in and Julie said, "There's your boyfriend."

Our eyes met and I excitedly walked over to him and hugged him.

"I'm glad you told me to come," I said. "It feels good to be with friends."

We kissed, then walked over to the couch to snuggle. Several people gathered around us asking us about our relationship.

"We fight all of the time," I confessed.

"Oh, Mike and I did that, too. For the first six months we fought the whole time. Now I can see that we were just working through things that most couples just ignore."

This is different, I thought to myself. *I can't imagine Jake transforming into someone I want to be with. He makes everything so hard.*

As we were sitting on the couch snuggling, Joel walked in. I felt my whole body tense with fear. Scared that I wouldn't have solid enough boundaries with Joel to satisfy Jake's jealousies, I froze, not knowing how to behave. From my place on the couch next to Jake, I casually said, "Hello."

A few minutes later, Jake went to the bathroom and Joel opened his arms to give me a hug. He whispered in my ear, "Come give me some of that sweet lovin'." Trying to have clear boundaries and to please Jake, I put my hands on Joel's stomach to stop him, and said "No."

"Are you ready to go, Harmony?" Jake asked when he returned from the bathroom.

"You just got here. I thought we could stay a bit longer."

"I'm ready to go."

I was confused but grabbed my things and said goodbye to our friends.

"What's happening?" I asked when we got to the car.

"I'm too triggered to talk about it."

"Please tell me. I want to know what's happening."

"Will you please respect me and my 'No.' I'm too triggered to talk."

On the quiet drive home I wanted to tell him about Joel but he didn't want me to speak. After fifteen minutes of loud silence, anxiety and insecurity permeated my system spread by my fear of this unknown trigger. When we got to his house, he asked me if I could get his world without personalizing what was happening for him. Knowing that I have the capacity to stay curious about other people and see them clearly, I believed that I would be able to gain understanding about where he was coming from without making it about me.

"Yes, of course," I replied to his request.

"I was in the bathroom thinking about how silly it was that you didn't even hug Joel. I wanted to come out of the bathroom and tell you that you should give him a hug. But when I came out you were hugging him."

"I know. I wanted to come tell you. It seemed so sneaky the way he waited until you were in the bathroom. He whispered in my ear and I told him 'no' and put my hands up. I thought you'd be proud of me for setting a boundary."

"I thought you were going to get my world. Did you even hear what I said?" Jake asked, clearly annoyed and triggered.

"Yes. I wanted to tell you this for so long. I thought this information would help."

"I don't need you to try to make this better for me! I need to know you heard what I said!"

"Okay. It sounds like you thought it was silly that I didn't give Joel a hug, and you wanted to tell me that I should. But when you came out of the bathroom I was hugging him."

"No! That's not what I said."

"Okay. What did I miss?"

"Do you need me to say it again? You're not even listening to me!"

"I feel scared and unsure of what to do. I thought I heard what you said."

"Now you're making it all about you! You were supposed to be getting my world!"

"It seems like I can't say anything right. I'm right here and I'm trying and I care. I want to know."

"It's too late. You should go."

Deep shame for being not enough caused me to energetically collapse. Unconsciously believing I was responsible for Jake's pain, I personalized his trigger about my apparent inadequacies to be the way he thought he needed me to be. There was a very particular way Jake wanted me to behave, speak, and be with him. He thought that if I did these things he would feel safe in our connection. I believed it to a degree, too. I thought that I should be what he wanted because he was an image of my sister and this wound was triggered in our connection. But it was never enough. There were always more triggers that caused him to demand that I contort and change and manage myself for his sense of security and stability.

I felt tension around my throat, as if I were being strangled. Our relationship was strenuous at best, and I had to remind myself daily that I was choosing to be with him, that I could end the context at any moment. With this awareness, I also knew that I had choice about how I wanted to show up. Without being attached to having this be a lifelong partnership, I felt free to choose something different, to not follow the impulse to contort myself to try to be what he thought he needed me to be.

A few days later, Jake came over to watch a movie at my house. We had been fighting nonstop, and this was our effort at reconnection. We agreed to keep the mood light and to not process anything, but when Jake walked in he seemed stoic and brooding. He barely spoke to me and kept looking at his phone. I kept trying to ignore his cold, stern presence and stay connected to the levity I felt inside myself as I made popcorn and tea.

"Sit here so I can rub your shoulders," Jake said as I walked into the living room. His tone sounded more like a demand than an invitation, so I didn't feel like being close to him.

"I prefer to sit in this chair for now. I'll come over in a little bit."

Jake didn't respond and we started watching the movie. After about twenty minutes, I said "I'm available for touch now if you still want to rub my shoulders."

"You can touch me if you want," he said in a gruff tone.

"Okay. Do you want to sit on the ground?" I asked, pointing to the place he had wanted me to sit.

"No. Over here," he said as he moved the corner of my L-shaped sofa.

His muscles seemed tense and his face appeared angry. I moved next to him but couldn't massage him from the position I was in, so I rested my hand on his arm in an awkward position.

"Do you want touch?" I asked.

"I said I did, Harmony! If I didn't want it I would have said 'No!'" he exclaimed.

"I'm having a hard time reaching you. Can you move down a bit?" I asked, trying to keep connection.

"No. If you want to touch me you have to touch me like this."

"I'm done with this," I said. "I am trying everything I can to keep connection with you and you seem to be trying everything you can to challenge our connection."

"What do you think it's like to be me right now?" he asked.

"You want me to get your world? Okay, you seem angry that I didn't want your touch, and now you seem to want touch while staying closed off to me."

"No, that's not it! Try again!" he yelled.

"I don't know what's happening with you, but I feel scared and confused and I'm starting to get angry."

"Now it's all about you again."

"I am a 'no' to this, Jake. I am tired of you telling me what to say or how to get your world or that what I'm doing is wrong. I will not do this with you."

"You don't even care about me. Listen to you. You only care about yourself. You're so selfish!"

"I am a 'no' to this," I said more firmly.

"If I leave now I am never coming back. I mean it, Harmony."

"I understand that and I'm totally okay with that. I am not willing to participate in this dynamic with you anymore. I am done."

"You agreed to three months! You can't end this now!"

"I did not agree to be treated this way. I am a 'no,'" I said.

Jake got up and stood by my front door for several minutes. Eventually I got up and walked over to him.

"I'm sorry," he said. "I don't know how to do this with you. I love you so much. I am so sorry. Can we have a proper goodbye?"

We hugged and cried as we stood in my doorway talking about why this relationship doesn't work.

"Being with you takes all of my focus off of work, kids, fitness, and self-care. This is too much for me. This dynamic is painful for me," I said.

"I hope you find a really solid man who can meet you."

When he said this, I burst into tears. Each time I have broken up with someone in the past, they have told me that I'd never find another man who loved me as much as them. I felt deeply loved by Jake when he expressed wanting more for me than he could give.

"Everyone in the community says we go together like peanut butter and jelly. We seem more like oil and vinegar to me," I said.

"I think we're amazing together," Jake said. "You are too much for me, and I think I'm too much for you. But I never knew that a woman could meet me in the way you do. Your strength has me seeing my shadow more clearly and I'm so grateful for that."

"I feel like I'm being strangled in our relationship."

"I feel like I can breathe. Like you give me a reason to live," he said.

After a beautiful goodbye, Jake left and I felt freedom return to my life. It was as if a dark cloud had been lifted. Saying "No" to this dynamic with Jake allowed me to trust myself. For the first time in my life, I protected myself and in that self-protection my energetic system softened.

Trying to stay in connection with someone who is volatile, controlling, and explosive is a trauma response. It's easy to blame the other person for not being kind or gentle, but when we don't set a boundary we are not being kind and gentle to ourselves. We trust ourselves more when we set boundaries with people who treat us poorly. The young ones within us who were traumatized and conditioned to enable other people's meanness are given the safety and protection they always needed. This allows us to soften in our energetic systems, and it allows us to trust ourselves to open to real love and real intimacy.

Understanding that people act out in anger and violence because they're suffering can cause us to be compassionate for others even at the cost of our own well-being. However, setting solid boundaries in such interactions is the kindest thing we can do for ourselves and for others, who are able to see themselves more clearly when we don't absorb their projections. A boundary can be the most honoring thing for all people involved.

CONSCIOUS CHOICE

A few weeks after we broke up, Jake texted me and asked to meet for coffee. Hopeful that I would have my dear friend back in my life, I eagerly agreed.

We met at The Laughing Goat on Pearl Street, and we caught up on the past two weeks. Easily dropping back into our connection, I forgot about all of the turmoil I had experienced being with him. We gazed into each other's eyes, and I felt my heart and my love for him.

"It feels so good to spend time with you," I said.

"I've missed you, Harmony," he shared.

"I can't believe how challenging it was. We love each other. I don't understand why it was so hard to be together."

"Maybe we don't need to understand that right now," he said as he placed his arms around me.

Taking a few deep, regulating breaths, I surrendered into his arms. I felt like I was home with him, but what I couldn't see was that he was a reflection of the dysfunctional home I grew up in. His dismissive and self-absorbed nature was representing a home I didn't want to go back to even though it was familiar. Being with him was tugging on the wounded young one in me who wanted to earn love and approval by being perfect. I needed to learn how to take care of my inner 5-month-old and 4-year-old and let them know that they were important to me and that I'd always love them no matter what.

"Do you want to come over and watch a movie tonight?" he invited.

"Yes!" I said eagerly.

Jake had a wisdom and openness about him that was so seductive and sexy to me. Being with him after having some space, I could feel that all of my attraction to him was present again and I wanted to be as close to him as possible. Believing that he would treat me differently because of the previous boundary I set, I willingly opened up to him without any hesitation.

When I arrived at his apartment later that same day, he had a big smile on his face and he was visibly happy that I was there. We hugged in his doorway as I stood on my toes to kiss him.

Jake walked over to the living room to put on a movie. As he searched for a movie on Netflix, he was disappointed that the one he wanted to watch with me wasn't featured.

"Let's just snuggle," I said as grabbed his hand and pulled him into his room.

"You want to snuggle? I thought we were going to watch a movie."

"I want to feel you close to me," I said.

Jake smiled as he lay down in his bed. When he grabbed me to pull me closer, we started kissing passionately. I immediately knew I wanted to have sex with him. We had been managing sexual energy between us for over eighteen months, with the prior month having been extremely thick with sexual tension and desire.

"I want to make love with you," I said.

"I want that, too. I'm ready," he said.

That night, we made love all night long. Looking into each other's eyes, I wept as my heart opened to him over and over again. For the first time in my life, I surrendered in the presence of a man, which caused me to feel more expansive and full. What I couldn't see at the time was that I surrendered with Jake not because of him, but because I trusted myself because I had set a firm boundary. With deep love moving through my body, I had waves of bliss and pleasure and opening come on stronger and stronger over the course of four hours. My whole system felt softer, more expansive, and more aligned with Source. It was transcendent lovemaking with deeper intimacy than I ever knew was possible.

Each time I cried, Jake held me close and said, "I'm right here, and I love you. I love you so much. I'm right here."

I'd look into his sweet brown eyes and feel completely held and loved, which made me cry more and more.

As we made love, Jake became more solid in himself. He described feeling a solid rod down the center of his body. Stronger, more tree-like, he held me in his masculine power while I expanded and opened in my soft feminine.

"I am so in love with you," I said.

"This is the intimacy I've always wanted," Jake said. "You are more beautiful than anything I have ever seen. Your openness and vulnerability are so incredibly amazing."

At 3 AM, I drove home to get some sleep before my 9 AM client. That entire morning, the ecstasy that I had felt the night before was still pulsating through my body, and I continued to walk around in a state of bliss for the next seven days.

Enjoying one another, following our desire, and being in our love together felt delightful. There was an ease in our connection for the first time, and I thought that having sex was the element missing from our prior attempt at being together.

"It seems like we needed to get the tension out sexually," I joked.

"I think so, too," Jake agreed.

We started working together and planning for our future together. Jake didn't spend time with my children, but we started talking about what that might be like and when that would happen. Jake would frequently arrive at my house carrying several bouquets of flowers and my favorite chocolate. He put tremendous effort into our connection, and I reserved every spare moment I had without children or clients to being with him.

The fighting came on slowly, and we were able to navigate it more quickly and easefully at first. I started noticing a pattern where Jake seemed to only be able to hold it together for two or three days before blowing up in a fit of explosive anger. His emotional maturity was reminiscent of a 2-year-old throwing a tantrum, which surprised me given how his emotional capacity seemed so great when we were friends.

Since his career wasn't thriving, Jake put all of his attention onto me. He seemed obsessed with me, as if his thick, dark, twisted energetic tentacles were wrapped around my soul, trying to suck me dry of my joy and vitality so he could feel okay. With his intense rage and lack of professional ambition, Jake made my ex-husband Jason look like a knight in shining armor.

I watched myself trying to keep connection with him, feeling my frightened young one in her trauma response attempting to make everything better so he wouldn't leave me. I was perpetually walking on eggshells to try to keep balance in the relationship. I wanted to appease his suffering so I tried to be perfect for him. This was my unconscious attempt at trying to change him, which came from my disowned desire and subversive control. This pattern was causing me to feel small and came from a belief that his experience was more significant than mine.

In this dynamic, Jake became the "bad guy" who didn't treat me the way I want to be treated, and I became the "crazy woman" who didn't understand what he was needing. His unhealthy masculine was angry and domineering, and my unhealthy feminine was collapsed around my power—like two puzzle pieces that fit together perfectly. Neither of us was good or bad—we were simply meeting from our wounds, not our wholeness. Playing out old trauma with one another, neither of us felt loved and safe in our relationship.

I eventually realized that true harmony is expansive enough to make room to unify darkness and light, to welcome conflict and to hold both "Good" and "Evil." Where before I wanted conflict and darkness to go away, during this relationship I was able to see that the old paradigm of "me against him" or "good vs. bad" or "men against women" was keeping us at war, just as it keeps the world at war. I started to shift to the new paradigm of "you are just another me," where I stopped otherizing him and built the capacity to see him in his suffering. Knowing that the way I treated him was quite literally the way I treated myself, I started respecting his process with dignity and giving him space to come through it on his own. No longer personalizing his pain, I knew I wasn't responsible for fixing it or making it go away. This empowered me with conscious choice about how I wanted to be with him.

In relationships, it's common to look at our partner as our point of reference. When we lean on our partner for security and safety, we leave our alignment with Source. When we are out of alignment with the core of our being, it is nearly impossible to meet our relationship with clarity, agency, and autonomy. The work is about staying in ourselves. Staying in our connection with Source. Standing in our sovereignty as whole, integrated human beings.

Jake and I broke up and came back together a few more times. Each time that we broke up, I felt relieved and at peace. Happiness and joy returned to my life. It was as if he were an energetic vampire and having him gone made it so I could breathe again. Then we would meet to talk or run into each other in the community and he would express how he still wanted to be with me. I would become seduced by his sexy vulnerability and masculinity. My young one wanted him to want me, so I'd follow the impulse of my wound once again.

"There's something here, Harmony," he said one afternoon. "And I'm not ready to walk away. I want to be with you."

Hearing this, I felt fear come up in my body. I felt an armor of self-protection surround my heart. "So much has happened. I can't just jump back into a relationship with you," I replied.

Seeing him want me, feeling the intensity of his desire for connection with me, I ignored my impulse to protect myself. Every time, the first few days were blissful, and then his anger, fear, defensiveness, and volatility would be ignited and he'd project it all onto me again. Criticizing me and blaming me for his suffering, he was antagonistic at every turn. At first my young one would do anything to keep connection, but I would come back to myself more quickly as I began to see the pattern more clearly.

"I'm on my way." I texted one day when we had plans to watch a movie. "I'm feeling soft and sweet. Are you open to snuggling or soaking in the hot tub before we watch a movie?" I asked.

I had just left an intense session with an energy healer, and I was feeling more like my True Self than I had since Jake and I got back together. In the session, I had worked on transforming the pattern of how I make myself small, wanting to claim my power and my voice. It was a powerful session and I was feeling more aligned with essence. Even still, before I sent this text, I had a feeling it would set Jake off, so I almost didn't send it. Wanting a partnership where I feel free to ask for what I want (especially snuggles), I chose to send the text and let him decide how he wanted to respond. Prior to this day, Jake had yelled at me numerous times for taking choices away from him when I hid my desire, so this simple text seemed like a step in the right direction for us.

"I'm open to discussing options. I'm feeling protective of my desires," he replied.

I felt fear jolt through my body when I read this. I sensed he was triggered, but I was still hopeful he might be sensible and say "Yes, I'd love to snuggle before we watch a movie!" Or "No, I'm not available for that right now. I really just want to zone out."

When I arrived at his house I saw flowers and chocolates awaiting me on the table. It sounded like Jake was in the shower so I went to peek in and say hello.

"Hi, sweetheart," I said with a smile, happy to see the flowers and excited to give him a hug.

"Get out! I'll be done in a minute." Jake seemed grumpy, and I felt unwanted and pushed out of the house altogether.

I sat in the living room on the sofa, still luxuriating in the goodness I felt from my energy session. Jake came in and started putting his shoes on.

"Will you walk with me around the lake?" he asked in a gruff and intimidating tone.

"I'm feeling really soft and slow right now. I don't feel like going for a walk."

"Will you just walk with me, Harmony? This is what I need to work through this."

"Work through what? Are you mad at me for asking to snuggle?"

"I'm not available for anything until we walk. Walk with me!" he demanded.

"Do you want me here? It seems like you don't want to be near me at all."

"Are you listening to me? Fine, I'm going for a walk."

He started to walk out the door and I grabbed my purse so I could go home. "I think it's best I go home. I just want to take a bath and snuggle up."

"You are so controlling! I know I'm being controlling here, but you are so controlling!"

"It sounds like you want me to do what you want."

"Yes! I want to know that what I want matters! You are so selfish. You only care about yourself. This is all about you. What about me? What about what I want?"

"It sounds like I'm a horrible partner," I reflected to him in the midst of his tirade. I was feeling surprisingly neutral to his volatility.

"What? No. That's not what I'm saying," he seemed surprised by my attempt to get his world rather than defend myself.

"No, really, if you are hurting that badly in this relationship with me, it sounds like you would be better off without me."

"That's not what I'm saying! Can't you just hear me? You don't even see me. You don't get me at all!"

"And that seems really painful for you, to not be gotten by me."

As he became more volatile, I stayed regulated and autonomous. My wound was not triggered by his wound's expression, and in that state I felt compassion for his tantrum but uninterested in trying to be what he thought he needed me to be. I was being myself, soft and snuggly, and he was being himself, triggered and demanding. Totally individuated from him, I did not match his frequency. My whole system knew that he didn't own me, that I didn't need to be an object for him, and that I was important. And from this place where I was no longer willing to play this game with him, he started spiraling.

After he yelled at me for several more minutes, I said, "Since you're still standing here, I'm imagining that you really want to feel connected to me."

"Yes! That's all I want!"

"I'm not available for this type of connection. I'm feeling soft and snuggly. I do not want to fight with you."

"I don't want to fight either! I want to be there for you. That's why I want to take the walk. So I can be there for you."

It seemed that Jake felt loved by me during the times I tried to keep connection with him when he was volatile because that's what his scared and wounded young one within wanted. When I stopped colluding in that, Jake was able to see his controlling, narcissistic behavior more clearly. Children are inherently narcissistic. It's an important developmental milestone for children to know that they're important and that the people around them care about what they need. When that isn't provided in a healthy, boundaried way, a child can get stuck thinking they don't matter. The result is either codependency (like me) or narcissism (like Jake). My codependency may have had me looking like the "good" one in a relationship, but both tactics were unhealthy and expressions of our wounds.

Knowing that I was not my attachment wound, I no longer felt responsibility to fix or heal Jake's wounded parts. I knew that what I wanted mattered, that feeling soft and snuggly was okay. More importantly, I knew that I could land on my own two feet when he wasn't there when I reached out for him. My inner 5-month-old felt loved and held by me, knowing that I was there for her when she wanted to snuggle, that I cared about what she needed. No longer projecting my old experience of my dad onto Jake, I felt more whole, more integrated, and more aligned with Source as I navigated this encounter.

I realized that I didn't trust Jake with my kids, just like I didn't trust my sister to have a relationship with them. Jake wasn't capable of being loving and kind to the young one in me for any consistent amount of time, and I knew that he wasn't a safe person to have in my children's lives in any close capacity. Had I chosen him, I would have been repeating the patterns that I played out with Jason, and I was done with that antiquated dynamic.

When my projections were the veil of illusion that guided my interactions, I attempted to rewrite the past with outdated ways of engaging with others. As I continued to grow and evolve, I was able to meet Jake from my mature self and recognize that this relationship wasn't about me being different for him or him being different for me. This relationship was a crucible of deep personal growth from which I emerged more aligned with the core of my being.

Jake was a Type 6 on the Enneagram, which is the most fearful type. Type 6 individuals want security, support, and guidance from their relationships in an attempt to soothe the constant underlying fear that is always there within them. They often test their partners to see if they will stay with them when they have angry outbursts. They are the most tender and mean type, with a polarity in their personality that can be extremely confusing for their partners. Jake had been extremely hurt by those who were supposed to love him and keep him safe, which had him projecting his fear of intimacy and desire for safety onto me. I could see his pain and wounding, but with my diligent attempts to help make him feel better, my Type 2 shaping colluded with Jake's Type 6 anxiety. I worked hard to fit into a box small enough for him to feel safe, trying to be perfect. This was a task that had no end in sight, and at my core I knew that it was not my job to do that for him. I was too full of life to kill parts of myself and be boxed in by fear. My True Self was too expansive and vast to play small for some guy—even when I loved that guy dearly.

The philosophy of the Enneagram framework is that each type has different personality expressions based on level of health. Characteristics of each type have certain collusion patterns; however, the level of health of each person in a relationship is more important than finding the right type to match your type. Jake's level of health was low, and it triggered in me the exact level of old pain that I was ready to heal. Had I been at a lower level of health, I would have continued to try to appease him ad nauseam. However, since I was committed to my own growth and evolution every step of the way— where my focus was on who I wanted to become, rather than how I could keep him as my person forever—I became more aligned with my True Self for having been in this relationship.

With beautiful moments and painful moments, being with Jake was a great gift of learning the difference between real love and the game of love. The game of love is what we play when we meet our partners from our conditioned self, using old patterns to try to get the love we think we're lacking. Real love is when we align with the Source of love and embody this energy, empowered with conscious choice about how we want to engage in relationships.

Real love never hurts another or violates boundaries. Real love never tries to manipulate or control another, and it never contorts or changes to try to fit what's happening. Real love feels safe and doesn't come from fear. It's endlessly abundant and feels like a welcoming cloud of pure, soft energy. Real love is inclusive, so loving myself is an important part of the full experience. When I embody love, I don't quiet myself, hide my pain, or allow others to mistreat me. I know that I am important and I set clear boundaries with people who treat me in a way that is not loving when I embody real love.

Honoring myself, I told Jake that I wasn't okay with the way he treated me and that I didn't want to be with him. He was surprised and felt blindsided hearing this; he had thought we were doing well. I was in disbelief that I had behaved in a way that communicated to him that I was okay with the way he treated me. This highlighted for me the way I was so skilled at making things look good even when they weren't. Because our connection was deep and profound, ending the relationship was extremely painful. I lost my best friend, the best lover I'd ever had, the only man who had ever met me in the depth of my emotional range, and the person who I wanted to partner with professionally. Even with all of that goodness and beauty, I was not available to be the punching bag for his projections of his mother-wound.

Similar to the first time I ended things with Jake, I went home alone but I went home with my dignity. If I were to choose Jake, I would be choosing from my wound, not my wholeness. Knowing that I am so much bigger than my conditioned self and old trauma, I aligned with my essence and became ready to love from my wholeness. My trauma was no longer guiding my actions in relationship to his irrational, explosive rage. My True Self was the guide and my wholeness was the vessel.

This was the most successful relationship I had ever had. It wasn't healthy. It was not a happily ever after story. And it was not the fantasy relationship my mind had imagined. As a lifelong learner I measure success by how much I learn and grow from life's experiences. I garnered tremendous learning and growth from this relationship, and I navigated this connection in a new and empowered way. Never looping in old patterns too long, I continually tried something different. I tried the truer, more loving thing until that thing was to say goodbye.

LESSONS LEARNED

In the spiritual community, people have told me that it was my karma to learn these lessons about myself with men. I have been told that I had a sacred contract with them, and all I had to do was get through the experiences and my contract would be complete.

In the psychology community, I have been told that I was codependent and needed to go to Al-Anon. I have been called an enabler to abusive behavior, and I am seen as the victim in this scenario. Although I don't see myself as a victim, I think both theories hold some truth: I have serious karma with men and I have codependent tendencies.

I've had several past life memories of most of the men I've had challenging relationships with. I remember being a sex slave, a Holocaust fatality, an indigenous slave, a witch, and a child prostitute in some of my lives. This pattern of overcoming the oppression of toxic masculinity has been one I've tried to overcome for centuries.

Aside from past lives and codependent tendencies, the thing that I look at is how I became identified with my conditioned self. Before my experiences of this lifetime, I was unified with Source. Pivotal experiences along the way conditioned me to believe that I was separate from Source. In that fragmentation, I created misbeliefs about who I was: that it was my responsibility to make other people happy; that I needed to quiet my dissonance or discontent; that I had to be okay with scraps of love; that it was vital for me to quickly abandon my preferences for what other people want; that I had to be manipulative to earn love; and that I had to keep giving and working to make things okay even when they're not.

When my identity was wrapped up in my conditioned self, I felt powerless and insignificant. The work here wasn't about creating happier thoughts or a healthier conditioned self; the work here was about cultivating an identity with the truest version of myself. When I know that who I really am is vast, wise, and divinely powerful, I embody my essence in a way that is unwavering.

The outer world is a holographic expression of our inner world, which is why relationships are such potent teachers. If I reflect my wound out into the world, believing that my fragmentation and wounds are real, then I see others as a reflection of my pain. Any unhealed part in me is reflected by those closest to me. When I cultivate an inner crystalline palace of health and self-love, then I reflect that out into the world and the people in my life reflect that back to me. It's not about bypassing the wounds; it's about inviting them back into the vast, sparkling ocean of wholeness. The more we all cultivate this inner health and beauty, the more we see the entire world around us come back to a state of full health and restoration.

17
EMERGENT BEING

"Step into the fire of self-discovery. The fire will not burn you, it will only burn what you are not."—Mooji

DIFFERENTIATING FROM PAIN

Having experienced such early trauma, I spent much of my life clinging to my pain-body, believing that the pain was me, that I was it, that life and love were painful. I was experiencing all aspects of my life through the lens of my wound, which led me to repeat outdated patterns and reinforce false beliefs. As I gathered more and more evidence that life and love were painful, I became doubtful that I would ever be happy.

As a roadmap for how to navigate the world, I carried my stack of evidence that I was unworthy of love, that being in a body was painful, and that my needs didn't matter. These misbeliefs informed my thoughts about myself and others, and as long as I was identified with my pain I kept looping through that old script. Even though that script was irrelevant to the current circumstances of my life, I couldn't see beyond the hardened casing of my old wounds.

Feeling powerless to create any lasting or satisfying change, my interactions with the world were coming from my conditioned self. With a character structure firmly in place, my accommodating personality caused me to abandon myself. Being angry at others for not giving me the thing that I was unable to give myself meant that all of my relationships were based on a game where love was a commodity.

When I started becoming curious about who I would be in the world if I didn't abide by the rules of my character structure or follow the path of my outdated roadmap, my life started to change. By doing the different thing from what my conditioning wanted me to do, I started differentiating from my attachment wounds and taking my power back from the old stories. The universe quickly started showing me that when I don't follow the impulse of my conditioning, beautiful things happen. Life opened up and abundant goodness started coming my way once I stopped matching the frequency of my old wounds.

When we wrap our sense of self in experiences from the past, we disempower ourselves by meeting the world from our distortion. When we feel small and insignificant, our relationship with ourselves, our loved ones, and the world suffers. We come at life in so many different ways, but everything seems effortful and we feel impotent to ignite the goodness we long for. It can be hard to see the wounds we are identified with because they become so much a part of the lens that we see the world through. Our wounds become part of the water that we swim in, and it can be challenging to even see that there is a different option for us.

The work of aligning with the core of our being in the presence of our pain can allow us to shift our identity to our powerful, expansive True Self almost immediately. Much of the work I did in breathwork was practicing being the witness of my pain-body without clinging to it. This potent practice allowed me to move the old trauma out. Since I wasn't clinging to my pain, it moved more easily. In its place I filled my energetic body with new breath, new life, and new vibrancy. This gave me room to update my psyche with a new story of what it's like to be me as a divine being and to see the world through fresh eyes.

Witnessing our wounds allows us to easefully differentiate from them. Our relationship to our wounds shifts, and we give them more space as the witness. This spaciousness allows us to feel powerful and expansive in the presence of our pain. Pain is like icicles within the ocean of the energetic body. Inviting these frozen energy blocks back into the vast and sparkling wholeness of the energetic body brings more fullness and life to the entire system. The result is more fluidity in the physical body, emotional body, energetic body, and mental body. Ease and flow guide us through life from this place, as the attention that's been used to resist the pain is freed up to align with Source.

When I was identified with my wounds, I oriented toward men who were identified with their wounds. Because the world is like a hologram and the universe brings us partners who embody the thing that we have disowned and cannot see within ourselves, my partners reflected my pain.

Now identified with my divinity—my wholeness, my bigness, my power, and my sovereignty—I orient toward men who reflect that. Because I evolved into the wise, mature woman who speaks her truth and claims her power, I can now recognize integrated men who embody the True Self as a protector and a king. I can see my sparkly spirit reflected in the men in my life, and from the depths of my soul, I now know that I am worthy of such a man. I now know that I am enough because I embody the love that I used to long for.

In the past, my weak boundaries merged with others to achieve connection. My attachment wounds had me matching the frequency of others and lowering my vibration. When my vibration is low, I am codependent and try to make everything better. From the outside, it looks as if the people in my life have the lowest level of health, but if I believe that, I keep myself the victim. I am now clear on what it feels like to be me: my values, my beliefs, my emotions, and my energetic vibration. And I can now see others clearly, without the lens of my projections. From this place, I can do the dance of relationship without entanglement convoluting our connection. I can care for others without leaving myself and I can set boundaries with them when appropriate. I stay individuated from my intimate partners, which is in service of real connection.

In my daily life, I attend a weekly authentic relating practice group where I continue to build the muscle of speaking my truth with conviction. This reminds the younger versions of me that I am important and my voice matters. Beyond projections, I know I'm speaking my truth when my words are about me and I'm succinctly giving voice to a part of my experience that is less obvious. My stories about others aren't my truest truth. My observations about relational dynamics are not my vulnerable reveal. My explanation about what's happening for me is a defense, not my truth. My truth lives in the present moment, usually is signified by a physical sensation (like pleasure, tightness, softness, and so on). Then the context I reveal about that sensation or feeling are in line with my truth—as long as my words are about me. Revealing is a powerful way to take our power back from our distortion.

Learning to give voice to our inner world with ownership and clarity invites us to differentiate from the wounds of our conditioning and cultivate real intimacy. Our conditioned self tells us to speak from a distorted place. Not wanting to offend someone or disrupt connection, we often hide our truest truth. But when we hide our truth for someone else, our interactions with them are distorted. There's an artistry to learning how to speak our truth with integrity, and we might be messy when we first try. But, being messy is more desirable than being distorted, and we need a training ground to practice.

In the authentic relating practice groups that I attend, I practice saying things that I'd otherwise censor, like my dissonant perspective or aversion to another person. Each time I do this, I feel more mature, integrated, and aligned for having practiced staying in myself in relationship with others. Another gift of these groups is that I witness men vulnerably give voice to their inner world, own their desires, and stay in touch with their compassionate heart. Each time I witness a man hold compassionate space for a woman who is in emotional pain or sit in awe of a woman owning her power, my old story about men becomes ever more outdated.

I love men, and I want to feel safe with them. I don't want to project my old stories onto them just as I don't want them to project their old stories onto me. Shifting these old stories is a collective effort, and each time we see one another as a mystery to get acquainted with rather than an image from our past, we take our power back from our conditioning and trauma.

Trusting ourselves to own our truth, we can soften into vulnerability. Knowing that we will land on our own two feet if the people in our lives are unable to meet us in our tenderness or our power, we differentiate from our attachment wounds. The very first step is to become clear on the mystery of our own way of being. We rarely see ourselves as clearly as we think we do, and this keeps us identified with the very patterns we want to separate from.

ALIGNING WITH SOURCE

Previously, I wanted to find "my person" and keep him in my life forever. With this as my motive, I would hide parts of myself to try to keep him happy so I could keep connection. I was aligning with my conditioning and trauma, and I was making men Source while simultaneously playing "God" as I tried to control various aspects of life. This painful pattern had to come to an end, and I needed to learn how to live in integrity with the core of my being.

Meditation was integral in learning how to attune to my connection with the Source that beats my heart. In the silence between my thoughts, I was able to drop into the most profound state of oneness. This is the way we train the mind to attend to our expansive self and cultivate an identity with this vast openness. No longer contracted around our pain, we can easily surrender to Source when we access our inner expansion. This is where true power rests.

Giving words to my intention to live from Source was also essential in cultivating my alignment. Simply saying aloud "Please guide my actions and make clear the way" began a wonderful practice of surrender. Asking my higher self to hold hands with Source as I moved through the day, my objective was to stay aligned with the core of my being. Anchoring this alignment down to the core of the earth, I learned how to embody the True Self at every turn. Using the world as a playground for my spiritual development, I kept coming back to my home base over and over again until it became natural to meet the world from my alignment.

Standing ever more solid in my sovereignty, I set clear boundaries as I make conscious choices from my higher self. Trusting in the process of life, I allow my relationships to unfold in the way they naturally want to, with no need to control the outcome. Without attachment to being with someone forever, my relationships are given breath and life, which paradoxically nurtures a healthy connection. Love does not hold possession, and any clinging to another person comes from the small self. Love can breathe when we allow it space to grow into the expression it wants, without projections from our wounds or conditioning.

When we are aligned with Source, the deep bliss of sexual intimacy is always available to us. When we feel pleasure with another human being, we mistakenly assign that pleasure to them. But the pleasure is ours, it always has been. Just like our anger is ours, our fear is ours, our sadness is ours, our bliss is ours to own and experience. True pleasure comes when all of our energy systems down the midline of the body are clean, open, and aligned. Continual breath keeps the energy of the bliss moving as we need to be fully in our life urge to experience the full range of pleasure.

Our original state is bliss. We all come from orgasm. When we do the work of healing, we come back to our original state and surrender into the bliss of our orgasms without effort.

Where I once performed for men and didn't care about my own pleasure, I now receive from men and go into my pleasure without shame. My body is mine, and sharing myself with a man is a gift. When I am treated with respect as a divine being, this is when I know I want to let my lover in. I owe him nothing and I do not belong to him, so I can stop anytime I want. I am safer saying "No" than enduring something I am not a "Yes" to experiencing—which is to say that I am safer embodying my True Self than playing small for a man.

When I honor myself in this way, I am able to honor my lover in the deepest way possible. Seeing him in his divine masculine strength, I generously bring him pleasure and willingly allow him to honor me as a goddess.

Embodying the healthy feminine, I nurture the healthy masculine in the world. My old way of manipulation, setting myself up for victimization, and fearing the masculine perpetuated an old story that is no longer relevant. Updating that story and embodying my full health and power, I set boundaries, I engage from my wise, mature self, and I see men beyond the illusion of my projections. This gives us the opportunity to meet one another from our wholeness and cultivate true intimacy. This is an essential component to the healing of the planet, where there is harmony between the masculine and feminine energies of the world. This is part of evolution.

I feel the joy of being in a body when I align with my True Self. I no longer compare my body to others. I no longer criticize my body or shame myself for my body. I no longer overeat or undereat, overexercise or underexercise. I no longer fret over what to wear or whether I'm beautiful. I feel beautiful from the inside, and I radiate that. I move in ways that feel good and bring me deeper into my bliss. I treat my body as a sacred vessel, and I can see my physical self as a radiant gift, giving me the opportunity to be here in this lifetime embodying Source.

We live in a world of illusion when we follow our conditioned self around believing that it's real. In the forefront of the mind, our conditioning creates persistent thoughts, projecting our beliefs about ourselves and the world onto what is happening. When we do this, when we believe the thoughts of our conditioned self, we allow ourselves to get pulled away from that part of us that is truly in alignment with Source. When we live from this small place, the life we create is out of alignment with our highest and best good. We feel disempowered and miserable while we're living from our conditioning.

Knowing the pattern of our conditioning and recognizing that we are so much more than that pattern is the first step in taking our power back from it. Once we recognize this, we can turn toward the young one within and hold her close—we can give ourselves what we've always longed for and stop projecting those unmet needs onto others. This creates an inner world that is integrated and developed. Cultivating a relationship with our essence as who we really are anchors us in our expansive, True Self. This gives us a home base to come back to when we get pulled off-center by the events of our life, no matter how big or small. Our breath keeps us in our body, so using our breath to embody our alignment with Source is imperative in staying centered in our midline.

Learning how to give voice to our truest truth helps us to bring our essence into all areas of life. Speaking from our persona is second nature; it's what we've been doing our whole lives. Learning the language of the True Self allows the essence of our being to impact all of our interactions with the world. Our words are powerful, and when our words distort or hide our truth, our interactions with the world lack integrity. Expanding our capacity to welcome the full range of our being, we hold ourselves in our wholeness. From here, we're able to give voice to our truth in a way that resonates with those around us. This is the gift of vibrating at a higher frequency than our conditioning and trauma. The energy behind our words builds connection and bridges because we no longer come from a place that is divisive and otherizing.

In meeting our pain and darkness and distortion consciously, we become more solid in ourselves while also becoming softer and more expansive. We need every single life experience that we've had in order to come back into alignment with Source. It's not about being perfect and having the perfect life; it's about embodying the truest version of ourselves at each step of the journey of continual evolution and learning. It's about being authentic and real and human. It's about undoing our distortion and learning to live in our wholeness. It's about creating an inner crystalline palace and reflecting that out into the world.

Revealing your essence to the world is an act of bringing more divine energy onto the planet. The world needs this. The world needs you to be in your full expression, aligned with essence and loving from wholeness. Your growth and evolution are in service of planetary restoration. Your inner peace and healing bring peace and healing to the planet. That is how important you are.

EMBODIED WHOLENESS

Awake to my True Self, I surrender to the unfolding of life. Where before I habitually tried to control life to try to find safety, my alignment with Source has me trusting and flowing at every turn. No longer asleep to who I really am, there's no need to play small and believe I'm powerless. Although the tendency to follow the impulse of my conditioned self still arises, I am now more aligned with the core of my being than with those old patterns. From time to time, the young one within me still tries to use old tactics find safety and connection, and I am able to hold this part in love and tenderness as I honor her truth and claim my power. Solidly connected to the essence of my True Self, I know that the misbeliefs of my younger self are outdated and my distortion no longer guides my thoughts and actions.

Because I was raised in a family of healers, I kept trying alternative and holistic therapies to support me in shifting my oppressive and unhealthy patterns. I began to recognize that real medicine and healing always brings us back to our original state of wholeness, undoing the hardness that our humanity has caused in our energetic bodies. In this epiphany, I started to learn how to use conscious awareness, breath, sound, and homeopathy to elevate my vibration and cultivate wholeness within myself. Remembering that my true nature is divinely powerful, I began to heal all of the ways I had been hurt during this lifetime.

Having a system that is inherently whole and healthy, I notice right away when anything mistunes my energetic field. When I follow the impulses of my distortion, my level of health goes down almost immediately. I can feel the twist, the heaviness, and the tightening in my energy, and there is a ripple effect throughout my whole system. If I don't go back to amend and atone the distorted behavior, my system suffers. I can become ill, angry, and resentful, and I feel small when even the slightest thought or behavior is out of alignment with Source.

With this awareness, I am committed to speaking my truest truth to all people who cross my path. By not matching the frequency of those identified with their conditioning, my presence shifts the way they think the system works. Sometimes it seems like hiding truth and putting on a face of happiness is the path of least resistance, but we all pay the price when our interactions with the world are distorted. Looking through the lens of distortion, life is a struggle. We feel disempowered when we live from our distortion and everything is effortful. Seeing the world through the eyes of our wholeness and alignment with Source, everything has an ease about it. Even when life is challenging, that challenge is met with ease. From here, our actions have a completely different impact on the world. Everything we do is life-affirming and in service of the highest good when we're in alignment with Source.

In my alignment with the True Self, I embody my sacred essence and bring this powerful goodness to all areas of my life. When we heal, our life starts to change from the outer circle of our world inward. This means that the way I showed up in my community shifted first. Simple shifts, such as holding a compassionate stance for the grocer who was grumpy, being understanding of the driver who was riding my tail, and contributing to worthy community efforts were the first places I noticed a shift in my interactions with the world. Feeling safer in the world, I engaged in a dance community, was more confident at social gatherings, and stopped judging other peoples' conditioned self.

Then, as I continued to do my work, my friendships with other women began to go deeper. Authenticity, care, and reciprocity characterize my friendships. Surrounded by other healers and goddesses, the sisterhood I feel with the women in my life is solid and genuine. Encouraging one another, holding space for one another, and enjoying the sweet feminine connection of being with other powerful women flow in my friendships.

Next, my work with clients began to thrive. No longer concerned if my clients liked me, I started speaking to the distortion I was seeing, gently nudging people to own their darkness in service of integration and wholeness. Giving voice to what my metaphysical eyes were seeing, I supported my clients in excavating old pain and updating younger parts. The more integrated I became, the more my clients could see themselves clearly in my presence. My metaphysical eyes can see both their wholeness and their distortion, and they are able to see this about themselves, too. Once I embodied my essence, I began to teach my clients how to do the same. Leaving my office feeling integrated, empowered and aligned with Source, the positive impact on their lives occurred almost immediately.

My relationships with my family of origin also began to change. I started setting clear boundaries, no longer willing to be triangulated in dysfunctional patterns or engage in drama. I began to speak my truth more and more with my dad, and he was able to hear me because it came from the truest version of myself. I told him the impact of the fall; I told him the impact of his denial of emotional validity; and I told him the impact of his womanizing. We became closer and more connected with each and every reveal. Still talking on the phone every Sunday morning, the love and sweetness between us is more profound than I could have ever imagined it would become.

My relationship with my children became joyous and beautiful. Once I was able to heal and integrate my attachment wounds, I was able to meet my children in deep ways, loving them unconditionally. With the capacity to make room for their darker emotions, I developed the skills to stay in connection with them, set boundaries with them, and hold space for them in the full range of their human experience. Seeing them for their truest self, I empower them at every turn and trust their wisdom and dignity. Creating a secure attachment with my children has been one of the biggest gifts from doing this work, knowing that I am not passing down my pain and trauma. I used to wish that I had done this work before giving birth to them, but now I can see that they are the mirrors I needed to see myself more clearly to transform.

Lastly, my intimate relationships with men were the final frontier of my growth and evolution. When I stopped seeing men through the lens of my wounded self, I stopped behaving as if they were potential perpetrators or absentee fathers. When I stopped wearing the attitude of victim, I stopped behaving like one and started using my voice. Never giving my will over to a man, I have nothing to resent. When I am in conscious choice, I am a victim to no one. When I passively follow the patterns of my conditioning, I am a victim to my own mind.

Men no longer induce my inner victim, just as I no longer induce their inner perpetrator. My conditioned self finally stopped colluding with theirs, and I can now meet them from my wholeness. I recognize that I am far too powerful to be a victim, and owning the shadow of my unhealthy feminine expression has allowed me to integrate and embody my healthy feminine essence. Where my wound used to cause me to hide my pain and contort my truth, my wholeness allows me to reveal my authentic experience and trust myself to own my "No."

It takes strength and autonomy to ask for what we want in a vulnerable and open way, without expectations or demands. When I suggest this to clients they often ask, "But what if he doesn't change?" If we ask for what we want so that someone will change, we're communicating for control. The act of vulnerably sharing our inner world and desires with someone is done so that we feel more connected to them. This is intimacy. And since we're in a relationship with another autonomous individual, we cannot control them. They get to choose how they want to show up, and we get to decide if we want the connection given their response.

This is the dance of mature relationship. Sovereign people with different desires, negotiating how to be with one another without contorting for the connection. The key here is to share our desire and sit with the feelings that arise within should our partner be unwilling to meet that desire.

As a woman, I was conditioned to disown my desire, and this cultivated an unhealthy feminine expression. I was taught that what a man wanted was important and my desire was inconsequential. My inner young one wants to hide inside of the closet in my heart that she built to escape vulnerability. Giving love and attention to my younger parts while standing solid in my alignment with Source, I'm okay with rejection. In my sovereignty, I'd rather have my partner reject me for what I want than stay with me for being in my distortion.

Honoring my desires and holding myself in the feelings that arise, I give the young one within me what she never got. I validate my own feelings, love myself in my experience, and welcome everything about my inner world, even the parts that are harder to claim. From this place, I am attracted to and attract men who also care about what I need and how I feel. The old puzzle pieces of wounding no longer fit once I fully embody the healthier, more integrated version of myself.

EMOTIONAL SELF ATTUNEMENT

Historically, the patriarchal dominant view has deemed emotions as bad and invalid. We've been told that emotions are weak and if we were truly present and without expectation we would not have negative emotions. We're also taught that we can choose to be happy and that it's a character flaw when we are chronically unhappy. I wholly and completely disagree with this stance. Every single experience within us is a valid part of our humanity. Our emotions are communicating to us important information and it's our job to turn toward ourselves to discover what our deep unconscious wants us to become aware of. This does not mean that we wallow and loop in our emotions. This simply means that we use this emotional information to excavate old energy, increase our awareness, and be in discovery about where our connection with Source was ruptured.

When we are emotionally self-attuned, we are better able to self-regulate. Resisting, suppressing, and disenfranchising our emotions causes them to come out sideways in unhealthy expressions. Disowned emotions cause the mind to loop in distorted stories. While our emotions are always valid, the stories that our mind makes up when we're emotionally triggered are likely not. Identifying with our emotional story is when we start to go down a rabbit hole of pain and suffering. Stopping the stream of thoughts, attuning to the physical sensations of emotions as they are expressed in the body, and welcoming everything we feel, we take our power back from the distortion of the mind and draw closer to our True Self.

Step 1: When you notice your mind is looping, stop the stream and ask yourself "What am I feeling?" From here you are already one step removed from your conditioned self.

Step 2: Label this emotion accurately. Is it fear, anger, grief, sadness, insecurity, envy etc.?

Step 3: Ask yourself where you feel this emotion in your body. Turn your focus inward and search your inner world for the sensations associated with your feelings. When you're tracking yourself at the level of sensation, you cannot also be identified with your mind at the exact same moment.

Step 4: Breathe with tenderness and love into the emotional sensations, welcoming them without resistance.

Step 5: Ask yourself, "What does this feeling need?" This is specifically is about what the young one within needs from you, so one else. This will help you become more in touch with your desire and what is beneath the feeling, meeting your young one from your wise, mature self.

We cannot be identified with the thoughts of our mind and attuned to the emotional experience in our body at the exact same moment. So staying with ourselves at the level of sensation is imperative in taking our power back from our conditioned self and aligning with Source during a trigger reaction.

What is this feeling? What is the feeling under the feeling? What is underneath that layer of feeling?

Looking for the least obvious experience brings us to the deeper truth of what's happening within us. Emotions get a bad reputation because typically a younger part is running the show when we're triggered. Casting aside our young one and suppressing our emotions does not nurture health and evolution. We elevate our self-awareness when we attune to our emotions in this way, rather than discharging them in backwards and sideways outlets. The work is to not distort and project our emotions or our thoughts onto others. The most effective way to stop projecting is to stay really curious about ourselves.

All healthy relationships have emotional intelligence at their core. Self-emotional attunement nurtures our relationship with ourselves, which ultimately is in service of our relationship with everyone.

Resisting our inner world is futile. In the resistance, we give the thing we don't like power over us and we perpetuate a fragmented state. In the welcoming of our emotions, we become empowered to move through the experience with awareness and regulation. This allows us to respond to life from our mature, wise self. We move forward with embodied wholeness when we welcome the full range of our inner world.

Our words are powerful, and revealing our authentic truth is a great act of self-love and deep integrity. The artistry of choosing words that are in alignment with our wholeness and our truest truth is worthy practice that will allow all of our interactions with the universe to be clean and clear. Emotional self-attunement is the first step in cultivating the self-awareness that will empower us to reveal.

FINAL THOUGHTS AND WISHES

Before your conception, your spirit easefully rested in the universal bliss of oneness. Expansive and inherently wise, you needed to do nothing to earn love or find safety. This was the unconditional state of existence.

In an instant, you came into this dimension as your body started to form. In the womb, you were already picking up on the murky energy of unhealed wounds of ancestral trauma. This old, acquired pain started to become yours to process. Then, as you were birthed as a separate being, the people around you saw you as separate. Preoccupied with their own drama, pain, and conditioned stories of how to be a human, the people around you didn't see the full range of your being. They projected their beliefs and pain onto you, and they only saw you for a minuscule part of who you were. Over time, you started to believe you were small, too.

Where before there was oneness, now there were rules to play by to get an inkling of the security that had been an inherent part of your reality. The people around you unknowingly taught you about power, desire, safety and love as your personality developed to organize this information. You disowned parts of yourself to present an acceptable face to the world, and your distortion was reinforced by the way people treated you as if you were your conditioned self. This habituated way of being became normal, it became part of the proverbial water that you swam in.

Matching the vibration of those around you, you developed strategies to find safety and connection. But all along you knew there was more to yourself. You knew they weren't seeing the most important part of you because they were not aligned with this part of themselves.

Then you forgot, just like them. You forgot your true nature, and you even forgot that you had forgotten.

You became so skilled at using these tactics to navigate this world that you didn't recognize they were not in integrity with the core of your being. Far from your true nature but not even knowing that this was the case, you navigated the world from your identification with your conditioned self.

A glimpse of light appeared, showing you a sliver of your True Self. Invigorated with excitement, you tried to return to your true nature before you fell asleep to it again, which you did. The conditioned ways came back online and once again you forgot, and once again you even forgot that you had forgotten. But the remembering came back more frequently, and over time the spaces of sleep got shorter. It became easier to stay awake to the True Self when you recognized that your identity was undeniably united with the Source that beats your heart.

Stripping away the layers of everything you are not and integrating disowned part, you begin to come back to the place in you that is untouched by the experiences you've had in this life. Unchanged, the experience of universal bliss and wholeness lives within you beneath the layers of your conditioned self. The pain, trauma, and misbeliefs that you've acquired in this life are not part of your true nature, they are not who you really are. Aligning with the Source that beats your heart and embodying the wholeness that is your birthright, you bring the essence of vitality, love, generosity, health, creativity, and curiosity into all areas of your life. With dignity and humility, you stand your sacred ground.

My wish for you is that the recognition of oneness come easefully into your awareness. I wish that the light of consciousness allows you to remember who you really are, and that you have the dignity to embody your True Self. May your alignment with Source emerge naturally, and may you lovingly and tenderly honor the young one within you, giving her the thing she's always longed for. From the depth of your soul, may you remember that you were made for this—that you belong in this world. You are here to be in your full expression where you let your wholeness shine unapologetically. Playing small for no one, may you always vibrate at the frequency of your True Self.

BOOK CLUB QUESTIONS

CHAPTER 1: THE LOST SELF

1. Do you remember when you started living from your conditioning and fell asleep to your True Self?

2. What were the circumstances of your life during that time?

3. What was the unconscious motive to follow the impulse of your conditioned self? (i.e. Connection, Safety, Something else?).

CHAPTER 2: SEARCHING FOR THE LIGHT

1. What ways did you feel disempowered as a child?

2. What was it that you were wanting and needing to feel unconditionally loved?

3. What ways did you feel empowered and big in the world as a child?

CHAPTER 3: LAPSE IN POWER

1. Who taught you about yourself as a sexual being? What was the impact on your developing sense of sexuality?

2. Was your first sexual experience empowering and pleasurable? Awkward and painful? Something else?

3. How did you feel about yourself and your body after exploring your sexuality?

Get the complete list of questions, along with access to the free masterclass *Embody the True Self*, at www.harmonykwiker.com.

REFERENCES

Bailey, P. (1995). *Homeopathic Psychology: Personality Profiles of the Major Constitutional Remedies.* North Atlantic Books: Berkeley, CA.

Brown, B. (2012). *Daring Greatly: How the Courage to be Vulnerable Transforms the Way We Live, Love, Parent, and Lead.* Penguin Group: New York, NY.

Caldwell, C. (1996). *Getting our Bodies Back: Recovery, Healing, and Transformation through Body-Centered Psychotherapy.* Shambala Publications: Boston, MA.

Campbell, S. (2001). *Getting Real: Ten Truth Skills you Need to Live an Authentic Life.* HJ Kramer/New World Library: Novato: CA.

Chodron, P. (2000). *When Things Fall Apart: Heart Advice for Difficult Times.* Shambala Publications. Boulder, CO.

D'Adamo, P. (2002). *Eat Right for your Type: The Individualized Blood Type Diet Solution.* Berkley Publications. Berkley, CA.

Epstein, M. (2013). *Thoughts without a Thinker: Psychology from a Buddhist Perspective.* Basic Books: New York, NY.

Feuerstein, G. (1998). *Tantra: The Path of Ecstasy.* Shambala Publications: Boulder, CO.

Gottman, J. & Schwartz Gottman, J. (2007). *And Baby Makes Three: The Six-Step Plan for Preserving Marital Intimacy and Rekindling Romance After Baby Arrives.* Three Rivers Press: New York, NY.

Halifax, J. (2008). *Being with Dying: Cultivating Compassion and Fearlessness in the Presence of Death.* Shambala Publications. Boston, MA.

Kurtz, R. (1990). *Body-Centered Psychotherapy: The Hakomi Method.* Life Rhythm. Mendocino, CA.

Levine, A. & Heller, R. (2010). *Attached: The New Science of Adult Attachment and How it can Help you Find—and Keep—Love.* Penguin: New York, NY.

Orr, L.D. (1988). *Breaking the Death Habit: The Science of Everlasting Life.* Frog: San Antonio, FL.

Perls, F. (1978). *The Gestalt Approach and Eye Witness to Therapy.* Bantam Books: New York, NY.

Riso, D., and Hudson, R. (1999). *The Wisdom of the Enneagram: The Complete Guide to Psychological and Spiritual Growth for the Nine Personality Types.* Bantam Publications: New York, NY.

Rosenberg, M. (2015). *Nonviolent Communication: Life-Changing Tools for Healthy Relations*, 3rd Ed. Rosenberg Publications: New Mexico.

Made in the USA
Middletown, DE
14 March 2019